Theological and Philosophical Premises of Judaism

JUDAISM AND JEWISH LIFE

Editorial board
Geoffrey Alderman (University of Buckingham, Great Britain)
Herbert Basser (Queens University, Canada)
Donatella Ester Di Cesare (Università "La Sapienza," Italy)
Roberta Rosenberg Farber (Yeshiva University, New York),
Series Editor Associate
Simcha Fishbane (Touro College, New York), Series Editor
Meir Bar Ilan (Bar Ilan University, Israel)
Andreas Nachama (Touro College, Berlin)
Ira Robinson (Concordia University, Montreal)
Nissan Rubin (Bar Ilan University, Israel)
Susan Starr Sered (Suffolk University, Boston)
Reeva Spector Simon (Yeshiva University, New York)

Theological and Philosophical Premises of Judaism

Jacob Neusner

Boston
2009

Copyright © 2009 Academic Studies Press
All rights reserved

ISBN 978-1-934843-54-3

Book design by Yuri Alexandrov

Published by Academic Studies Press in 2009
28 Montfern Avenue
Brighton, MA 02135, USA
press@academicstudiespress.com
www.academicstudiespress.com

Contents

Preface vii

THREE THEOLOGICAL PREMISES OF JUDAISM

1. SPEECH: An eye that sees an ear that hears 3
   i. Know before whom you are going to give a full account of yourself . . . 3
   ii. Oaths 5
   iii. Vows and the Nazirite Vow in Particular 14

2. TIME: "Considerations of Temporal Priority or Posteriority Do Not Enter
   into the Torah" 35
   i. Temporal Sequence Does Not Apply to the Torah. 35
   ii. The Present-Tense Past: Scripture Re-Presented in the Immediacy of
       the Moment. 37
   iii. How are events treated, if not as unique indicators of the movement
        of history? Patterning Events. Mishnah-tractate Ta'anit 4:6–7 44
   iv. History in the Torah and in the Mishnah 47
   v. How the Mishnah Configures Israel in the Context of History Defined by
      God. How the Destruction of the Temple Figures in Mishnah-tractate
      Rosh Hashanah 4:1–3 49
   vi. Patterning the History of the Sacrificial Cult: Mishnah-Tractate
       Zebahim 14:4–10 51
   vii. A Messiah in the Mishnah: Mishnah-tractate Sotah Chapter Nine 55

3. SPACE: The land of Israel is holier than all lands 59
   i. The Locative Dimension. 59
   ii. Taking life to Sustain Israel's life: Hullin 68
   iii. The Domestic Table Compared with the Temple Altar 70
   iv. The Particular Laws of Mishnah-Tractate Hullin 72
   v. Gradations of Sanctification 80
   vi. Why Hullin in Particular? 82
   vii. Location, Occasion, the Character of the Encounter, in God's Context,
        of God and the Israelite 84

The Philosophical Premise of Judaism

4. ANALYSIS: Hierarchical classification and the Law's Philosophical
   Demonstration of Monotheism 89
   i. Hierarchical classification. 89
   ii. Aristotle and the Mishnah's Deductive Reasoning 97
   iii. Message: The Taxonomic Power of Human Intentionality 100
   iv. The Judaism behind 116

5. MIXTURES 117
   i. The Three Types of Mixtures 117
   ii. Zebahim 123
   iii. Hullin 125
   iv. Temurah 125
   v. Miqvaot 125
   vi. Makhshirin 127
   vii. Mixtures in the First Division of the Halakhah: Bikkurim 128
   viii. Conclusion 149

6. ANALYSIS: Intentionality 150
   i. Defining Intentionality, Attitude 150
   ii. Intentionality and Freedom of Will 160
   iii. The Manipulation and Application of power 166
   iv. The point of differentiation within the political structures, supernatural
       and natural alike, lies in the attitude and intention of a human being 171
   v. The Sources of Power: The Will of God and the Will of Man 175

Integral Judaism

7. Integrating the System 179
   i. At the Center of the System 179
   ii. Defining Zekhut 184
   iii. Specific Meanings of Zekhut in Particular Contexts 186
   iv. Zekhut in Genesis Rabbah 193
   v. Deeds that Generate Zekhut 199
   vi. Relationships 203

8. Living in the kingdom of God 206
   i. The Rationality of the Israelite Social Order 206
   ii. Approved Emotions 211
   iii. Competition for the Status of "Being Israel" 215
   iv. From Philosophy to Religion: The Kingdom of Heaven and
       the City of God 218
   v. The Question of History Once Again 227

Index of Ancient Sources 235
Index of Subjects 242

Preface

Classical Judaism imagined the people Israel's situation in three aspects to be unique among the nations of the earth. The nations lived in unclean lands contaminated by corpses and redolent of death. They themselves are destined to die without hope of renewed life after the grave. They were prisoners of secular time, subject to the movement and laws of history in its inexorable logic. Heaven did not pay attention to what they did and did not care about their conduct, so long as they observed the basic decencies mandated by the commandments that applied to the heirs of Noah, seven fundamental rules in all.

That is not how Israel the holy people was conceived. The Israel contemplated by Rabbinic Judaism lives in sacred space and in enchanted time, all the while subject to the constant surveillance of an eye that sees all and an ear that hears all and a sentient being that recalls all. Why the divine obsession with Israel? God yearned for Israel's love and constantly contemplated its conduct. The world imagined by the Rabbis situated Israel in an enchanted kingdom, a never-never-land and conceived of God as omniscient and ubiquitous.

Here I show that in its generative theology Rabbinic Judaism in its formative age invoked the perpetual presence of God overseeing all that Israelites said and did. It conceived of Israel to transcend the movement of history and to live in a perpetual present tense. Israel located itself in a Land like no other. And it organized its social order in a hierarchical structure ascending to the one God situated at the climax and head of all being. The sanctification of Israel, the people, endures [1] in the absence of the cult and [2] in alien, unclean territory and [3] whatever the source of the food that Israel eats. Israel's sanctity is eternal, un-contingent, absolute. The sanctification that inheres in Israel, the people, transcends the Land and outlives the Temple and its cult. Since the sanctity of Israel, the people, persists beyond the Temple and outside of the Land, that sanctity stands at a higher point in the hierarchy of domains of the holy that ascend from earth to heaven and from Man to God.

That theological construction (Chapters One, Two and Three) gained support from a science and a philosophy (Chapters Four, Five, and Six) that accomplished the hierarchical classification of nature and of the social order. Nature and society arose from the complex to the simple, and conversely the many descended from the one. These represented the theological givens, sustained by the philosophical premises, of Judaism. The law constructed its propositions upon generalizations that pertained universally, so bringing the Israelite norms into accord with natural law. This emerges in the way in which the law sorted out mixtures by their types, fully in line with the Stoic theory of mixtures. The philosophical categorization and classification of the power of intentionality, shaded over into the consideration of classes of causation and responsibility in the Aristotelian manner — from deliberate to inadvertent.

But how does Judaism integrate into a coherent system its premises, the theological propositions, and its recurrent analytical protocols, the philosophical principles. I set forth the integrating conceptions in Chapters Seven and Eight. The philosophical and theological components are integrated in an encompassing composition.

An earlier exercise in a different way pursued the question raised here, namely, the premises of the Rabbinic canon. There I asked about the convictions that animate the classical documents but are not necessarily articulated in them. But the approach and issues taken up here do not intersect with the prior exercise.

The Judaism Behind the Texts. The Generative Premises of Rabbinic Literature. I. *The Mishnah*. A. *The Division of Agriculture*. Atlanta, 1993: Scholars Press for South Florida Studies in the History of Judaism.

The Judaism Behind the Texts. The Generative Premises of Rabbinic Literature. I. *The Mishnah*. B. *The Divisions of Appointed Times, Women, and Damages (through Sanhedrin)*. Atlanta, 1993: Scholars Press for South Florida Studies in the History of Judaism.

The Judaism Behind the Texts. The Generative Premises of Rabbinic Literature. I. *The Mishnah*. C. *The Divisions of Damages (from Makkot), Holy Things and Purities*. Atlanta, 1993: Scholars Press for South Florida Studies in the History of Judaism.

The Judaism Behind the Texts. The Generative Premises of Rabbinic Literature. II. *The Tosefta, Tractate Abot, and the Earlier Midrash-*

Compilations: Sifra, Sifré to Numbers, and Sifré to Deuteronomy. Atlanta, 1993: Scholars Press for South Florida Studies in the History of Judaism.

The Judaism Behind the Texts. The Generative Premises of Rabbinic Literature. III. The Later Midrash-Compilations: Genesis Rabbah, Leviticus Rabbah and Pesiqta deRab Kahana. Atlanta, 1994: Scholars Press for South Florida Studies in the History of Judaism.

The Judaism Behind the Texts. The Generative Premises of Rabbinic Literature. IV. The Latest Midrash-Compilations: Song of Songs Rabbah, Ruth Rabbah, Esther Rabbah I, and Lamentations Rabbati. And The Fathers According to Rabbi Nathan. Atlanta, 1994: Scholars Press for South Florida Studies in the History of Judaism.

The Judaism Behind the Texts. The Generative Premises of Rabbinic Literature. V. The Talmuds of the Land of Israel and Babylonia. Atlanta, 1994: Scholars Press for South Florida Studies in the History of Judaism.

The Judaism the Rabbis Take for Granted. Atlanta, 1995: Scholars Press for South Florida Studies in the History of Judaism.

Jacob Neusner
Distinguished Service Professor of
the History and Theology of Judaism
Senior Fellow, Institute of Advanced Theology
Bard College

Three Theological Premises of Judaism

1.
SPEECH:
An eye that sees an ear that hears

> *"Know what is above you: An eye that sees, and an ear that hears, and all your actions are written down in a book."*
>
> Abot 3:20

I. KNOW BEFORE WHOM YOU ARE GOING TO GIVE A FULL ACCOUNT OF YOURSELF

God's is the eye that sees and the ear that hears. Life subject to ubiquitous supervision by the all-powerful supernatural authority, watching and listening to everybody all the time and everywhere ought to have left little occasion for free agency. The individual in such a universe could scarcely withstand God. But the individual Israelite's power of will made all the difference in the world, for God cared about what the Israelite man ate for breakfast and how the Israelite woman carried out her professed intentionality. Attitude and intentionality, the most subjective components of the human condition, lay beyond God's control and therefore engaged God's attention. He could see into the heart of everyone, and he craved the freely given love of each one. And for that reason — the power at one's own will to obey or disobey God — the individual mattered most of all.

The sages of Judaism in the formative age, the first six centuries C. E., adopted as the fundamental, implicit premise of human affairs that they lived in a world subject to a single will, that of the one God, creator of heaven and earth, who from on high oversaw all human affairs. He bore witness to the conduct of every living creature and responded to what he saw. The record of life on earth accounted for the conduct of heaven. The issue I address here is, to what extent does this conception of supernatural judgment to which every human being is subject actually govern the normative law of Judaism? Where in concrete contexts and secular transactions does God intervene in this world? And how does he do so?

Where does the Judaism of the sages imply that God sees all and hears all and records all, so that heavenly oversight extends to each individual? The world of the Israelite is subject to perpetual supervision. God sees all, hears all, and records all. Nothing is forgotten, nothing escapes notice. The important point in what follows is that each person is going to give

THREE THEOLOGICAL PREMISES OF JUDAISM

a full account of himself before the one God who knows and responds to everything:

- A. Aqabiah b. Mehalalel says, "Reflect upon three things and you will not fall into the clutches of transgression:
- B. "Know (1) from whence you come, (2) whither you are going, and (3) before whom you are going to have to give a full account [of yourself].
- C. "From whence do you come? From a putrid drop.
- D. "Whither are you going? To a place of dust, worms, and maggots.
- E. "And before whom are you going to give a full account of yourself? Before the King of kings of kings, the Holy One, blessed be he."

Abot 3:21

Not only does God know what people say and do, but he foresees what they are going to do. Still he judges them only in accord with their deeds, not their plans:

- A. "Everything is foreseen, and free choice is given.
- B. "In goodness the world is judged.
- C. "And all is in accord with the abundance of deed[s]."

Abot 3:15

Finally, the process of recording action and thought, for which one bears responsibility, accumulates credits and debits, which are brought into balance:

- A. He would say, "(1) All is handed over as a pledge,
- B. "(2) And a net is cast over all the living.
- C. "(3) The store is open, (4) the storekeeper gives credit, (5) the account book is open, and (6) the hand is writing.
- D. "(1) Whoever wants to borrow may come and borrow.
- E. "(2) The charity collectors go around every day and collect from man whether he knows it or not.
- E. "(3) And they have grounds for what they do.
- G. "(4) And the judgment is a true judgment.
- H. "(5) And everything is ready for the meal."

Abot 3:16

The record of one's deeds and deliberations reaches its climax in the summary-judgment to which each person is subject. These didactic statements describe the human situation of people subject to constant oversight. In these statements God is conceived as a preoccupied busybody, who invades the private thoughts and concealed actions of everybody all the time. God's relates to humanity with ultimate concern, and he displays his engagement with humanity by his preoccupation with the thoughts and deeds of his handiwork:

> [A] R. Hananiah b. Aqashia says, "The Holy One, blessed be he, wanted to give merit to Israel.
> [B] "Therefore he gave them abundant Torah and numerous commandments,
> [C] "as it is said, 'It pleased the Lord for his righteousness' sake to magnify the Torah and give honor to it (Is. 42:21)."
>
> *Mishnah-tractate Makkot 3:15*

The commandments impose rules on eating, sexual activity, conduct at specified times and occasions — a whole panoply of areas of concern.

I asked just now how in concrete terms God intervenes in this world. Now let us consider where in the exposition of the law God's all-seeing eye and all-hearing ear provoke him to intervene in what we should classify as secular, this-worldly affairs. The first inquiry concerns oaths, which involve Gods name: how does the law of oaths and vows embody the view that God sees all and hears all?

II. OATHS

Oaths and vows, as well as the special vow of the Nazirite (Num. 6) entail invoking God's name to validate a particular claim. Present at the occasion of the oath in all the times and places in which people take oaths, God hears his name and pays attention. Taking a false oath is an act of blasphemy and is subject to punishment by Heaven. Mishnah-Tosefta tractate Shebuot covers several classes of oaths:[1] [1] oaths of adjuration; [2] the rash oath; [3] the false claim in connection with bailments. The topic of the tractate is the definition of binding words and the consequence for violating commitments; the religious dimension emerges, as we shall see, when God's stake in the formulation of commitments enters into the matter. That is where the one possessed of the ear that hears becomes an active participant in the human situation. So, in all, we move from actions and their consequences — crime or sin and the penalty therefor — to the effects of saying certain words, starting with the word, God, properly formulated in context.

---

[1] Vows should not be confused with oaths. They represent a very different category and are dealt with in the setting of the household, in tractate Nedarim.

Where God intervenes is determined by where man's eye is not present to see, his ear to hear. The law takes account of transactions to which man bears adequate witness and differentiates them from those to which God is the principal witness. God alone knows what man does in the privacy of his heart, while to some sins or crimes man attests. Take for example Sanhedrin-Makkot, which deals with public deeds that violate the law, both those of omission and those of commission. Sanhedrin-Makkot addresses deeds that man has witnessed and to which he attests in court. Rules of evidence provide for man to establish the facts and for the earthly court to act upon those facts. But what man says to which God alone bears witness requires its own protocol. The premise of the perpetual, ubiquitous divine witness takes over in Shebuot, where human testimony is not called for.

The Halakhah of oaths, which fills the greater part of the tractate Shebuot, then defines types of oaths and the counts on which, in the taking of an oath that turns out to be false or that is violated, one incurs culpability. The first issue involves all oaths in general. It concerns the assessment of the divisibility of a mental condition: how many counts of guilt does one incur within a single oath by multiple acts in violation thereof? The answer derives from a close reading of the language that is used; if it is partitive, treating as distinct each component of the oath ("wine, oil, and honey"), each action is culpable, forming a distinct classification. If it is inclusive, treating as a group a variety of categories ("many different beverages"), all actions fall into the same classification and are penalized under a single count.

From rules pertinent to all oaths, we proceed to the subdivision of oaths into four categories, rash oath, vain oath, oath of testimony and oath of bailment. A separate category of oaths, those imposed by the judges as part of a court proceeding, is taken up in due course. These four principal types obviously fall into two distinct categories as well, the former being oaths of a private character, the latter involving public policy—the courts, the protection of property. Once more we distinguish inadvertent taking of such an oath, in which case an offering suffices, from deliberately doing so, in which case the sanction is corporal. Taking the former two types of oath is itself culpable, in the latter cases, violating the oath or taking the oath under false pretenses is culpable, an important difference. The rash or vain oath takes effect as a general statement, the oath of testimony or of bailment must be particular to the case at hand. One is not penalized for taking a true oath of testimony or oath of bailment, but one is automatically subject to sanctions for taking a rash or a vain oath. That difference accounts also for the character of the rules that define the application of the law: men and women, relatives and otherwise, and the like. Oaths pertaining to the court matter only when taken by those qualified to give testimony, e.g., men not women, unrelated parties but not relatives of the litigants, and the like. That explains, also, why for these categories of oaths only taking a false oath is penalized. In these cases, too, the oath must be particular to the case, e.g., imposed on specific, named persons.

The judges investigate the case before them by imposing oaths. These form their own category, involving not only private persons but the agency of the community at large. The judges exercise the power to impose an oath upon contesting parties, in the certainty that Israelites will not take a false oath, involving God's name or Presence. Here the character of the claim and the concession governs. If the defendant denies that he owes anything, he is exempt from having to take an oath; if he concedes the facts but quibbles about details, he is required to do so. And once he does, he prevails and pays no more than he has conceded. That indicates the power of the oath in court. Five classes of claimant take the oath and collect what they claim. The oaths as they affect bailments are subdivided in terms of the character and quality of the guardianship promised by the bailiff, the unpaid bailiff being held to a lower standard than the paid bailiff, and so on. Here the oath proves effective where there are no witnesses as to the facts.

If the sages wished to make the statement that man's word is comparable to God's and that, for man as for God, words form media of sanctification, they could find no more suitable occasion for doing so than in their discussion of the oath. And if, further, they wanted to say, God is everywhere present, a sentient being who pays close attention to everyone all the time, to what people say, not only to what they do, and, especially, to what they say upon the invocation of God's presence in particular — if that is what they wanted to say, then Shebuot provides not the ideal occasion but the only really appropriate one.

That is for two reasons. First, the oath by definition calls God to witness the transaction; the person who takes the oath invokes God's name and calls upon God to confirm his allegation. So the consequence of asking God to join in one's claims and certify them, the conviction that God is everywhere, all the time, when he is called upon, forms the foundation of all else. Second, the oath represents a purely verbal transaction, not ordinarily confirmed by concrete action, not commonly subjected to the supervision of all parties. It is the transaction that in the end depends upon the integrity of the person who makes the statement in God's name, "By an oath, I shall not eat," for who is going to keep watch to see that the man even in secret does not eat?

The religious premise of oath-taking accordingly involves an assessment of man's and of God's character. God oversees all things; he will know when his name has been taken in vain. Man is possessed of character and conscience; he does not need to be subjected to supervision by a this-worldly force outside of himself, when, having invoked God's name, he has subjected himself to God's oversight. So to language sages impute remarkable power, specifically the capacity to change a transaction, through intangible but powerful formulations, by the introduction of an interest on God's part into an arrangement otherwise between men alone. These religious convictions come to full expression in the Halakhah at hand, stating in concrete language and norms the conviction that God responds when his name is invoked and is not to be deceived — ever. That conviction provides ample motivation for a detailed definition, in norms of speech, of the circumstances and formulas that engage God's interest and participation, respectively.

The oath represents the use of words for an inviolable and utterly dependable result: if I take an oath, I invoke God's name, and in doing so, I declare myself completely truthful — "so help me God." God hears the oath and records it. However many people take an oath at the same moment, God hears them all and holds them all to account if they break their oaths. But God not only enforces the oath, having a personal stake therein. God himself takes oaths and binds himself thereby, Scripture being rich in divine oath-takings, e.g., Gen. 22:15, "By myself I have sworn and oath, says the Lord, because you have done this and have not withheld your son, your only son, I will indeed bless you..." In formulating matters in that way, God undertakes a perpetual blessing for Abraham's heirs, the taking of the oath securing credence from Abraham and imposing an iron-clad obligation upon God. The upshot is, the oath possesses an integrity, an autonomy of power, such that God as much as man is bound. Words properly formulated therefore exert extraordinary power, and that is why, from deeds that represent sins or crimes, the Halakhah now turns to words. It follows that the Halakhah will carefully define the formula by which words take on the power to bind or loose, by which God himself is engaged in the transaction among men. But, as we already realize, the Halakhah also focuses its attention upon the power of the oath here at home, within Israel's interior transactions, in relationships between one Israelite and another. That is not how the Aggadah frames its discussion of the same matter.

The oath involves the name of God, and at the foundation of the Halakhah is the fourth of the Ten Commandments, "You shall not take the name of the Lord your God in vain, for the Lord will not hold him guiltless

1. SPEECH: An eye that sees an ear that hears

who takes his name in vain" (Ex. 20:7). The view of the Halakhah that at issue in the fourth commandment is the inviolability of oaths is stated explicitly in the following:

1. A. R. Hiyya taught, "(The statement, 'Say to all the congregation of the people of Israel' (Lev. 19:2)) teaches that the entire passage was stated on the occasion of the gathering (of the entire assembly.)
   B. "And what is the reason that it was stated on the occasion of the gathering (of the entire assembly)? Because the majority of the principles of the Torah depend upon (what is stated in this chapter of the Torah)."
   C. R. Levi said, "It is because the Ten Commandments are encompassed within its (teachings).
   D. "'I am the Lord your God' (Ex. 20:2), and here it is written, 'I am the Lord your God' (Lev. 19:2).
   E. "'You shall have no (other gods)' (Ex. 20:3), and here it is written, 'You shall not make for yourselves molten gods' (Lev. 19:4).
   F. "'You shall not take (the name of the Lord your God in vain)' (Ex. 20:7), and here it is written, 'You shall not take a lying oath by my name' (Lev. 19:12)."

Leviticus Rabbah XXIV:V

The principles of the Torah may be derived from a few basic statements, which yield them all, and the Ten Commandments serve as the source for the rest. Here the way in which the oath forms a fundamental component of man's relationship to God is made explicit. In taking the oath, man is like God; God binds himself by an oath, so does man. There is one difference between God and man. God supervises man. God needs no supervision; he is truth. That is what the Aggadah, building upon the facts of the Written Torah, sets forth as the theology implicit in oaths, and that is what the Halakhah, organizing both the facts of the Written Torah and the facts produced by logical reflection, defines as the action-symbols, the norms expressed in concrete ways, of that same theology.

But the difference between the Aggadah and the Halakhah when addressing the oath is not to be missed. The Aggadah speaks to the larger world of humanity, the Halakhah to the inner life, the domestic transactions, of Israel at home, within its own social frontiers. The Aggadah takes for granted the power and probative capacity of the oath, the Halakhah, for its part, embodies that power, defining how it is invoked and exercised. The Aggadah speaks of the power of the oath at large, the Halakhah the concrete force of the oath in workaday transactions in Israel's inner life. The Halakhah then bears the message that the language Israelites use among themselves in the engagement with God's name affects not only the intangibles of transcendent faith but the palpable results of ordinary activities: acts of faith and faithlessness, acts of honesty and dishonesty, acts of integrity and deceit — all of them measured by the criterion of truth established in what is said and in the way it is formulated. Using God's name in certain contexts brings God into the here and now, and that represents a power that language, rightly used, possesses. No wonder sages find the topic so richly engaging.

The Halakhah always centers on the oath as man is affected by it. Here is how the Aggadah expresses the conception that God is bound by the oath:

X:I.1. A. "[The Lord said to Moses,] 'Take Aaron [and his sons with him, and the garments, the anointing oil, the bull of the sin offering, the two rams, and the basket of unleavened bread, and assemble all the congregation at the door of the tent of meeting]'" (Lev. 8:1–3).
B. (Gen. R. 39:6:) "You love righteousness and hate wickedness, [therefore God, your God, has anointed you with the oil of gladness above your fellows]" (Ps. 45:7).
C. R. Yudan in the name of R. Azariah interpreted the verse to speak of Abraham, our father:
D. "When [Abraham] was pleading for mercy for the people of Sodom, he said before him, 'Lord of the world! You have taken an oath that you will not bring a flood upon the world.'
E. "That is in line with the following verse of Scripture: 'For this is like the days of Noah to me; as I swore that the waters of Noah should no more go over the earth, so I have sworn that I will not be angry with you and will not rebuke you' [Is. 54:9].
F. "'Now [Abraham continued], it is a flood of water that you will not bring, but a flood of fire you will bring! Then you turn out to practice deception with regard to the oath.
G. "'If so, you will not carry out the obligation of your oath.'
H. "That is in line with the following verse: 'Far be it from you to do such a thing!' [Gen. 18:25].
I. "He said before him, 'Far be it from you . . . shall not the judge of all the earth do justly' [Gen. 18:25].

Leviticus Rabbah X:I–III.1

What emerges is that the language of the oath is deemed precise and determinative, so that Abraham can read God's oath concerning the flood to be exclusionary, not a flood of water but of some other flood; that would represent an act of deception, violating the oath in spirit if not in letter.

How in the Aggadah does an oath figure? It is to impose upon oneself restrictions or limitations, to strengthen one's own resolve to avoid sin. For example, these three invoked an oath so as to avoid temptation by the impulse to do evil, specifically, sexual sin:

1. SPEECH: An eye that sees an ear that hears

1. A. Said R. Yosé, "There were three who were tempted by their inclination to do evil, but who strengthened themselves against it in each case by taking an oath: Joseph, David, and Boaz.
   B. "Joseph: 'How then can I do this great wickedness and sin against God' (Gen. 39:9).
   E. "David: 'And David said, "As the Lord lives, no, but the Lord shall smite him" (1 Sam. 26:10).'
   J. "Boaz: 'As the Lord lives, I will do the part of the next of kin for you. Lie down until the morning.'"

Ruth Rabbah LXXII:III.1

To avoid sexual sin, the three principals take the oath, thus gaining fear of God as a buttress against sin. Now these are private transactions, so the oath brings God's oversight into the conduct of the named saints even when they are all by themselves. The oath here governs God's relationship to individuals, as much as the oath as taken to Abraham governs God's relationship to Abraham (and his seed). In the Halakhah, by contrast, matters are otherwise; there the oath is invoked to regulate man's relationship to man, God being asked to validate the commitment therein undertaken.

Further, in the Aggadic representation of the world, the nations are adjured as much as Israelites, and in the same transaction. By an oath, God imposes the arrangement that the gentiles must not rule Israel so harshly that Israel will rebel, and Israel must not rebel against the gentiles but must accept their government as punishment for sin:

1. A. R. Yosé b. R. Hanina said, "The two oaths [Song 2:7: 'I adjure you, O daughters of Jerusalem,' and Song 3:5, 'I adjure you, O daughters of Jerusalem, by the gazelles or the hinds of the field'] apply, one to Israel, the other to the nations of the world.
   B. "The oath is imposed upon Israel that they not rebel against the yoke of the kingdoms.
   C. "And the oath is imposed upon the kingdoms that they not make the yoke too hard for Israel.
   D. "For if they make the yoke too hard on Israel, they will force the end to come before its appointed time."

Song of Songs Rabbah XXIV:II.1

The upshot is simple. The Aggadic representation of the oath in no way prepares us for the issues that will predominate in the Halakhic treatment of the same topic. In the Aggadah the setting for the oath proves either entirely private and personal or on the other extreme wholly public and political. It affects an individual's relationship with God and Israel's collective relationship with the gentiles. The intermediate ground, between

Israelites all by themselves and Israel's outer frontiers with the nations, is taken up by the Halakhah.

In the Aggadah the oath figures as a medium of securing a stable relationship between God and man, a mode of setting and maintaining the rules that will govern. God binds himself and imposes bonds upon man, all through the medium of words. When man takes an oath, for his part, the concern is an equivalent transaction of power. Nothing in the Aggadah prepares us for what is at stake in the Halakhah, which is trustworthy relationships, effected through verbal formulas, between man and man. The upshot is, God's relationship with man, defined and regulated by the use of language to impose an oath, forms the model of man's relationship to man. If God is bound by the oath that he takes by his own name, man all the more so is bound by the oath that he takes in God's name; man is like God, and man's words matter just as God's words matter; the same formulas pertain. To that principle of theological anthropology the laws in detail attest, even though the principle itself remains implicit, being articulated only in the Aggadic setting.

What then is at stake in the four types of oath that people impose upon themselves, the rash, the vain, the oath of testimony, the oath of bailment? The rash oath attracts attention because it is one that in the end is going to be violated willy-nilly: the oath not to do something that one is highly likely to do. The vain oath is one that is contrary to fact or condition, e.g., an oath that one has seen what is impossible, or an oath not to do what one is commanded to do. These oaths misuse, abuse language; they represent the utilization of the formula of the oath in inappropriate ways, asking by an oath that people believe one will do the impossible or believe the implausible. In the context of the Halakhah, we require two things: a definition of the sin or crime, and a specification of the penalty for deliberate and for inadvertent commission of the sin or crime. The Halakhah then identifies those whose oaths bear consequences. In the present instance anyone may take such an oath, anyone may be affected by it: men and women, persons not related and those related, and the like. But what distinguishes the classification is that the oath represents an act of one's own volition.

The other two types of oath — oath of testimony, oath of bailment — by contrast may be imposed by the court or by the law, but pertain only to those who to begin with are able to give testimony. Men not related to the parties to the conflict suitable to bear witness, are subject to the oath of testimony. Gentiles, women, children, and others invalid to testify in a court of Judaism are not. The oath of testimony then serves the process of the courts in the administration of law, imposing the requirement to testify upon reluctant witnesses. The oath of testimony is particular to the person on whom it is imposed; it cannot form a generalized imprecation applicable to all who hear it. The transaction moreover takes a highly personal form, the oath being imposed by the party that requires the testimony upon the party that is supposed to know pertinent facts. The oath of bailment has no bearing upon court transactions, so anyone may take it. It must pertain to something of value. Its terms and consequences are defined by the diverse definitions of responsibilities for bailments. The oath imposed by the judges, finally, embodies Scripture's disposition of the conflicting claims to property, e.g., the claim of an undischarged debt in specie or in kind, but one that is tangible and not personal or theoretical (ownership of land), e.g., to money but not slaves, to movables but not real estate.

How, then, do oaths figure in the Halakhah? They represent media for engaging God in the resolution of conflict, the more important cases all involving competing claims of one kind or another. The oath of the judges, the oath of testimony, and the oath of bailment all serve to introduce the criterion of truth and to exclude the exercise of force. The claimant seeks a just restoration of his property or compensation for his loss, the defendant insists upon a fair adjudication of the matter. For that purpose, words backed up not by deeds but by divine supervision serves. But contention precipitates also the taking of the vain and rash oath. The rash oath involves securing credence for a preposterous allegation — one that others deny. The vain oath asks people to believe one will carry out an implausible resolve, again bearing within itself the implicit motive to secure credibility where there is none. So one way or another, the oath serves, within the Israelite polity, to engage God's participation within the transactions of man, to involve God in Israel's points of inner conflict, to ask God to impart certainty to the points of stress and strain.

The power imputed to the oath, the context in which the oath exercises its controlling authority, the cogency of the details of the types of oaths — all work together to say in concrete and detailed ways precisely the implicit, abstract theological statement that the sages wish to express. That is God's intimate, eternal, and on-going engagement with what Israelites say to one another within Israel's interior social order. If sages wanted to say, God listens carefully to what people say and pays attention to the details of what they do, God knows what you promise and observes how you carry out your promise, God oversees what no man witnesses, God lives among us and abides with us — if sages wished to underscore the perpetual presence of God within Israel's everyday life, they could have accomplished their goal no more effectively than by setting forth the laws of Shebuot in the way that they have. And, as we have seen in our brief consideration of the oath in the Aggadah, it is in particular through the interior spaces given structure by the Halakhah that they sages have framed for themselves.

III. VOWS AND THE NAZIRITE VOW IN PARTICULAR

The Halakhah deems language the mirror of the soul; the words that are used expose the heart, articulate and give effect to intentionality. The key to the entire system comes to expression in the language, "An act of consecration done in error is not binding [consecrated]." And from the viewpoint of the Torah's Halakhah, what man intends makes all the difference: God responds to what man wants, more even than to what he does, as the distinction between murder and manslaughter shows in an obvious way. For the critical dialectics of the Torah embodies the conflict between God's and man's will. That focus upon the definitive, taxonomic power of intentionality explains, also, why if a man says to a woman, "Lo, you are consecrated...," and the woman acquiesces, the intentionalities matching, the woman is thereby sanctified to that man and forbidden to all others; the act of intention formulated in words bears the power of classification upon which the entire system builds. But—self-evidently—not all intentionality finds Heaven's approval, and that is so even though Heaven confirms and acquiesces therein. And that brings us to the vow, which realizes in words the intentionality of the person who takes the vow and imposes upon himself restrictions of various kinds. And, inseparable from the vow, in sequence comes the special vow of the Nazirite.

The dismissive judgment of the Halakhah upon the vow is fully exposed in the rule, "He who says, 'As the vows of the suitable folk' has said nothing whatsoever. Such a statement does not constitute a euphemism for a vow. Why not? "Because suitable folk (*kesherim*) do not take vows." And the rest follows. But most people do take vows, and they are particularly common in the life of the household, meaning, in relationships between husband and wife. For, as we shall see, the vow is the weapon of the weak, the way by which the lesser party to a transaction exercises power over the greater. If the wife says to the husband, "By a vow, I shall not derive benefit from you," or "What food you feed me is Qorban," she removes from herself her husband's control, so too, the guest to the intimidating host. But the vow also stands for the release of discipline, it is an expletive and an outcry, an act of temper, and no wonder sages do not respect those that take vows! Now let us see matters in more general, theoretical terms.

The power of the word to change the status of persons and things defines and sustains the household above all, which rests in the last analysis upon the foundations of commitment, responsibility, and trust — all to begin with embodied and effected in language. Classifying vows as a chapter in the life of the household, with special reference to the sanctification of marriage, therefore presents no surprise. The sanctity of one's word forms a corollary of the proposition that the language we use bears the power of classification, and, in the present context, of therefore effecting sanctification. If, after all, by declaring a woman consecrated to a man, or an animal to the altar or a portion of the crop to the priesthood, one brings about the sanctification of the woman or the beast or the grain, then what limits to the power of language to affect the everyday world are to be set? In that same framework, after all, God communicates and is communicated with: in the present age, with the Temple in ruins, worship is through prayer, which takes the form of words whether spoken or not.

But why locate vows within the household (in the received organization of the Mishnah, within the division devoted to the family), when vows can take place in the larger framework of the Israelite social order, the market or the village? Not only so, but another form of effective language, the oath, indeed finds its location in the tractates that deal with the social order, with public transactions of movable property, for example. So while oaths, which are public and juridical in effect, belong to the account of the social order, vows, which are personal and private, belong to the exposition of the inner life of the household. In the Halakhah of Ketubot the affect of vows on the marital bond receives ample consideration, and in particular, the effects of the woman's taking a vow and so encumbering herself. Scripture imposes its judgment on the point, within the social order, at which vows become pertinent when it presents the matter as a dimension of the life of wives with their husbands or daughters with their fathers.

That fact emerges from the pertinent verses of Scripture, which are as follows (Numbers 30:1–16):

> Moses said to the heads of the tribes of the people of Israel, "This is what the Lord has commanded. When a man vows a vow to the Lord or swears an oath to bind himself by a pledge, he shall not break his word; he shall do according to all that proceeds out of his mouth.
>
> "Or when a woman vows a vow to the Lord and binds herself by a pledge, while within her father's house in her youth, and her father hears of her vow and of her pledge by which she has bound herself and says nothing to her, then all her

vows shall stand, and every pledge by which she has bound herself shall stand. But if her father expresses disapproval to her on the day that he hears of it, no vow of hers, no pledge by which she has bound herself, shall stand; and the Lord will forgive her, because her father opposed her. And if she is married to a husband while under her vows or any thoughtless utterance of her lips by which she has bound herself, and her husband hears of it, and says nothing to her on the day that he hears, then her vows shall stand, and her pledges by which she has bound herself shall stand. But if, on the day that her husband comes to hear of it, he expresses disapproval, then he shall make void her vow which was on her and the thoughtless utterance of her lips, by which she bound herself; and the Lord will forgive her. But any vow of a widow or of a divorced woman, anything by which she has bound herself, shall stand against her.

"And if she vowed in her husband's house or bound herself by a pledge with an oath, and her husband heard of it, and said nothing to her and did not oppose her, then all her vows shall stand, and every pledge by which she bound herself shall stand. But if her husband makes them null and void on the day that he hears them, then whatsoever proceeds out of her lips concerning her vows or concerning her pledge of herself shall not stand; her husband has made them void. But if her husband says nothing to her from day to day, then he establishes all her vows or all her pledges that are upon her; he has established them, because he said nothing to her on the day that he heard of them. But if he makes them null and void after he has heard of them, then he shall bear her iniquity."

These are the statues that the Lord commanded Moses, as between a man and his wife, and between a father and his daughter, while in her youth, within her father's house.

The generalization, that a person is not to break his word but keep "all that proceeds out of his mouth," meaning, his vows, immediately finds its amplification in the framework of the household.

The Halakhah of vows (drawing in its wake the Halakhah of the special vow of the Nazirite) concerns matters of personal status: what may a person do or not do by reason of a self-imposed vow? And that matter turns out to define the core of what the Halakhah has to say about the conduct of a marriage — the operative chapters, for the middle of the marriage, after the beginning, before the end — in the Halakhah of Ketubot as well. The Halakhah so reveals what it finds especially interesting in marriage, which is, relationships: shifts and changes in the relationship of the wife to the husband. That is consistent with the points pertinent to the status of a woman in relationship to a man at which the Halakhah begins and ends: the creation of the marriage through Heavenly action (the Halakhah of Yebamot) or human intervention (Qiddushin, Ketubot, as we already have seen); the cessation of a marriage through Heavenly action (death) or through the writ of divorce (Gittin). Now we raise the question

1. SPEECH: An eye that sees an ear that hears

about the interplay between responsibilities to Heaven, on the one side, and to the husband, on the other, that the woman takes upon herself — the gray area in which the woman owes fealty to Heaven and to husband alike. Here we find ourselves in dialogue with the three pertinent chapters of the Written Torah that all together address the matter, Numbers Chapter Five for the woman investigated for faithfulness; Numbers Chapter Six for the Nazirite vow; and Numbers Chapter Thirty for the ordinary vow.

The most general statement of matters then invokes the matter of relationships with Heaven that affect relationships on earth, that is, the woman's vow to Heaven that affects her relationships with her husband and family. That is what is at stake in the Halakhah of Qiddushin and Gittin as well — only now in the reverse. Acts of consecration involve declarations made on earth and confirmed in Heaven, e.g., consecration of a woman to a particular man. Here we address the effects of declarations made to Heaven that shape a woman's status and relationships on earth, and that means, in the nature of things, with her father before marriage and with her husband in marriage. God listens in to conversations between husbands and wives.

The presentation of the Halakhah starts with the definition of a vow and proceed to consider the affects of a vow upon what a person may or may not do, mainly, eat. We conclude with close attention to how one may gain absolution from a vow, releasing its binding character by reason of diverse grounds or pretexts. That is the whole story, beginning, middle, and end, a structure that is simple and logical. That vows principally locate themselves within the household — the premise of the Scripture's statements and the Halakhah's presentation throughout — guides the articulation of the details of the law. But Scripture treats the matter as principally one involving women — wives and daughters — while the Halakhah presents it as a sex-neutral one, involving vows by man or woman alike. Rather, the Halakhah wants to know about the language that makes the vow effective, the results of vows, the release of vows — topics implicit, but not explored, within the Scripture's account of the matter.

The first important problem taken up by Nedarim concerns language and its meaning. The Halakhah spreads a broad net over the language people use, treating every sort of euphemism as effective in imposing the vow. The Halakhah of definition yields no problematics I can discern, only a principle richly instantiated that any sort of language that resembles the language of a vow takes effect. The essay on language that the Halakhah embodies proceeds to language that is null, because the euphemism itself contradicts reality, such as "the dough-offering of Aaron," for the priesthood does not separate dough-offering; hides pierced at the heart fall into the category of idolatry, which is null; double-negatives do not count. Language that refers to idolatry is not effective. More to the point, there are entire categories of vows that are null, meaning, types of language that do not bear the authority of the vow. These are vows that to begin with represent language of no effect or language used without adequate reflection, e.g., vows of incitement, on the one side, vows of exaggeration, on the other. In both cases the vow does not follow much thought. Or, more to the point, the intention behind the language is inappropriate. Vows of incitement — to purchase an object at a given price — embody inappropriate intentionality; they are meant to influence the other only. Vows made in error, like acts of consecration made in error, do not stand for the intentionality of the speaker, and so are null. Finally, vows broken under constraint are null. Along these same lines, one may intentionally take a false vow to save life or limb or to deceive the thief and the tax-collector (regarded as one and the same thing).

The second important problem is philosophical and concerns classifying things. It provides a systematic exercise in differentiating the genus from the species, embodied in the distinction between a vow against deriving benefit from the genus, which encompasses all the species of that genus (the genus, house, the species, upper chamber), and a vow against deriving benefit from a particular species, which leaves available the other species of the same genus (upper chamber, house). That exercise is worked out in vast detail, repeating the same point throughout. The difference between genus and species (wool, shearings) and between two distinct genera (clothing, sacking) accounts for a broad range of the issues dealt with here, and the matter of speciation covers much of the rest. Thus we differentiate cooking from roasting or seething. So too, language that is general is interpreted in minimal ways, "pickling" applying only to vegetables. In all, the exercise of speciation and its effects accounts for many of the concrete Halakhic problems that are set forth, and a few generalizations, even given in abstract terms, would encompass much of the Halakhah in its details.

If speciation explains a broad range of rules, the matter of causation accounts for another. Specifically, the third type of problem addressed by the Halakhah concerns the effects of vows, e.g., the result of general statements about deriving benefit for specific types of benefit. A vow against deriving benefit from his friend leaves the friend free to perform certain general actions, e.g., paying the man's half-sheqel tax to the Temple and restoring what he has lost. The distinction between forbidden and permitted benefit is subtle, and so far as I can see rests upon the difference in the taxonomy of causation between efficient cause and proximate cause, benefit deriving from actions in the category of efficient causes being forbidden, the other kind permitted.

That that distinction governs is shown, among other cases, by the rule that allows the fellow, forbidden by the man's vow to give him any benefit, to hire a storekeeper to give what the man cannot directly give himself. The rule is worth reviewing: The fellow goes to a storekeeper and says, "Mr. So-and-so is forbidden by vow from deriving benefit from me, and I don't know what I can do about it." And the storekeeper gives food to him who took the vow and then goes and collects from this one against whom the vow was taken. [If] he against whom the vow was taken had to build the house of the one prohibited by vow from deriving benefit, or to set up his fence, or to cut the grain in his field, the fellow goes to the workers and says to them, "Mr. So-and-so is forbidden by vow from deriving benefit from me, and I don't know what I can do about it." Then the workers do the work with him who took the vow and come and collect their salary from this one against whom the vow was taken. Clearly, the difference between direct and indirect action governs. But if we differentiate indirect from direct cause, we also focus upon direct cause in its own terms, e.g., fruit, what is exchanged for the fruit, what grows from the fruit. So from an exercise on the difference between genus and species we here proceed to one on the difference between direct and indirect causation.

Vows are remitted or lose effect when the conditions specified in them have been realized or proved null. They also are remitted when the purpose of the vow is shown spurious, e.g., "Did you not speak only to do me honor? But this [not taking your wheat and wine for my children] is what I deem to be honorable!" Further, vows cannot in the end take effect so as to bring about the violation of existing obligations or contracts. A vow against what is written in the Torah is null; one that violates the marriage-contract is ineffective; one that requires dishonoring parents is null. Vows that contradict the facts explicitly invoked in making them are null. The point is then obvious: language takes effect only when the facts embodied in the language to begin with are valid.

The power of the husband or the father, as the case may be, to annul the vows of the wife or the daughter presents no surprises. We deal with the familiar range of cases, e.g., the interstitial status of the betrothed girl, over which both father and husband enjoy power. Once the woman is on her own, it goes without saying, no man may nullify her vows. The husband may annul the vows of the wife once she comes into his domain. The action must take place on the spot, through the day in question; it cannot be done in advance. The Halakhah clearly makes provision for the autonomous woman, not subject to father or husband, and treats as valid whatever vows she makes on her own account.

The fact is, the Halakhah recognizes no important difference in substance between stating a certain formula and writing down a certain formula into a document. In either case, the relationship of a woman to the generality of mankind is drastically restricted. The range of relationships of that same woman to a particular man is drastically expanded. Stating other formulas of words effect important changes, permitting or prohibiting activities and relationships. The vow in general, and the vow to be a Nazirite in particular, share the principle that words enchant, affect relationships, effect change in the world. Before proceeding in this discussion of the religious principles of Nedarim and Nazir, let us now turn to the law of the Nazirite, both male and female. With both bodies of Halakhah in hand, we shall identify the single and cogent religious statement that sages propose to make concerning vows and the special vow of the Nazirite.

Nedarim and Nazir form profound reflections on the meaning and affects of language. If a man or woman says a certain set of words, Heaven hears. The man or woman thereby adopts certain restrictions or prohibitions, whether, as in Nedarim, not to eat certain foods of any sort or to derive benefit from a given person, or, as in Nazir, not to eat grapes in particular, cut hair, or attend funerals (something the husband cannot ever prevent the wife from doing, but the Nazirite vow prevents the Nazirite from doing). These restrictions, that language, serve to provoke Heaven's interest in, and intervention into, the conduct of the man or the woman. That is why Nedarim and Nazir form a continuous exposition of the Halakhah, even though, in Scripture, the framer of the book of Numbers does not recognize continuity between the Nazirite vow, Num. 6, contiguous with the woman accused of unfaithfulness, Num. 5, and the vow in general, Num. 30. But from the perspective of the Halakhah, with its focus upon the sanctifying power of language, it is no surprise that Nedarim and Nazir fit together as well as they do, or that both belong comfortably within the framework of the division of women, or, within the category-formation of this study, life within the walls of the Israelite household.

Scripture finds two points of interest in the present topic, the prohibitions upon the Nazirite, the offerings that come as the climax of the vow. The Nazirite then is comparable to a *kohen* or priest: subject to certain prohibitions and is assigned a particular position in the conduct of the Temple cult. The priest cannot serve if he is drunk or contaminated by a corpse or bald (a bald-headed man is invalid to serve as a priest, so

1. SPEECH: An eye that sees an ear that hears

M. Bekh. 7:2A). A single paradigm pertains, a single analogy governs. From the perspective of Scripture, once the Nazirite vow takes effect, prohibitions are invoked against wine, hair-cutting, and corpse-uncleanness; the other point of interest is the offerings that are required if the Nazirite is made unclean with corpse-uncleanness and when the Nazirite completes the vow in a state of cleanness. All this the Halakhah both takes for granted and in the main simply ignores. What Scripture holds does not require detailed analysis, by contrast, is the process by which the woman or man becomes a Nazirite, that is to say, the vow itself. To that problem fully half of the Halakhah as defined by the Mishnah with the Tosefta is devoted.[2] So while the triple taboo is merely restated by the Halakhah, it is the exposition of the vow that defines the tough problems, generates interesting conundrums, and entails the rich exposition that the Tosefta and two Talmuds would ultimately provide.

But the Halakhah, for its part, characteristically ignores what is securely classified and instead takes up interstitial problems, generated by intersecting rules or classes of data. In the present case, the Halakhah focuses upon not the black-and-white language that invokes the vow, but on euphemisms that may or may not pertain, just as with Nedarim. Language that is similar in sound or in sense takes effect. What about stipulations that might affect the vow, conditions under which the vow is or is not invoked, the taking of sequences of Nazirite-vows at a single moment? That is the next problem. The duration of the vow, undefined in Scripture, occupies attention. Then comes the intervention of the husband into the applicability of the vow his wife has taken. We turn, further, to designating the diverse animals that are to serve as the Nazirite's offerings at the end of the vow, with special attention to situations in which the animals are not used in accord with the original language of sanctification.

The Halakhah, then, finds acute interest in the working of euphemisms. But that is not only because of the unclear status of euphemistic language — does it mean what it seems or not? A deeper consideration constantly comes into play. Language, the Halakhah recognizes, conveys sense and meaning in many ways. Language stands for what is intensely personal and private. But language also conveys meanings of general intelligibility. It is by definition a public act. With what result for the

---

[2] As usual, the contribution of the Talmuds to the formulation of Halakhah proves negligible. Their interest is in analysis, not legislation. The Yerushalmi's formulations show little augmentation of the law, much amplification; I give no indication of the speculative problems explored therein, which are as usual imaginative and rich, but add nothing to the Halakhah in its classical formulation except refinements.

Halakhah? What is private (mumbled, unintelligible, gibberish) bears no consequence, but what is intelligible by a common-sense standard takes effect. That is how the Halakhah sorts matters out. Thus, when it comes to euphemisms, all of them take effect; for what matters about language is not adherence to the governing formula, though it matters. What makes all the difference is the perceived and publicly comprehensible intent. If the intent conveyed by the language is clear and unmistakable, then the language has done its task of embodying intentionality. And then the language is affective. If the intentionality is not vividly conveyed, however indirectly, then the language is null. The power of language lies in its capacity to convey, to embody, inchoate intentionality, to realize in the shared world of public transactions the individual and private attitude or intentionality that motivates action.

And that accounts for the Halakhah's recognition of the special status of a Samson-Nazirite: the language that is used signals the intentionality to accept the Nazirite vow in the model of Samson, and hence fully exposes the will of the one who takes the special vow. Whether or not the Halakhah has invented the category of the Samson-Nazirite to build upon the implications of its theory of the relationship of language to intentionality — the necessary connection between language and intention, public metaphor and private attitude and will — we cannot surmise. It is the simple fact that once the important questions pertinent to the topic at hand center upon the power of language to embody and realize, confirm and convey the attitude, the (mere) details of language will precipitate the formation of specificities of the Halakhah. The main problem addressed by the Halakhah pertaining to the language of the vow to be a Nazirite is how to standardize matters, so that private meanings and personal stipulations do not corrupt discourse. Then the prevailing solution is to identify what is general and intelligible and dismiss the rest. One example serves. That is why if someone specifies a detail as incumbent, then all the details of a Nazirite vow pertain to him. Nothing remains private, personal, idiosyncratic, once language serves. Even what affects the household in particular is framed for effect for all Israel.

The Tosefta's contribution to all this is, predictably, expansive: Just as euphemisms for Nazirite-vows are equivalent to Nazirite-vows, so euphemisms for Samson-vows are equivalent to Samson-vows. The vow applies in the Land and abroad, to hirsute and bald alike, and — it goes without saying — whether or not the Temple is standing. The intention is the key, not the limitations of circumstance. And that same governing principle accounts for the interpretation of the language, "I will be a Nazir like the hairs of my head" or "like the dust of the earth." That is taken to mean, for an unlimited period of time. The net effect of the Halakhah is to generalize upon specific and idiosyncratic usages. Individual conditions are null, e.g., If one said, "Lo, I am a Nazir on condition that I shall drink wine and become unclean with corpse uncleanness," lo, this one is a Nazir. But he is prohibited to do all of these things that he has specified as conditional upon his vow. If he said, "I recognize that there is such a thing as Naziriteship, but I do not recognize that a Nazir is prohibited from drinking wine," lo, this one is bound by the Nazirite oath. But legitimate stipulations bear consequences, e.g., conditions that do not violate the law of the Torah: "...if my wife bears a son" or "a daughter."

Because the husband has the power to nullify the vows of the wife (or the father of the daughter), the Halakhah attends to the case of nullification. But I see nothing of special interest in the laws, except that while the husband may nullify the wife's vow, he may not nullify his own. If his vow is contingent upon her vow, by contrast, neither is subject to the Nazirite rule. Limits are set upon intentionality; if one intended to violate the vow but in fact was not subject to the vow, there is no penalty: If her husband annulled the vow for her, but she did not know that her husband had annulled it for her and nonetheless continued to go around drinking wine and contracting corpse uncleanness, she does not receive forty stripes. So too, someone who violated the vow but had a sage annul it is not penalized; the vow never took effect. Here intention to violate the vow is insufficient to precipitate sanctions; the actualities intervene. Or, to put it otherwise, improper intention not confirmed by improper deed is null. Mere intention on its own is null — language and action decide everything, and, when it comes to the vow, the language constitutes the act.

When it comes to the offerings of the Nazirite, the Halakhah takes special interest in the interstitial case of the beast that has been consecrated but cannot be offered in fulfillment of the intent of the sacrifier: what to do with a beast designated for a given purpose that no longer is needed for that purpose? That involves the general rules that pertain. If a beast is designated as a burnt offering, it is presented in that designation; so too, a peace offering, differentiated from the Nazirite's peace-offering as to accompanying gifts. When it comes to the disposition of the coins that are designated for the purchase of an animal to be consecrated for the stated purpose, the rules follow the same lines. The upshot is, the language that is used to designate the animal or the coins takes effect, even though the purpose for which the animal or coins is required is nullified by circumstance. What is the stopping point? It is the tossing of the blood. At that point, the vow has been fully carried out and can no longer be annulled.

When it comes to the restrictions upon the Nazirite that the Torah has defined, the Halakhah devotes its exposition to the familiar problem of differentiating among a sequence of actions of a single type, that is, the general theme of the many and the one, the one and the many, that preoccupies the Halakhah in one topic after another. This routine problem comes to expression in the language, "A Nazir who was drinking wine all day long is liable only on one count. If they said to him, 'Don't drink it! Don't drink it!' and he continues drinking, he is liable on each and every count [of drinking." The problem is particular to the topic, the resolution and consequent rule are not. So too the conundrum about the high priest and the Nazirite, both of them subject to the same restriction against corpse-uncleanness, who share the obligation to bury a neglected corpse requires us to hierarchize the sanctity of each in relationship to that of the other. This too represents a particular form of a general problem of the Halakhah in its work of hierarchical classification, here of competing sanctities: who is holier than whom, and so what? For the same reason, we need not be detained by the Halakhah covering cases of doubt. They merely illustrate prevailing principles on how cases of doubt are to be resolved; another tractate provides the systematic statement of governing principles of the matter, the present one, merely concrete problems for solution.

The Halakhah of Nedarim-Nazir accordingly takes up the theme, the power of language to impose changes in status. That is a common theme of the Halakhah, paramount in the Halakhah of Israel's relationships with God as much as that of Israel within the household walls. In words a magic dwells. That is because God hears and answers what he hears, remembering everything everywhere all the time. In relationship to God what is at issue is the designation of what belongs to God or God's surrogates. Here at stake is personal status. The former then concerns how language affects the tangible world of wine and grain and oil, the latter, the intangible but very real world of a person's standing in the sight of Heaven and Israel alike. By using certain language, a man or woman effects an alteration in his or her condition, e.g., in relationships with other people, or in food that may or may not be eaten, or situations that may or may not be entered into. In both realms of being words affect the world of tangible substances and real relationships. Here, as we noted earlier, by words a man declares himself analogous to a priest — and his actions confirm his intention, realized in language.

What the vow does is to call down Heaven's sanctity upon the benefit, material or otherwise, that the donor wishes to give over for the sake of Heaven. No wonder then, that in analyzing vows, we call upon the conceptions of the gift to Heaven that form the center of Holy Things. The intention of the farmer to consecrate the beast, expressed in the proper language, is confirmed: the beast enters the status of sanctification even before it is set on the altar and slaughtered, its blood tossed at the corners of the altar. "Qorban," "Nazir," and other effective language—these form a single classification, words that transform by reason of the intent with which they are spoken, which they realize because they are spoken.

To state matters in more general terms: at stake in the vow and in the special vow of the Nazirite is the realization of intention brought about through the use of language. But language used for vows, so sages portray matters, does not sanctify, it contaminates. That language ought to express reflected-upon intentionality—like the designation of an animal to expiate an inadvertent, newly-realized sin—but it conveys the outcome of temper and frustration. Designating a beast as consecrated realizes a noble, godly intention; designating the benefit one receives from one's spouse as "Qorban" uses language to embody a lowly and disreputable intention, one to humiliate and reject and disgrace the other. Sages' message registers that language is dangerous because it realizes intentionality, which had best, therefore, be expressed with probity and restraint. And these virtues form the opposite of the traits of mind and character of the vow-taking Israelite, wife or husband, host or guest, salesman or customer.

Why treat the matter within the framework of the household? The reason is that all of the consequences of the use of special language—the illustrative materials of both bodies of Halakhah, Nedarim and Nazir—concern relations of husbands and wives, or parents and children, or the localized transactions of the household and the service-economy round-about (the shop-keeper for example), thus the household and the conduct of life therein. Only rarely does the language of the vow or of the special vow of the Nazirite, spill over into the public affairs of Israel in general. Being private, the vow and the Nazirite vow have no consequences for the relationship of Israel to God in general; breaking the vow or failing to observe what is pledged concerns the individual and God, the community being a bystander to the transaction and bearing no stake therein. The category-formations involved in vows and Nazirite vows do not encompass transactions within the social order, never alluding to a Nazirite's cow that gored the cow of a woman, or a man subject to a vow who struck another and injured him; the compensation for torts and damages is unaffected by the status of the Nazirite or the person who has taken a vow, in the way in which compensation is shaped by the status, e.g., of the slave, the minor, or the idiot:

THREE THEOLOGICAL PREMISES OF JUDAISM

A. A deaf-mute, idiot, and minor — meeting up with them is a bad thing.
B. He who injures them is liable.
C. But they who injure other people are exempt.
D. A slave and a woman — meeting up with them is a bad thing.
E. He who injures them is liable.
F. And they who injure other people are exempt.

M. Baba Qamma 8:4

No such provision in public law takes account of the status of the Nazirite or the person subject to a vow; these do not define classifications of persons for which the social order publicly makes provision. The exemplary cases in Nedarim-Nazir reinforce the essentially private circumstance of matters, their restriction to the household or the village formed by households. The matter of accepting gifts or hospitality hardly registers as a social event. In two of the three dimensions of Israel's world order, its public relationship with God and the conduct of its social order, vows and special vows make no material difference.

But language on its own is a public event, not subject to private manipulation. Language matters because of what it represents and conveys, which is, the solemn intentionality of the one who uses the language, and that is the key to all else. Language makes public and attracts public attention to the intentionality of the private person, forms the point of intersection ("the interface") between the individual and the community. So the classification of the law at hand within the framework of the Israelite household, while appropriate, somewhat misleads. For when it comes to the theme and problem at hand — the interplay of intentionality and language — the Halakhah uniformly explores the matter in its impact upon Israel's relationship with God, Israel's social order, and Israel's life within the household, all three. But sages' category-formation, setting Nedarim-Nazir in the framework of home and family finds ample justification.

That is because the Halakhah of Nazir carries us deep into the recesses of Israel in its tents, within the walls (whether tangible or otherwise) of its households — there alone. Intentionality matters in many category-formations of the Halakhah, but in connection with vows and the Nazirite vow in particular sages localize their statement on the matter. Here they state, people bear direct, personal responsibility for what they say, and while statements made in error are null, those made in jest bear real consequences. That is why euphemisms form so central a concern. There is no fooling around with God, no language exempt from God's hearing. What makes the Nazirite vow effective is language that an individual has used, and it is the power of language to bring about profound change in the status of a person that forms the one of the two centers of interest of the Halakhah of life within the walls of the Israelite household — the focus of sanctification. That formal fact explains the topical pertinence.

Sages work with analogy and contrast: something is like something else, therefore belongs in its classification, or it is not like something else, therefore belongs in the opposite to its classification. And sages furthermore classify matters through matching opposites: the traits of the one, the diametrically opposed, mirror-image traits of the other. In the present case, in the Halakhah of the household, sages compare and contrast language, which realizes intentionality and which leads to sanctification, and the opposite of language and intentionality, which is what comes about of necessity and not as an act of will. What joins these matched opposites is their point of origin, which is man: his intentional words sanctify, his unintentional emissions of another sort contaminate. When we move from sanctification as the sacred takes over the household of Israel to contamination as the unclean affects the household of Israel, the problematic of the Halakhah shifts from the power of intangible language to sanctify, to the power of tangible excretions — morphologically the counterparts to and opposites of language — to contaminate or bring about uncleanness. Both proceed from the body of man or woman, words and excretions alike, the one intangible, the other palpable. The one sanctifies, the other marks a person (or object) as unclean. The one in the form of language attracts Heaven, the other in the form of bodily excretions repels Heaven.

An act of sanctification matches a woman to a particular man, and the act must involve language, documentation, correct formulas, all a fully-exposed statement of will. Where do we locate the basis for the power of language? Words exercise the power to sanctify through the articulation of will. When he speaks and things come about, man acts like God, who as at creation confirms through language that his deed represents his will and through language sanctifies the result. Specifically, God creates and sanctifies the world with words, and, like God, man or woman sanctifies himself or herself with words. With language special tasks are undertaken, particular acts of self-classification take place. The whole then forms an exercise in volition and in the articulation of volition.

Then what about the counterpart and opposite, other things that proceed out of the body of man or woman? The opposite of sanctification, uncleanness, comes about whether or not it is wanted, and it comes about in a purely physical event, e.g., death or bodily excretion. The whole set of transactions—sanctification of table and of bed, on the one side, contamination of the table or the household, on the other—takes place within the walls (for instance, as with death, under the roof) of the household. Take the case of uncleanness by reason of flux, that source of uncleanness flowing from the body of man or woman to which Leviticus 15 makes reference. Here the Halakhah is explicit that it comes about whether by an act of will or not by an act of will, for it is by an act of nature.

Sanctity comes about as an act of will, flux such as is invoked at Leviticus 15 comes about precisely not as an act of will but through inadvertence—naturally, not by intent but under compulsion: "Any flux which happens inadvertently is unclean." The Mishnah-paragraph that pertains is explicit on that matter.

- A. All are susceptible to uncleanness through flux,
- B. even converts,
- C. even slaves, whether freed or not freed,
- D. a deaf-mute, imbecile, or minor,
- E. a eunuch by castration and a eunuch by nature.
- F. As to a tumtom and androgyne—they place upon them the stringencies that apply to man and the stringencies that apply to woman: (1) they are susceptible to uncleanness through blood, like a woman, (2) and through white [flow], like a man. (3) And their status as to uncleanness remains in doubt.

Mishnah-tractate Zabim 2:1

- A. In seven ways do they examine the Zab before he is confirmed as to flux [to make certain that the flux is caused by nature and not by some artificial cause]:
- B. (1) as to what he had eaten, (2) as to what he had drunk, (3) and as to what he had carried;
- C. (4) as to whether he had jumped, (5) as to whether he was ill;
- D. (6) as to what he had seen, and (7) as to what he had fantasized—
- E. [if] he fantasized before he [actually] saw, or saw before fantasizing.
- F. R. Judah says, "Even if he saw cattle, beast, and fowl engaged with one another [in sexual relations], even if he saw a woman's colored garments."
- G. R. Aqiba says, "Even if he had eaten any sort of food, whether bad or good, or drunk any sort of liquid."
- H. They said to him, "Henceforth, there will be no Zabim [for we shall find ample evidence to dismiss as artificial, not natural, fluxes of all kinds]."
- I. He said to them, "Responsibility for Zabim is not yours [and you do not have to see to it that Zabim multiply in Israel]!"
- J. Once one is confirmed as to flux, they do not examine him [further].
- K. [Any flux which happens] inadvertently, and any that is subject to doubt, and his semen [all] are unclean,
- L. for there is now a basis for the matter [of deeming them unclean].

Mishnah-tractate Zabim 2:2

1. SPEECH: An eye that sees an ear that hears

The gentile, the minor, the slave—these and others of their class do not have the power of will or intentionality; they can contract zob-uncleanness, but they cannot by their language sanctify a beast for the altar or a woman for the bed. Their will is null; the slave's will is that of his master, the minor's that of his father. Here, then, when it comes to uncleanness, intentionality is null, therefore language bears no consequences whatsoever. The language still more directly pertinent to our case is at M. Zabim 2:2K: flux that comes about inadvertently and unintentionally is contaminating. The contrast between sanctification and cultic uncleanness then is clear. The status brought about through the act of sanctification and comparable acts such as those involving vows or the vow of the Nazirite come about by intention and express through language the inner attitude and desire of the man or the woman who speaks the language. The counterpart and opposite, the status of uncleanness, comes about willy-nilly, through excretions of the body, the physical counterpart and opposite of words spoken with intent.

What God hears effects the classification of the speaker: the Halakhah of Nedarim-Nazir investigates the power of a person through invoking the name of Heaven to affect the classification in which he or she is situated and so his or her concrete and material relationships with other people. This is done by stating, "May what I eat of your food be prohibited to me as is a sacrifice prohibited to me," all conveyed in the word "Qorban." Having said that, the person may not eat the food of the other. The reason is that the other person's food has been declared by the individual who took the vow to be in the status of a sacrifice. We know that what makes an ordinary beast into a holy beast, subject to the laws of sacrilege and set aside for the alter, is a verbal designation as a sacrifice. Here too what makes ordinary food into food in the status of Holy Things, so far as the given individual is concerned, is the verbal designation of that ordinary food as Holy Things. The difference is that designating an animal as a beast for sacrifice is a public act, affecting society at large. No one then can make use of said animal. Declaring that a dish of oatmeal is in the status of a Qorban by contrast, has no affect upon the cereal, except for the person who made that declaration.

Sages revere the language that brings about sanctification of a woman to a man, and they treat with great punctiliousness the language of the marriage-contract, which, indeed, they subject to the closest exegetical processes of reading and interpretation. If they wished to say, language bears its own power (for the reason stated earlier, its capacity to embody intentionality), they could have no superior choice of topic than the

Halakhah of betrothals and divorce: Qiddushin and Ketubot and Gittin. But what if they wanted to say, language bears power even for purposes of which we (and Heaven) disapprove? And what if their intent was to warn, watch what you say, hold your tongue and keep your temper, because in expressing intentionality, your words give effect to your will, and you will be unable to retract? In other words, if sages wanted to make the point that people had best use in a wise and astute manner the power of language, how would they best say so?

Within the framework of the Halakhah, vows, inclusive of the special vow of the Nazirite, present the particular and appropriate medium for such a message. That is not only because sages want to tell people to watch their words and not pretend to joke when it comes to matters where intentionality makes a difference as to personal status. That is also because sages to begin with take a negative view of vowing. While of oaths taken in court with full deliberation, invoking the name of God, they approve, vows they despise. They are explicit on that matter: people who take vows show their weakness, not their strength. Vows represent the power of the weak and put-upon, the easy way to defend oneself against the importunities of the overbearing host, the grasping salesman, the tormenting husband or wife. But sages do not honor those who take the easy way, asking God to intervene in matters to which on our own we ought to be able to attend.

Sages do not accord respect to the person who takes vows. Vow-takers yield to the undisciplined will, to emotion unguided by rational considerations. But intentionality must (ideally) take form out of both emotion and reflection. Vows explode, the fuel of emotion ignited by the heat of the conflict, the occasion. "Qonam be any benefit I get from you" hardly forms a rational judgment of a stable relationship; it bespeaks a loss of temper, a response to provocation with provocation. Right at the outset the Halakhah gives a powerful signal of its opinion of the whole: suitable folk to begin with do not take vows, only wicked people do. That explains in so many words why, if one says, something is subject to "the vows of suitable folk," he has said nothing. Distaste for vowing and disdain for people who make vows then characterize the law. People who take vows are deemed irresponsible; they are adults who have classified themselves as children. They possess the power of intentionality but not the responsibility for its wise use. That is why they are given openings toward the unbinding of their vows; they are forced at the same time to take seriously what they have said. Vows are treated as a testing of Heaven, a trial of Heavenly patience and grace. Sanctification can affect a person or a mess of porridge, and there is a difference. Expletives are not admired.

1. SPEECH: An eye that sees an ear that hears

But because the Halakhah begins and ends with the conviction that language is power, the Halakhah also takes account of the sanctifying effect of even language stupidly used. That is the message of the Halakhah, and it is only through the Halakhah at hand that sages could set forth the message they had in mind concerning the exploitation and abuse of the power of language. It is a disreputable use of the holy. And language is holy because language gives form and effect to intentionality — the very issue of the Halakhah at hand!

That is why we do admit intentionality — not foresight but intentionality as to honor — into the repertoire of reasons for nullifying vows, as we note in the Halakhah of Nedarim:

> In a matter which is between him and his mother or father, they unloose his vow by [reference to] the honor of his father or mother.
>
> *Mishnah Nedarim 9:1*

> They unloose a vow for a man by reference to his own honor and by reference to the honor of his children. They say to him, "Had you known that the next day they would say about you, 'That's the way of So-and-so, going around divorcing his wives,' "and that about your daughters they'd be saying, 'They're daughters of a divorcée! What did their mother do to get herself divorced' [would you have taken a vow]?" And [if] he then said, "Had I known that things would be that way, I should never have taken such a vow," lo, this [vow] is not binding.
>
> *Mishnah Nedarim 9:9*

The normative law rejects unforeseen events as a routine excuse for nullifying a vow; foresight on its own ("had you known...would you have vowed?") plays a dubious role. But when it comes to the intentionality involving honor of parents or children, that forms a consideration of such overriding power as to nullify the vow.

So sages' statement through the Halakhah of Nedarim-Nazir is clear. Vows are a means used on earth by weak or subordinated person to coerce the more powerful person by invoking the power of Heaven. They are taken under emotional duress and express impatience and frustration. They are not to be predicted. They do not follow a period of sober reflection. They take on importance principally in two relationships, [1] between friends (e.g., host and guest), [2] between husband and wife. They come into play at crucial, dangerous points, because they disrupt the crucial relationships that define life, particularly within the household: marriage, on the one side, friendly hospitality, on the other. They jar and explode. By admitting into human relationships the power of intentionality, they render the predictable — what is governed by regularities — into a source of uncertainty, for who in the end will penetrate what lies deep in the heart, as Jeremiah reflected, which is beyond fathoming? But language brings to the surface, in a statement of will best left unsaid, what lurks in the depths, and the result, Heaven's immediate engagement, is not to be gainsaid. That is why vows form a source of danger. What should be stable if life is to go on is made capricious. So far as marriage is concerned, vows rip open the fabric of sacred relationships.

Language represents power, then, and it is a power not to be exercised lightly. In the cases examined in Ketubot as those laid out here, the weaker side to the party is represented as taking a vow — whether the milquetoast husband, whether the abused wife. It is the wife against the husband, the harried guest against the insistent host, the seller against the buyer, the boastful story-teller against the dubious listener, the passive against the active party, that the vow is taken. The strong incites, the weak reacts, and the language of reaction, the vow, contains such power as is not to be lightly unleashed even against the one who gives and therefore dominates, whether in sex or food or entertainment. Vows then are the response: the mode of aggression exercised by the less powerful party to the relationship. The weak invoke Heaven, the strong do not have to. A vow will be spit out by a guest who has been importuned to take a fourth portion in a meal he does not want to eat. A wife will exclaim that she will derive no benefit whatsoever from her husband. A whole series of cases emerges from a vow taken by a person not to derive benefit from his friend, with the consequence that the friend, who wants to provide some sort of support for the dependent person, does so through a third party. The dependence then is less obtrusive. So, once more: who gives, dominates, and the vow is the instrument to escape earthly domination in the name of Heaven.

As usual, what the Halakhah states in its way, the Aggadah expresses in its manner too. Here is the Bavli's topical composite on losing one's temper, which is deemed the basis for taking vows:

> Said R. Samuel bar Nahman said R. Yohanan, "Whoever loses his temper — all the torments of Hell rule over him: 'Therefore remove anger from your heart, thus will you put away evil from your flesh' (Qoh. 11:10), and the meaning of 'evil' is only Hell: 'The Lord has made all things for himself, yes, even the wicked for the day of evil' (Prov. 16:4). Moreover, he will get a belly ache: 'But the Lord shall give you there a trembling heart and failing of eyes and sorrow of mind' (Deut. 28:65). And what causes weak eyes and depression? Stomach aches."
>
> B. Ned. 3:1A–D I.14/22A

1. SPEECH: An eye that sees an ear that hears

Said Rabbah bar R. Huna, "Whoever loses his temper — even the Presence of God is not important to him: 'The wicked, through the pride of his countenance, will not seek God; God is not in all his thoughts' (Ps. 10:4)."

B. 3:1A–D I.16/22b

A. R. Jeremiah of Difti said, "[Whoever loses his temper] — he forgets what he has learned and increases foolishness: 'For anger rests in the heart of fools' (Qoh. 7:9), and 'But the fool lays open his folly' (Prov. 13:16)."

B. R. Nahman bar Isaac said, "One may be sure that his sins outnumber his merits: 'And a furious man abounds in transgressions' (Prov. 29:22)."

B. 3:1A–D I.17/22b

Said R. Ada b. R. Hanina, "If the Israelites had not sinned, to them would have been given only the Five Books of the Torah and the book of Joshua alone, which involves the division of the Land of Israel. *How come?* 'For much wisdom proceeds from much anger' (Qoh. 1:18)." [Freedman, *Nedarim, ad loc.*: The anger of God caused him to send prophets with their wise teachings.]

B. 3:1A–D I.18/22b

Sages leave no doubt as to their view of matters, which they express with the usual explicit clarity.

The same negative view pertains to the Nazirite vow. It is a mark of arrogance. The special vow of the Nazirite arrogates to the person who takes it the special status of a holy man or woman, even though Heaven has not endowed him or her with that status by nature, by birth. The priest by birth cannot function drunk or subject to corpse-uncleanness. The Nazirite takes on himself the same prescriptions and beautifies himself with abundant hair, held by sages to form a mark of pride.

A. Said Simeon the Righteous, "In my entire life I ate a guilt-offering of a Nazir only one time.

B. M'SH B: "A man came to me from the south, and I saw that he had beautiful eyes, a handsome face, and curly locks. I said to him, 'My son, on what account did you destroy this lovely hair?'

C. "He said to me, 'I was a shepherd in my village, and I came to draw water from the river, and I looked at my reflection, and my bad impulse took hold of me and sought to drive me from the world.

D. "'I said to him, 'Evil one! You should not have taken pride in something which does not belong to you, in something which is going to turn into dust, worms, and corruption. Lo, I take upon myself to shave you off for the sake of Heaven.'

E. "I patted his head and kissed him and said to him, 'My son, may people like you become many, people who do the will of the Omnipresent in Israel. Through you is fulfilled this Scripture, as it is said, 'A man or a woman, when he will express a vow to be a Nazir, to abstain for the sake of the Lord'" (Num. 6:2).

T. Nazir 4:7

But the Nazirite is one who lets his hair grow long, cutting it only at the end of the process, when the vow has been fulfilled. So the Nazirite has undertaken important restrictions incumbent on the priesthood and beautified himself with long hair. Only at the end does the Nazirite make himself praiseworthy, in line with Simeon's judgment, by cutting off all the hair. In line with this statement of matters, sages treat the Nazirite vow as they treat vows in general, as a mark of inferior character or conscience, here, of pride.

What is at stake, then, in the Halakhah of Nedarim-Nazir? Sages build on the premise that God hears what man says and holds man to what he has stated. So what is at stake here is sages' interest in defining the source of the power of language. This they find in Heaven's confirmation of man's or woman's affirmation. By using formulary language man or woman invoke the response of Heaven more really by throwing up words toward Heaven and so provoking a response in Heaven. That is how patterns of behavior and relationship, such as are defined by the vow, the Nazirite-vow, the act of sanctification of a woman to a particular man or a marriage contract, are subjected to Heaven's concerned response. Relationships and deeds are subjected to Heaven's engagement by the statement of the right words. So the Halakhah explores the effects of words, and it is in the Halakhah —and not the Torah, with its powerful bias toward priestly concerns— that that exploration takes place.

The Halakhah answers the question, what can a man or a woman say so as to become obliged to do or not do a specified range of deeds? And the answers to that question respond to yet another, still more profound question. It is, how is Heaven mindful of man and woman on earth? The ornate essays into the trivialities of language and the use of language respond to that question. The Halakhah speaks large and simple truths in conveying a remarkable vision of humanity in God's image. Man and woman are so like God as to be able through what they say to provoke, and even encumber, God's caring and concern. That is because man and woman know how to say the ordinary words that make an extraordinary difference on earth and in Heaven. The message of the Halakhah is, we are responsible for what we say—there is no such thing as "mere words" — because God is listening to what we say. That statement of ours brings to full articulation what we want, words bearing the burden of intentionality. After all, the first act of creation is contained in the statement, "And God *said*..."

2.
TIME:
"Considerations of Temporal Priority or Posteriority Do Not Enter into the Torah"

I. TEMPORAL SEQUENCE DOES NOT APPLY TO THE TORAH

Rabbinic Judaism posits an Israelite world living in an eternal present tense and takes as its premise the simultaneity and fungibility of events superficially deemed sequential. In Rabbinic Judaism events are reversible and interchangeable; no fixed order governs. The commonplace, if flawed logic of sequence—first this, then that, therefore this caused that (post hoc ergo propter hoc)—plays no role. Under such conditions explaining the world as it is by reference to the past is impossible because, in an exact sense, it is unthinkable. That is to say, by means of thinking with principles such as we shall now examine, history—a mode of accounting for the social order by appeal to how things have been and have progressed—in the simplest and most conventional definition then cannot be conceived.[1] The Rabbinic conception of time does not yield a theory of history. The single most important fact in the consideration of the unity of time past and time present is simple: considerations of temporal order simply do not apply. We need not merely infer from what is implicit that that view served as a premise, since it is stated in so many words that considerations of temporal order do not apply to the sequence of Scriptural stories.

This is explicit in the exegesis of Scripture and also in the interpretation of history:

1. A. "And the Lord spoke to Moses in the wilderness of Sinai in the first month of the second year after they had come out of the land of Egypt, saying, ['Let the people of Israel keep the Passover at its appointed time. On the fourteenth day of this month, in the evening, you shall keep it at its appointed time; according to all its statutes and all its ordinances you shall keep it.']" (Num. 9:1–14):

---

[1] In fact, the Mishnah's portrayal of Israel's life ignores all considerations of time and place (other than holy time and enchanted place) and sets forth a utopian Israel, ruling out all considerations of historical time and circumstance. But for the present purpose, a survey of how the past and present are treated as a single span of time is what is required.

B. Scripture here expresses the disgrace of Israel, for they had been camping before Mount Sinai for eleven months [and had not yet observed the Passover].
C. And Scripture further serves to teach you that considerations of temporal order do not apply to the sequence of scriptural stories.
D. For at the beginning of the present book Scripture states, "The Lord spoke to Moses in the wilderness of Sinai in the tent of meeting on the first day of the *second* month in the second year after they had come out of the land of Egypt" (Num. 1:1).
E. And here Scripture refers to "the *first* month,"
F. so serving to teach you that considerations of temporal order do not apply to the sequence of scriptural stories.
G. Rabbi says, "Such a proof is not required, for Scripture in any event says, 'And the children of Israel ate manna for forty years, until they came to the border of the land' (Ex. 16:35).
H. "And at this point they had not eaten it? That statement thus service to teach you that considerations of temporal order do not apply to the sequence of scriptural stories."

Sifré to Numbers LXIV:I

The several proofs make the same point. Scripture narrates events in an other-than-temporal sequence: this happened first, then that second, then the other thing third, all without regard to the temporal order in which the things actually took place. Therefore, the framers of the passage maintain, the account of existence that Scripture portrays transcends considerations of temporal sequence altogether. It follows that, to begin with, sages reject history's conception of a linear and irreversible sequence of events, governed by the logic intrinsic in them: this cannot happen until that has happened, therefore this did not happen before that took place.

A further premise of all historical thinking is that the past has come to closure and awaits description, analysis, and interpretation. All data are in hand, the story now awaits telling. Without a clear point of conclusion historical inquiry cannot identify its data and must suspend its work pending further information. Not only so, but if history cannot identify that dividing point between past and present, it also cannot project that linear sequence of events, singular and irreversible, that forms its premise. For if past flows smoothly into present, then the reverse also commands consideration: the present flowing into the past (as indeed was commonplace in the paradigmatic mode of analyzing human events followed by the sages).

The upshot is simply stated. Rabbinic writings do not recognize the pastness of the past. For we do not observe a sense of distance and difference between the writers and the ancient events of Scripture that they consider. Scripture is rewritten to accord with contemporary convictions and conceptions; the present flows into the past, the past into the present, and at no point do we discern a trace of consciousness that the past is over and done with.

II. THE PRESENT-TENSE PAST: SCRIPTURE RE-PRESENTED IN THE IMMEDIACY OF THE MOMENT

It is the simple fact that Scripture was rewritten, its events recast, to suit the immediate requirements of the authors of compositions. Examples of the rewriting of Scripture fill the documents before us. Every one of them exhibits the same trait of indifference to the criterion of evidence, oblivion to the notion of testing allegations concerning the past against evidence deriving from, or even pertinent to, the age, prior to the present one, that is under discussion. Conversations are invented, events fabricated, the order of Scriptural history recast, in complete indifference to all considerations of historicity, evidence, and criticism. A single case suffices to show us how events in Scripture were rewritten:

1. A. "On the second day Nethanel the son of Zuar, the leader of Issachar, made an offering" (Num. 7:18):
   B. What does Scripture provide this information?
   C. It is because the tribe of Reuben came and entered a complaint, saying, "It is enough that Judah came before me [the elder] in the order of the tribal journeys. Let me give an offering in the sequence of the birth of the tribal ancestors [hence, first]."
   D. Moses rebuked him, saying, "It is directly from the mouth of God that the instructions have come to me to present the offerings in accord with the order in which the tribes are arranged for the journeys."
   E. So it is said, "...Offer," and that word bears the sole meaning that the Holy One, blessed be he, instructed him for the tribes to make their offerings in accord with the order in which they are arranged for the journeys.

Sifré to Numbers LII:I

There is a number of stories about events portrayed in Scripture, and, in a history of Israel from the beginnings to the present, stories such as these will have found a place along with the Scriptural narrative itself; in them, there is no pretense at joining the present narrative into the language or thought-patterns of Scripture.

Not only does the present flow into the past, the past is made to flow into the present. In the type of narrative given here, Scripture is updated in every possible way; new speeches are written, and no one pretends

THREE THEOLOGICAL PREMISES OF JUDAISM

these speeches were made long ago; new details are set forth without the slightest interest in formulating matters to conform to the style or discipline of Scripture:

1. A. "So Moses went out and told the people [the words of the Lord, and he gathered seventy men of the elders of the people and placed them round about the tent.] Then the Lord came down in the cloud [and spoke to him, and took some of the spirit that was upon him and put it upon the seventy elders; and when the spirit rested upon them they prophesied, but they did so no more.] Now two men remained in the camp, [one named Eldad, and the other named Medad]" (Num. 11:24–26):
   B. Some say that their names had remained in the lottery-box. For the Holy One, blessed be he, had said to Moses to choose seventy men for him. Moses replied, "How shall I do it? Lo, all of the tribes will get six representatives each except for two tribes, which will get only five. [Sixty from each of ten tribes, five from each of the other two.] Which tribe will agree to have only five selected from its midst?"
   C. Moses made an arrangement. He took seventy slips of paper and wrote on them the word "elder," and he took two further slips and left them blank and mixed them up and put them all into a lottery-box. He said to them, "Come and pick your slips."
   D. To everyone who chose a slip on which was written, "elder," Moses said, "The Omnipresent has already sanctified you."
   E. And to those who chose a slip on which was not written, "elder," Moses said, "It's from Heaven [and there is nothing I can do about it], so what can I do for you?"

Sifré to Numbers XCV:II

Procedures attested in Mishnah-tractate Tamid, e.g., for the division, by chance tossing of the priests' share in the offering, of the priestly sacrifices among the officiating priests are now retrojected into the remote past. No effort is invested into citing Scriptural evidence that the practice familiar from contemporary writings prevailed even long ago. That fact is simply taken for granted; past and present exist on the same plane. But more is at stake here than merely the atemporality of time. We shall now see how in the formative canon ancient times are fabricated out of contemporary materials.

Not only do scriptural stories up-dated and made to accommodate a reformulation in acutely contemporary terms, but sages invent chapters for the life of biblical figures, e.g., Abraham. Once more we find no interest in joining the story to Scripture's account; it is told entirely in its own terms, in the manner of a Rabbinic polemic-narrative. A single case suffices to make the point that, just as in the first set of documents, events are in-

2. TIME: "Considerations of Temporal Priority or Posteriority Do Not Enter into the Torah"

vented or totally recast, so in the second as much as in the first, considerations of the pastness of the past do not prevent fabrication of whole chapters in lives of saints. The premise once more is that the present is part of the past, and vice versa.

I have chosen for my illustrative case the matter of David. What is interesting is that, when David is reworked into the model of the sages, the conception that the conditions of David's life, as portrayed in scripture, and those of Torah study that rabbis recognized from day to day, were treated as uniform; here is a fine example of what I mean by obliterating the sense of the pastness of the past, while, at the very same time, insisting on the presence of the past in the time of the sages as well. No lines distinguished one age from the other, even while the account of Scripture, read in its own terms, is scarcely acknowledged as exhibiting points of contrast:

A. "O Lord, how many are my foes! Many are rising against me; many are saying of me, there is no help for him in God. Sela" (Ps. 3:2–3):
B. R. Samuel bar Immi and Rabbis:
C. R. Samuel bar Immi interpreted the verse to speak of Doeg and Ahitophel:
D. "'…many are saying of me,' refers to Doeg and Ahitophel. Why does he refer to them as 'many'?
E. "For they formed a majority in Torah-study.
F. "'..many are saying of me,' — They say to David, 'A man who has seized a ewe-lamb, killed the shepherd, and made Israelites fall by the sword — will he have salvation? There is no help for him in God.'
G. "Said David, 'And you, O Lord, have concurred with them, writing in your Torah, saying,' The adulterer and the adulteress will surely die' (Lev. 20:10).
H. " 'But you, O Lord, are a shield about me' (Ps. 3:4): For you have formed a protection for me through the merit attained by my ancestors.
I. " 'My glory' (Ps. 3:4): For your restored me to the throne.
J. " 'And the lifter of my head' (Ps. 3:4): While I was liable to you to have my head removed, you raised my head through the prophet, Nathan, when he said to me, 'Also the Lord has removed your sin and you will not die' (2 Sam. 12:13).' "

Pesiqta deRab Kahana II:I.1

The point hardly requires elaboration. David is now turned into something that Scripture's account does not adumbrate, a disciple of sages, and the politics of his court followed those of the academy. The flow from present to past and future is unimpeded. There is no differentiation among present, past and future.

A still more striking revision of times past into the framework of the rabbis' own times involves the rewriting of the story of Hezekiah and the Babylonians. Now the past forms a palpable component of the present.

THREE THEOLOGICAL PREMISES OF JUDAISM

What is important in this example is the provision of an elaborate, sustained narrative, in which history is invented through a process of invention of anecdotes or events; not a single indicator of the presence of a historical mentality can be located in this historical narrative — not one:

34. A. ["At that time Merodach Baladan, the son of Baladan, sent" (Isa. 39:1) — Spelling out the story to which allusion has just now been made:] he was a sun-worshipper, and he would ordinarily eat at the sixth hour and sleep to the ninth hour.
    B. But, in the time of Hezekiah, king of Judah, when the sun reversed its course, he slept through it and woke up and found it was dawn.
    C. He wanted to kill his guards. He accused them, "You let me sleep all day and all night long."
    D. They said to him, "It was the day that returned [the sun having reversed its course]."
    E. He said to them, "And what god reversed it?"
    F. They said to him, "It was the God of Hezekiah who reversed it."
    G. He said to them, "Then is there a god greater than mine?"
    H. They said to him, "The God of Hezekiah is greater than yours."
    I. Forthwith he sent letters and a present to Hezekiah: "At that time Merodach-baladan, son of Baladan, king of Babylonia, sent letters and a present to Hezekiah [for he had heard that he had been sick and recovered]" (Isa. 39:1).
    J. And what was written in them?
    K. He wrote him, "Peace to King Hezekiah, peace to the city of Jerusalem, peace to the Great God!"
    L. But when the letters had been sent, his mind was at ease, and he said, "I did not do it right, for I greeted Hezekiah before his God."
    M. Forthwith he arose and took three steps and retrieved the letter and wrote another instead, in which he said, "Peace to the great God, peace to the city of Jerusalem, peace to King Hezekiah."
    N. Said the Holy One, blessed be He, "You have risen from your throne and taken three steps in order to pay honor to me. By your life, I shall raise up from you three cosmopolitan kings, who will rule from one end of the world to the other."
    O. And who are they? Nebuchadnezzar, Evil-Merodach, and Belshazzar.
    P. But when they went and blasphemed, the Holy One, blessed be He, crushed their eggs out of the world [exterminated them] and set up others in their place.

Song of Songs Rabbah XXXVIII:II

The story is made up, beginning to end; Scripture's event is recast in a process of imagination, and we discern not the slightest interest in harmonizing the story with Scripture's data. The process of writing history in the model of the present, obliterating all lines of differentiation between past and the present age, made by illustrated by one final case. In the following the death of the prophet is given a reprise.

2. TIME: "Considerations of Temporal Priority or Posteriority Do Not Enter into the Torah"

Here, the story-teller retrojects the destruction of the second Temple into the events of the first, or, more to the point, finds no point in distinguishing one from the other. The two events fall into the same classification and are subject to the same rule.

- A. "This was for the sins of her prophets and the iniquities of her priests, who shed in the midst of her the blood of the righteous:"
- B. R. Yudan asked R. Aha, "Where did the Israelites kill Zechariah? Was it in the courtyard of women or in the courtyard of the Israelites?"
- C. He said to him, "It was neither in the women's courtyard nor in the Israelites' courtyard, but in the priests' courtyard.
- D. "But they did not dispose of his blood like the blood of a hind or a ram: 'He shall pour out the blood thereof and cover it with dust' (Lev. 17:13).
- E. "But here: 'For the blood she shed is still in her; she set it upon a bare rock; she did not pour it out on the ground to cover it with earth' (Ezek. 24:7).
- F. "'She set her blood upon the bare rock, so that it was not covered, so that it may stir up my fury to take vengeance' (Ezek. 24:8)."

2.
- A. Seven transgressions did the Israelites commit on that day: they murdered [1] a priest, [2] prophet, [3] judge, [4] they spilled innocent blood, [5] they blasphemed the divine name, [6] they imparted uncleanness to the courtyard, and it was, furthermore, [7] a Day of Atonement that coincided with the Sabbath.
- B. When Nebuzaradan came in, he saw the blood of Zechariah begin to drip. He said to them, "What sort of blood is this dripping blood?"
- C. They said to him, "It is the blood of oxen, rams, and sheep that we offered on the altar."
- D. He forthwith sent and brought oxen, rams, and sheep and slaughtered them in his presence, but the blood continued to drip.
- E. He said to them, "If you tell the truth, well and good, but if not, I shall comb your flesh with iron combs."
- F. They said to him, "What shall we tell you? He was a prophet who rebuked us. We conspired against him and killed him. And lo, years have passed, but his blood has not stopped seething."
- G. He said to them, "I shall appease it."
- H. He brought before him the great Sanhedrin and the lesser Sanhedrin and killed them, [until their blood mingled with that of Zechariah: "Oaths are imposed and broken, they kill and rob, there is nothing but adultery and license, one deed of blood after another (Hos. 4:2)].
- I. Still the blood seethed. He brought boys and girls and killed them by the blood, but it did not stop seething.
- J. He brought youngsters from the school house and killed them over it, but it did not stop seething.
- K. Forthwith he took eighty thousand young priests and killed them on his account, until the blood lapped the grave of Zechariah. But the blood did not stop seething.
- L. He said, "Zechariah, Zechariah, All the best of them I have destroyed. Do you want me to exterminate them all?"

M. When he said this, the blood forthwith came to rest.
N. Then he considered repenting, saying, "Now if one soul matters are thus, as to that man who has killed all these souls, how much the more so!" [He fled and sent a parting gift and converted.]
O. On the spot the Holy One, blessed be He, was filled with mercy and made a gesture to the blood, which was swallowed up in place.
P. To that Scripture refers when it says, "This was for the sins of her prophets and the iniquities of her priests, who shed in the midst of her the blood of the righteous."

Lamentations Rabbati CXIII.I.1

A final instance allows us to follow sages' bold recasting of the scriptural narrative, inventing dialogue, action, and motive, without the slightest interest in inserting any detail into the framework of the Scripture's picture. The following is invented out of whole cloth, no consideration is given to distinguishing the time of Moses from the time of the narrator; we detect not the slightest interest in identifying the sources of the story, e.g., in remote antiquity. History fabricated is simply not history; it is something else:

A. When our fathers stood at the sea, Moses said to them, "Get up and pass through."
B. They said to him, "We are not going to pass through until the sea is turned into passages." Moses took his staff and hit the sea, and the sea was turned into passages, as it is said," You have hit through with rods, the head of his rulers" (Hab. 3:14).
C. Moses said to them, "Get up and pass through."
D. They said to him, "We are not going to pass through until the sea is turned a valley before us." Moses took his staff and hit the sea, and the sea was turned into a valley before them, as it is said, "He made a valley of the sea and caused them to pass through" (Ps. 78:13), and it is said, "As the cattle that go down into the valley, so did you lead your people" (Is. 63:14).
E. Moses said to them, "Get up and pass through."
F. They said to him, "We are not going to pass through until the sea is cut into two parts before us." Moses took his staff and hit the sea, and the sea was cut into two parts before them, as it is said," To him who divided the Red Sea into two parts" (Ps. 136:13).
G. Moses said to them, "Get up and pass through."
H. They said to him, "We are not going to pass through until the sea is turned clay for us." Moses took his staff and hit the sea, and the sea was turned into clay, as it is said, "You have trodden on the sea with your horses, through the clay of mighty water"s (Hab. 3:15).
I. Moses said to them, "Get up and pass through."
J. They said to him, "We are not going to pass through until the sea is turned into a wilderness before us." Moses took his staff and hit the sea, and the sea was

2. TIME: "Considerations of Temporal Priority or Posteriority Do Not Enter into the Torah"

    turned into a wilderness, as it is said, "And he led them through the deep as through a wilderness" (Ps. 106:9).

K. Moses said to them, "Get up and pass through."

L. They said to him, "We are not going to pass through until the sea is turned into pieces before us." Moses took his staff and hit the sea, and the sea was turned into pieces, as it is said, "You broke the sea in pieces by your strength (Ps. 74:13).

M. Moses said to them, "Get up and pass through."

N. They said to him, "We are not going to pass through until the sea is turned rocks before us." Moses took his staff and hit the sea, and the sea was turned into rocks, as it is said, "You shattered the heads of the sea monsters" (Ps. 74:13). And where does one smash the heads of the sea monsters? One must conclude that they are shattered only on rocks.

O. Moses said to them, "Get up and pass through."

P. They said to him, "We are not going to pass through until the sea is turned into dry land before us." Moses took his staff and hit the sea, and the sea was turned into dry land, as it is said, "He turned the sea into dry land (Ps. 66:6), and further, But the children of Israel walked on dry land in the midst of the sea" (Ex. 14:29).

Q. Moses said to them, "Get up and pass through."

R. They said to him, "We are not going to pass through until the sea is turned into walls before us." Moses took his staff and hit the sea, and the sea was turned into walls, as it is said, "And the waters were a wall for them on their right hand and on their left" (Ex. 14:29).

S. Moses said to them, "Get up and pass through."

T. They said to him, "We are not going to pass through until the sea [stands up and is] turned into the shape of a bottle before us." Moses took his staff and hit the sea, and the sea was turned into the shape of a bottle, as it is said, "The water stood up right like a bottle containing liquid" (Ex. 15:8).

U. Fire came down and licked up the water between the parts, as it is said, "When fire caused that which melts to disappear, and the fire lapped up the water, to make your name known to your adversaries" (Is. 64:1).

V. And the bottles let out oil and honey into the mouths of infants, and they sucked from them, as it is said, "And he made them suck honey out of the rock" (Deut. 32:13).

W. And some say, "They produced fresh water from the sea and they drank it in the paths,

X. "(for sea water is salty),

Y. "[continuing W] as it is said, 'Flowing streams' (Deut. 32:13), and flowing streams refers only to sweet water, as it is said, 'A well of living water and flowing streams from Lebanon' (Song 4:15)."

The Fathers According to Rabbi Nathan XXXIII:V.1

The examples just now set forth can be duplicated many times over. They embody the fundamental attitudes toward historical time that characterize the Rabbinic literature throughout its formative age (and beyond).

To the past is imputed no autonomy; dividing between past and present no dividing line of any kind is conceived. Transcending the mere flaws of anachronism, the conception that time past and time present flow together yields the principle that events may be ordered in accord with a logic quite autonomous of temporal order. The point at which we started forms a fitting conclusion to this brief experiment in the testing of a null-hypothesis. Not only do we find not a trace of historical thinking, as that mode of thought is defined in the Hebrew Scriptures. We find expressions of a quite different mode of thought altogether.

III. HOW ARE EVENTS TREATED, IF NOT AS UNIQUE INDICATORS OF THE MOVEMENT OF HISTORY? PATTERNING EVENTS. MISHNAH-TRACTATE TA'ANIT 4:6–7

The Aggadic formulation of the premises of Rabbinic Judaism concerning time finds its counterpart in the disposition of events by the Halakhah. Stated in a few words: events were classified and hierarchized by their classes. They were interpreted as paradigms not as singular events, exemplary not unique. The Mishnah's sages surely mourned for the destruction and the loss of Israel's principal mode of worship, and certainly responded to the event of the ninth of Ab in the year 70. But in the Mishnah they did so in their characteristic way: they listed the event as an item in a catalogue of things that are like one another and so demand similar responses. Then the destruction no longer appears as a unique event. It is absorbed into a pattern of like disasters, all exhibiting similar taxonomic traits, events to which the people, now well-schooled in tragedy, knows full well the appropriate response. History yields rules, just as nature does, just as the Torah does. The work of regularization and ordering was not to be abandoned in the face of catastrophe, it was, rather, to be intensified and renewed.

So it is in demonstrating regularity that the sages reveal their way of coping. Then the uniqueness of the event fades away, its mundane character is emphasized. The power of taxonomy in imposing order upon chaos once more does its healing work. The consequence was reassurance that historical events obeyed discoverable laws. In this way Israel's ongoing life would override disruptive, one-time happenings. So catalogues of events, as much as lists of species of melons, served as brilliant apologetic by providing reassurance that nothing lies beyond the range and power of an ordering system and a stabilizing pattern. Here is yet another way in which the irregular was made regular, orderly, and subject to rules:

2. TIME: "Considerations of Temporal Priority or Posteriority Do Not Enter into the Torah"

Mishnah-tractate Ta'anit 4:6–7

M. 4:6

Five events took place for our fathers on the seventeenth of Tammuz, and five on the ninth of Ab.

On the seventeenth of Tammuz

(1) the tablets [of the Torah] were broken,
(2) the daily whole offering was cancelled,
(3) the city wall was breached,
(4) Apostemos burned the Torah, and
(5) he set up an idol in the Temple.

On the ninth of Ab

(1) the decree was made against our forefathers that they should not enter the land,
(2) the first Temple,
(3) the second [Temple] were destroyed,
(4) Betar was taken,
(5) the city was ploughed up [after the war against Emperor Hadrian led by Bar Kokhba, 132–135].

When Ab comes, rejoicing diminishes.

I include M. Ta'anit 4:7 to show the context in which the list of M. 4:6 stands.

M. 4:7

In the week in which the ninth of Ab occurs it is prohibited to get a haircut and to wash one's clothes. But on Thursday of that week these are permitted, because of the honor due to the Sabbath.

On the eve of the ninth of Ab person should not eat two prepared dishes, nor should one eat meat or drink wine.

The calamities catalogued in the list form groups, reveal common traits, so they are subject to classification. Then the laws (M. 4:7) provide regular rules for responding to and coping with these untimely catastrophes, all (fortuitously) in a single classification. So the raw materials of history are absorbed into the ahistorical, supernatural system of the Mishnah. The process of absorption and regularization of the unique and one-time moment is well illustrated in this passage from Ta'anit. The Mishnah's statement of the Halakhah is timeless and transcends change. The Halakhah regularizes the occasional and systematizes the episodic.

The Torah leaves no doubt that it is through historical events that Israel lives in the cosmic political context defined by God. The character of the events — what makes them eventful — is their grounding in issues of salvation: salvation from Egyptian bondage, salvation for restoration to the condition of Eden realized in the Land — the whole prefiguring salvation from the grave and entry into life eternal. The narrative of the Torah defines God's actions in terms of Israel's relationship to the Land, so history consists of chapters in that parlous connection. History recapitulates Israel's relationship to the Land, abandoned, recovered, lost, and restored.

It is the way of the Mishnah to respond to the Torah by regularizing the irregular. But these axial events, by their nature, cannot be regularized by the law of the Mishnah. They are one-time, to be remembered and memorialized, they are not accessible of everyday reenactment. On the negative side, then, they can define no topic for a tractate. That is because, as a matter of definition, world-historical happenings defy ordering. They disrupt the timeless serenity of everyday life and its orderly transactions of sanctification through purification. That is what marks such events as eventful: as history-making. The law of the Mishnah provides for the regular, orderly, predictable, reliable life of the Temple with its penumbra of sanctification encompassing the secure life of the Israelite household. But that life was lived above the serrated surface of history, with its irregular, disorderly, never-certain consequences for the Israelite social order.

Awaiting salvation, anticipating restoration, the Mishnah's framers could not ignore disruptive history. They formed the earliest generations after events of millennial consequence, whether viewed backward or (as we now know) forward. The loss of Jerusalem, confirmed in 135, defined the context of the Rabbinic sages' work. They had no reason to anticipate the near-term restoration of the sacrificial system that had functioned for many centuries and had defined Israel's service of God: the medium for atonement.

But momentous happenings express God's will — so the prophets, including Moses in the Torah, made clear — and therefore events define God's context for Israel. The law of the Mishnah could not ignore history. The issue for the Mishnah was how to process the consequential facts of history. Here, the sages embraced Scripture's convictions [1] that God has a plan for humanity, [2] that history has a purpose, and [3] that history leads to a foreordained conclusion, the coming of a Messiah at the end of days. Accordingly, salvation, not sanctification alone, presented to the sages of the Mishnah a program of inquiry. The high priest on the Day of Atonement, bringing about the sanctification of Israel through the atonement for sins effected by the rite and by the Day of Atonement itself, ministered through

2. TIME: "Considerations of Temporal Priority or Posteriority Do Not Enter into the Torah"

time without boundary, so long as history did not intervene. But history did intervene: the Temple was destroyed, its rites were abandoned.

IV. HISTORY IN THE TORAH AND IN THE MISHNAH

We may now generalize on the case of M. Ta. 4:6–7. In the Torah events bear unique meaning and deliver God's message and judgment. Every event, seen as singular, must be interpreted in its own terms, as significant in itself. What happens when God intervenes is identified as consequential, an event to be noted. The one-time event thus points toward lessons to be drawn for where things are heading and why. Events, being unique, do not conform to prior patterns. They however do *form* patterns. That pattern is preserved through the narrative of what has happened, and prophets and sages interpret the meaning of events, discern the pattern that events define.

So the writing of history served as a form or method of understanding prophecy, an applied theology. Just as prophecy takes up the interpretation of historical events, so historians retell these events in the framework of the prophetic theses. And out of the two—history-writing as a mode of reflection, prophecy as a means of theological construction—emerged a picture of future history, that is, what is going to happen. In short, history consists of a sequence of one-time events, each of them singular, all of them meaningful. These events move from a beginning somewhere to an end at a foreordained goal. History moves toward the end of history—the teleology of the narrative.

The Mishnah sets forth a system of thought that does not appeal to history as a sequence of one-time events, each of which bears meaning on its own. Rather, as we saw in the case of M. Ta. 4:6–7, the Mishnah seeks patterns. It undertakes to classify and hierarchize events, to discover not what marks them as unique but what they have in common. The framers of the Mishnah explicitly refer to very few events, treating those they do mention within a focus quite separate from what happened—the unfolding of the events themselves. They rarely create sustained narratives. More probative still, historical events do not supply organizing categories or taxonomic classifications. That is shown at M. Ta. 4:6–7, cited just now. We find no tractate devoted to the destruction of the Temple, no complete chapter detailing the events of Bar Kokhba, nor even a sustained celebration of the events of the sages' own historical life, biography for instance. These are matters alluded to episodically in the Mishnah, not foci of systematic analysis.

When things that have happened are mentioned, it is neither in order to narrate nor to interpret and draw lessons from the event. It is either to illustrate a point of law or to pose a problem of the law—always *en passant*, never in a pointed way. So when the sages refer to what has happened, this is casual, tangential to the main thrust of discourse. One example suffices. Famous events of enduring meaning, such as the return to Zion from Babylonia in the time of Ezra and Nehemiah, gain entry into the Mishnah's discourse only because of the genealogical divisions of Israelite society into castes among the immigrants (M. Qiddushin 4:1).

Moreover, where the Mishnah provides little tales or narratives, they more often treat how things in the cult are done in general rather than what in particular happened on some one day. It is sufficient to refer casually to well-known incidents. Narrative, in the Mishnah's limited rhetorical repertoire, is reserved for the narrow framework of what priests and others do on recurrent occasions and around the Temple. That staple of history, stories about dramatic events and important deeds, in the minds of the Mishnah's jurisprudents provide little nourishment. Events, if they appear at all, are treated as trivial. They may be well-known, but are consequential in some way other than is revealed in the detailed account of what actually happened.

The Mishnah's legal system is set forth outside of all historical framework. Considerations of priority and posteriority do not figure. Viewed whole, the Mishnah proper (in the sixty-two Halakhic tractates, omitting reference to tractate Abot) contains no story of its origin and authority; that story was left to one small tractate, Abot, to tell, and then in its own unusual way. Compare the Pentateuch's presentation of its law. The law codes of Exodus and Deuteronomy are set forth in a narrative framework, and the priestly code of Leviticus, for its part, appeals to God's revelation to Moses and Aaron at specific times and places. In the Mishnah we have neither narrative nor setting for the representation of law. The Mishnah admits no sustaining story, recognizes no before or after, begins in no particular locale and ends in middle of a legal exposition. And no narrative logic governs the ordering of its topics.

Instead of narrative, which as in Exodus spills over into case-law, the Mishnah gives an atemporal description of how things are done in general and universally, that is, it supplies out-of-specific context strictly descriptive cases. These are not episodic or anecdotal cases, but they form patterns that yield laws. Instead of reflection on the meaning and end of history, it constructs a world in which history plays little part. Instead of narratives full of didactic meaning, the Mishnah's authorship provides lists of events

2. TIME: "Considerations of Temporal Priority or Posteriority Do Not Enter into the Torah"

so as to expose the traits that they share and thus the rules to which they conform. The definitive components of a historical system of Judaism yielding a theory of the end of history and its goal are not set forth in the Mishnah. The law of the Mishnah rarely resorts to the description of events as one time happenings, to analysis of the meaning and end of events, and to interpretation of the end and future of singular events.

Then, how does history come to full conceptual expression in the Mishnah? History as an account of a meaningful pattern of events, making sense of the past and giving guidance about the future, begins with the necessary conviction that events matter because they form series, one after another. And when we put a series together, we have a rule—just as when we put cases together, we can demonstrate the rule that governs them all. The Mishnah's authors therefore dispose of historical events just as they sort out the traits of clay pots or the regularities of anything else of interest—the correct composition of contracts, the appropriate disposition of property, proper conduct on a holy day. The upshot is, all things imputed to specific events —exemplary anecdotes and concrete transactions, illustrative cases —are formed so that we can derive, out of the concrete, the abstract and encompassing rule.

That is why we may not find surprising the Mishnah's framers' reluctance to present us with an elaborate theory of events, a fact fully consonant with their systematic points of insistence and encompassing concern. Events do not matter, one by one. The Mishnah's philosopher-lawyers exhibited no theory of history either. Their conception of Israel's destiny in no way called upon historical categories of either narrative or didactic explanation to describe and account for the future. The small importance attributed to the figure of a Messiah as an historical-eschatological figure, therefore, fully accords with the larger traits of the system as a whole. If what is important in Israel's existence is sanctification, an ongoing process, and not salvation, a one-time event at the end, then no one will find reason to narrate history.

V. HOW THE MISHNAH CONFIGURES ISRAEL IN THE CONTEXT OF HISTORY DEFINED BY GOD. HOW THE DESTRUCTION OF THE TEMPLE FIGURES IN MISHNAH-TRACTATE ROSH HASHANAH 4:1–3

The Mishnah's system may be ahistorical and indifferent to temporal considerations, but concluding that it is non-historical or anti-historical could not be more mistaken. The Mishnah presents events in a different way, producing a different kind of history. Specifically, it revises the inherited conception of history and reshapes that conception to fit into its own system. Since the greatest event in the century-and-a-half, from ca. 50 to ca. 200, in which the Mishnah's materials came into being, was the destruction of the Temple in the year 70, we must expect the Mishnah's treatment of that incident to illustrate the document's larger theory of history: what is important and unimportant about what happens.

The destruction of the Temple thus constitutes a noteworthy fact in the history of the law, because various laws about rite and cult had to undergo revision on account of the destruction. The following provides a stunningly apt example of how the Mishnah regards what actually happened as simply marking changes in the law.

> The festival day of the New Year which coincided with the Sabbath — in the Temple they would sound the *shofar*.
> But not in the provinces.
> When the Temple was destroyed, Rabban Yohanan ben Zakkai made the rule that they should sound the *shofar* in every locale in which there was a court.
> Said R. Eleazar, "Rabban Yohanan b. Zakkai made that rule only in the case of Yabneh alone."
> They said to him, "All the same are Yabneh and every locale in which there is a court.
>
> *Mishnah-tractate Rosh Hashanah 4:1–3*

The Halakhic issue, predictably, concerns the hierarchical comparison of Jerusalem and Yabneh, the locus of Yohanan ben Zakkai's circle of disciples, continuators of the oral tradition. So in this version of matters, the center of Torah-study forms the counterpart to the center of divine service through sacrifice. Placed on a continuum with Jerusalem, Yabneh served as the embodiment of the tradition of Sinai, the activities of learning carried on there as the continuation of the divine service now suspended — an amazing claim.

It is continued in the following language:

> And in this regard also was Jerusalem ahead of Yabneh:
> in every town which is within sight and sound [of Jerusalem], and nearby and able to come up to Jerusalem, they sound the *shofar*.
> But as to Yabneh, they sound the *shofar* only in the court alone.

What about rites formerly carried on only in the Temple? The issue of how these are adjusted to the new age is raised in the following:

2. TIME: "Considerations of Temporal Priority or Posteriority Do Not Enter into the Torah"

> In olden times the *lulab* was taken up in the Temple for seven days, and in the provinces, for one day.
>
> When the Temple was destroyed, Rabban Yohanan ben Zakkai made the rule that in the provinces the *lulab* should be taken up for seven days, as a memorial to the Temple;
>
> and that the day [the sixteenth of Nisan] on which the *omer* is waved should be wholly prohibited [in regard to the eating of new produce] [M. Suk. 3:12].

The point is, the loss of the Temple requires adjustments in the rites, but does not justify dropping them altogether.

What we see is that the destruction of the Temple in the law of the Mishnah is recognized and treated as consequential — but only for the organization of rules. The event forms division between one time and some other, and, in consequence, we sort out rules pertaining to the Temple and synagogue in one way rather than in another. What we perceive is the opposite of an interest in focusing upon the one-time meaning of events. Now it is the all-time significance of events in the making of rules. Events are treated not as irregular and intrinsically consequential but as regular and merely instrumental.

VI. PATTERNING THE HISTORY OF THE SACRIFICIAL CULT: MISHNAH-TRACTATE ZEBAHIM 14:4–10

A still more striking example of the reordering of one-time events into all-time patterns derives from the effort to put together in a coherent way the rather haphazard facts that form the history of the cult as that history is inherited from the Torah, with sacrifices made here and there and finally in Jerusalem. Now, the entire history of the cult, so critical in the larger system created by the Mishnah's lawyers, produced a patterned, sensible and intelligible picture. This is, we now realize, typical of their disposition of events. Everything that happened turned out to be susceptible of classification once the taxonomic traits were specified. An exercise in sorting out periods and their characteristics took the place of narrative, to explain things in its own way: first this, and then that, and, in consequence, the other.

Everything was absorbed into one thing — all classified in its proper place and by its appropriate rule. Indeed, so far as the Mishnah's lawyers proposed to write history at all, they wrote it into their picture of the long tale of the way in which Israel served God: the places in which the sacrificial labor was carried on, the people who did it, the places in which the priests ate the meat left over for their portion after God's portion was set aside and burned up. This "historical" account forthwith generated precisely that problem of locating the regular and orderly that the philosophers loved to investigate: what happens when a given set of cases is governed by two distinct rules, so that we do not know how to classify the cases? We see the intersection of conflicting but equally correct, taxonomic rules in this passage from M. Zebahim. The passage is history, so far as the Mishnah's creators proposed to write history: finding meaning in the reduction of events to rules that form compositions of regularity.

I reproduce the entire exposition, even though it is of formidable length, because that is the only way for the reader to see the full extent of the pattern that is adumbrated. A single example will not serve, when centuries of history are reduced to a few taxic indicators, realized in a tiny repertoire of concrete actions; the whole then differentiated by whether or not a given action pertains to a given circumstance. What we have is a triumph of that process of ordering and regularization that transforms the chaos of the everyday into the patterned construction that the Mishnah's law seeks to bring into being.

Mishnah-tractate Zebahim 14:4–9

M. 14:4

Before the tabernacle was set up, (1) the high places were permitted, and (2) [the sacrificial] service [was done by] the firstborn [Num. 3:12–12, 8:16–18].

When the tabernacle was set up, (1) the high places were prohibited, and (2) the [sacrificial] service [was done by] priests.

Most Holy Things were eaten within the veils, Lesser Holy Things [were eaten] throughout the camp of Israel.

M. 14:5

They came to Gilgal.
The high places were prohibited.
Most Holy Things were eaten within the veils, Lesser Holy Things, anywhere.

M. 14:6

They came to Shiloh.
The high places were prohibited.
(1) There was no roof-beam there, but below was a house of stone, and hangings above it, and (2) it was 'the resting place' [Deut. 12:9].
Most Holy Things were eaten within the veils, Lesser Holy Things and second-tithe [were eaten] in any place within sight [of Shiloh].

2. TIME: "Considerations of Temporal Priority or Posteriority Do Not Enter into the Torah"

M. 14:7

They came to Nob and Gibeon.
The high places were permitted.
Most Holy Things were eaten within the veils, Lesser Holy Things, in all the towns of Israel.

M. 14:8

They came to Jerusalem.
The high places were prohibited.
And they never again were permitted.
And it was 'the inheritance' [Deut. 12:9].
Most Holy Things were eaten within the veils, Lesser Holy Things and second-tithe within the wall.

M. 14:9

All the Holy Things which one sanctified at the time of the prohibition of the high places and offered at the time of the prohibition of high places outside —
lo, these are subject to the transgression of a positive commandment and a negative commandment, and they are liable on their account to extirpation [for sacrificing outside the designated place, Lev. 17:8–9].

[If] one sanctified them at the time of the permission of high places and offered them up at the time of the prohibition of high places,
lo, these are subject to transgression of a positive commandment and to a negative commandment, but they are not liable on their account to extirpation [since if the offerings had been sacrificed when they were sanctified, there should have been no violation].

[If] one sanctified them at the time of the prohibition of high places and offered them up at the time of the permission of high places,
lo, these are subject to transgression of a positive commandment, but they are not subject to a negative commandment at all.

M. 14:10

These are the Holy Things offered in the tabernacle [of Gilgal, Nob, and Gibeon]:
Holy Things which were sanctified for the tabernacle.
Offerings of the congregation are offered in the tabernacle.
Offerings of the individual [are offered] on a high place.
Offerings of the individual which were sanctified for the tabernacle are to be offered in the tabernacle.
And if one offered them up on a high place, he is free.
What is the difference between the high place of an individual and the high place of the community?
(1) Laying on of hands, and (2) slaughtering at the north [of the altar], and (3) placing [of the blood] round about [the altar], and (4) waving, and (5) bring near.
R. Judah says, "there is no meal-offering on a high place [but there is in the tabernacle]" —

and (1) the priestly service, and (2) the wearing of garments of ministry, and (3) the use of utensils of ministry, and (4) the sweet-smelling savor and (5) the dividing line for the [tossing of various kinds of] blood, and (6) the rule concerning the washing of hands and feet.

But the matters of time, and remnant, and uncleanness are applicable both here and there [by contrast to M. 14:3F-I].

All possible cases are dealt with. A few comments suffice to highlight the pattern that imparts coherence and rationality to the particular rules.

In the first case, both sanctification and offering up take place at the time that prohibition of high places applies. There is transgression of a positive commandment and a negative commandment. The negative is Deuteronomy 12:13, the positive is Deuteronomy 12:14: "Take heed that you do not offer your burnt-offerings at every place that you see; but at the place which the Lord will choose in one of your tribes, there you shall offer your burnt-offerings..." The mixtures (M. 14:9) then go over the same ground. If sanctification takes place when it is permitted to sanctify animals for use in high places, but the offering up takes place when it is not allowed to do so (that is, the former for M. 14:4, the latter for M. 14:6), then extirpation does not apply (Lev. 17:5–7). When we reverse the order (as at M. 14:6 and M. 14:7) there is no negative (Deut. 12:13), but the positive commandment (Deut. 12:14) has been transgressed. However, matters do not stop there. The rule-making out of the raw materials of disorderly history continues unabated.

The inclusion of Mishnah Zebahim 14:9, structurally matching Mishnah Ta'anit 4:7, shows us the goal of the historical composition. It is to set forth in a system and pattern the rules that intersect and otherwise produce confusion. The typology may now be stated briefly. The authorship at hand had the option of narrative, but chose the way of natural philosophy: generalization through classification, comparison and contrast.

The Mishnah thus absorbs into its encompassing system all events, small and large, that it deems consequential. With what happens the sages accomplish what they do with is, that is, with everything else: an immense construction of the order and rules governing the classification of everything on earth and in Heaven. One-time events of ineluctable significance scarcely impress the Mishnah. The authors find no difficulty in showing that what appears unique and beyond classification has in fact happened before and so falls within the range of trustworthy rules and known procedures. Once history's components, one-time events, lose their distinctiveness, then history as a didactic intellectual construct, as a source of lessons and rules, also loses all pertinence. Instead, lessons and rules come from sorting things out and classifying them, that is, from the procedures and modes of thought of the philosopher seeking regularity.

For this labor of taxonomy, the historian's way of selecting data and arranging them into unique patterns of meaning to teach lessons beyond their own limits proves inconsequential. One-time events are not what matters. The world is composed of nature and supernature. The repetitious laws that count are those to be discovered in Heaven and, in Heaven's creation and counterpart, on earth. Keep those laws and things will work out. Break them and the result is predictable: calamity of whatever sort will supervene in accordance with the rules. But precisely because it is predictable, a catastrophic happening testifies to what has always been and must always be, in accordance with reliable rules and within categories already discovered and well explained.

The sages possessed not an anti-historical conception of reality but a deeply historical one, even though it is a different conception of the meaning of history—the study of the rules of the social order—not historical in the traditional sense of history-writing. For history-writing, what is important is to describe the unique and the individual, not what is ongoing and unremarkable. That explains the requirement of narrative: histories are the story of change, development, movement, not of what does not change, develop, or move. For the thinkers of the Mishnah, historical patterning emerges as today scientific knowledge does, through the classification, the ordering by rule of the unique and individual. Learning proceeds through the organization of change and movement within unchanging categories.

VII. A MESSIAH IN THE MISHNAH: MISHNAH-TRACTATE SOTAH CHAPTER NINE

The Mishnah's framers found it possible to present a statement of goals for their system entirely separate from appeals to history and eschatology, the theory of the end of days and the end of history. Theirs was a teleology without an eschatological dimension thereof. They would restore and renew Eden — the opposite of an eschatological teleology. Time and change, accordingly, took a subordinated role to enduring patterns, built upon the sanctification of Israel.

Since the Mishnah's sages certainly knew and even alluded to long-standing and widely held convictions on eschatological subjects, they from time to time utilized the language Messiah and Messianic. In the Mishnah the words "the" and "Messiah" violate the rules of semantics. "Messiah" referred to a classification of priest, for example, a Messiah anointed for war. There were several classifications of Messiahs, and any number of representatives within those classifications. Messiahs played a part. But these "anointed men" had no historical role. They undertook a task quite different from that assigned to Jesus by the framers of the Gospels. They were merely a species of priest, falling into one classification rather than another.

What if, then, we ask the Mishnah to answer the questions what of a Messiah; when will he come; to whom, in Israel, will he come; and what must, or can, Israelites do while waiting in order to hasten his coming? To these questions we find no answers. Answering these questions out of the resources of the Mishnah is not possible. As we saw in Rosh Hashanah, Ta'anit, and Zebahim, the Mishnah presents no large view of history. It contains no reflection whatever on the nature and meaning of the destruction of the Temple in 70 C.E., an event that surfaces only in connection with some changes in the law explained as resulting from the end of the cult. The Mishnah pays no attention to the matter of the end time. The word "salvation" is rare, but "sanctification" with its synonyms and antonyms (unfit, unclean) is commonplace.

In one of its few historical-narrative passages, the Mishnah sets forth the decline of generations, in which the destruction of the Temple and the death of great sages mark the movement of time and impart to an age the general rules that govern life therein. Here is how the Messiah-theme is treated by the Mishnah within an explicitly eschatological framework. The decline of generations leaves no choice but salvation through divine intervention:

> When R. Meir died, makers of parables came to an end.
> When Ben Azzai died, diligent students came to an end.
> When Ben Zoma died, exegetes came to an end.
> When R. Joshua died, goodness went away from the world.
> When Rabban Simeon b. Gamaliel died, the locust came, and troubles multiplied.
> When Eleazar b. Azariah died, wealth went away from the sages.
> When R. Aqiba died, the glory of the Torah came to an end.
> When R. Hanina b. Dosa died, wonder-workers came to an end.
> When R. Yosé Qatnuta died, pietists went away.

2. TIME: "Considerations of Temporal Priority or Posteriority Do Not Enter into the Torah"

When Rabban Yohanan b. Zakkai died, the splendor of wisdom came to an end.

When Rabban Gamaliel the Elder died, the glory of the Torah came to an end, and cleanness and separateness perished.

When R. Ishmael b. Phabi died, the splendor of the priesthood came to an end.

When Rabbi died, modesty and fear of sin came to an end.

R. Pinhas b. Yair says, "When the Temple was destroyed, associates became ashamed and so did free men, and they covered their heads.

"And wonder-workers became feeble. And violent men and big takers grew strong.

"And none expounds and none seeks [learning] and none asks.

"Upon whom shall we depend? Upon our Father in heaven."

R. Eliezer the Great says, "From the day on which the Temple was destroyed, sages began to be like scribes, and scribes like ministers, and ministers like ordinary folk.

"And the ordinary folk have become feeble.

"And none seeks.

"Upon whom shall we depend? Upon our Father in heaven."

With the footprints of the Messiah: presumption increases, and dearth increases.

The vine gives its fruit and wine at great cost.

And the government turns to heresy.

And there is no reproof.

The gathering place will be for prostitution.

And Galilee will be laid waste.

And the Gablan will be made desolate.

And the men of the frontier will go about from town to town, and none will take pity on them.

And the wisdom of scribes will putrefy.

And those who fear sin will be rejected.

And the truth will be locked away.

Children will shame elders, and elders will stand up before children.

For the son dishonors the father and the daughter rises up against her mother, the daughter-in-law against her mother-in-law; a man's enemies are the men of his own house" (Mic. 7:6).

The face of the generation in the face of a dog.

A son is not ashamed before his father.

Upon whom shall we depend? Upon our Father in heaven.

R. Pinhas b. Yair says, "Heedfulness leads to cleanliness, cleanliness leads to cleanness, cleanness leads to abstinence, abstinence leads to holiness, holiness leads to modesty, modesty leads to the fear of sin, the fear of sin leads to piety, piety leads to the Holy Spirit, the Holy Spirit leads to the resurrection of the dead, and the resurrection of the dead comes through Elijah, blessed be his memory, Amen."

Mishnah-tractate Sotah 9:15

What we learn from this elegy including its supplementary composition is that the Messiah-theme in the Mishnah does not stand at the forefront of the framers' consciousness. The framers of the Mishnah do not resort to speculation about a Messiah as a historical-supernatural figure. So far as that kind of speculation provides the vehicle for reflection on salvific issues or — in mythic terms — narratives on the meaning of history and the destiny of Israel, we cannot say that the Mishnah's philosophers take up those encompassing categories of being: Where are we heading? What can we do about it? That does not mean that questions found urgent in the aftermath of the destruction of the Temple and the disaster of Bar Kokhba failed to attract the attention of the Mishnah's sages. But they treated history in a different way, offering their own answers to its questions. So lessons and rules come from sorting things out and classifying them from the procedures and modes of thought of the philosopher seeking regularity.

3.
SPACE:
The land of Israel is holier than all lands

I. THE LOCATIVE DIMENSION

The Halakhah states concerning sacred space in so many words what it wants to know, which is, whether [1] the destruction of the Temple and cessation of the offerings, [2] the degradation of the Land of Israel, and [3] the exile of the holy people, Israel, from the Holy Land, affect the rules of sustenance in the model of the nourishment of God in the Temple, in the Land, among the holy people. The answer is, whatever the condition of the Temple and its altar, whatever the source — the Holy Land or unclean gentile lands — of sacrificial animals, and whatever the location of Israel the people, whether enlandised or not, one thing persists. The sanctification of Israel the people endures [1] in the absence of the cult and [2] in alien, unclean territory and [3] whatever the source of the food that Israel eats. Israel's sanctity is eternal, un-contingent, absolute. The sanctification that inheres in Israel, the people, transcends the Land and outlives the Temple and its cult. Since the sanctity of Israel, the people, persists beyond the Temple and outside of the Land, that sanctity stands at a higher point in the hierarchy of domains of the holy that ascend from earth to heaven and from Man to God.

How are we asked to hear that remarkable statement? The Halakhah to make its statement about the eternal sanctification of the people, Israel, explicitly responds to three facts: [1] Israelites live not only in the holy land but abroad, in unclean land; [2] the Temple in Jerusalem has been destroyed; [3] and, consequently, animals are slaughtered not only in the Temple in the holy Land but in unconsecrated space and abroad, and the meat is eaten not only in a cultic but in a profane circumstance. Anyone who wonders whether the Halakhah that applied to the Temple and the home when the Temple was standing and Israel was in the Land of Israel continues to apply with the Temple in ruins and Israel in exile here finds his answer. Although the sanctity of the Temple altar stands in abeyance, the sanctity of the Israelite table persists; although Israel is in exile from the Holy Land, Israel remains holy; although in the Temple rules of uncleanness are not now kept, they continue in force where they can be. Birds and animals that flourish outside of the Land when prepared for the Israelite table are regulated by the same rules that apply in the Land and even (where relevant) at the altar. So Israel, the people, not only retains sanctity but preserves it outside of the Land, and the sanctity of Israel transcends that of the Temple and its altar.

It is not difficult to take the measure of space, the locative dimension of Rabbinic Judaism. Space is measured in a hierarchy of locations. I cite the Mishnah in bold face type and the complementary Tosefta in regular type.

M. Kelim 1:6–9

M. Kelim 1:6 There are ten [degrees or levels of] holiness: (1) The land of Israel is holier than all lands. And what is its holiness? For they bring from it the omer, and the first fruits, and the Two Loaves, which they do not bring (thus) from all lands.
Tosefta Kelim B.M. 1:5 In three ways is Syria [subject to the same legal status] as the Land of Israel, and in three [ways is Syria subject to the same legal status] as foreign territory. Its dirt imparts uncleanness as [does dirt of] foreign territory. And he who brings a writ of divorce from Syria is like one who brings [a writ of divorce] from foreign territory. And he who sells his slave to [purchaser in] Syria is like him who sells [a slave] to [a purchaser] in foreign territory. [In] three [ways is Syria subject] to [the same legal status as] the Land of Israel, for he who purchases a field in Syria is like one who purchases [a field] in the suburbs of Jerusalem. And it [produce grown in Syria] is liable for tithes and for [the observance of] the Seventh Year. And if one can bring [something] into it in a state of cleanness, it remains in a state of cleanness.
M. Kelim 1:7 (2) The cities surrounded by a wall are more holy than it [the land]. For they send from them the lepers, and they carry around in their midst a corpse so long as they like. [But once] it has gone forth, they do not bring it back.
M. Kelim 1:8 (3) Space within the wall [of Jerusalem] is more holy than they For they eat there lesser sanctities and second tithe. (4) The Temple mount is more holy than it. For Zabim, and Zabot, menstruating women, and those that have given birth do not enter there. (5) The rampart is more holy than it. For gentiles and he who is made unclean by a corpse do not enter there. (6) The court of women is more holy than it. For a tebul-yom does not enter there, but they are not liable on its account for a sin offering. (7) The court of Israel is more holy than it. For one who [yet] lacks atonement [offerings made in the completion of his purification rite] does not enter there, and they are liable on its account for a sin offering. (8) The court of the priests is more holy than it. For Israelite(s) do not enter there except in the time of their cultic requirements: for laying on of hands, for slaughtering, and for waving.

3. SPACE: The land of Israel is holier than all lands

Tosefta Kelim B.M. 1:8 [If] lepers enter [the area] beyond the wall, they incur forty stripes. [If] *Zabin* and *Zabot*, menstruating women, and women unclean by reason of childbirth enter the Temple mount, they incur eighty stripes. One who is unclean by reason of corpse-uncleanness enters the Temple mount, and not one unclean by corpse-uncleanness alone have they said, but even the corpse itself, as it is said, "And Moses took the bones of Joseph with him" — with him into the camp of the Levites.

Kelim B.M. 1:9 The entire court is suitable for eating Most Holy Things and for slaughtering Lesser Holy Things. He who slaughters unconsecrated [animals] therein — they [the animals] are prohibited for [his] use. It was the courtyard of the tent within the veils which were in the wilderness.

M. KELIM 1:9 (9) [The area] between the porch and the altar is more holy than it. For those [priests] who are blemished or whose hair is unloosed do not enter there. (10) The sanctuary is more holy than it. For [a priest] whose hands and feet are not washed does not enter there. (11) The Holy of Holies is more holy than they. For only the high priest on the Day of Atonement at the time of the service enters there.

Tosefta Kelim B.M. 1:10 All unclean people who entered [the area] from Nicanor's Gate and inward, even if they have not yet completed atonement, lo, they are liable, [if they did so] deliberately, for extirpation, and, [if they did so] inadvertently, for a sin-offering. And one does not have to say [that the same rule applies to] those who have immersed and await sunset [the Tebul Yom]. And as to all other unclean people who entered beyond their limits, lo, they are subject to warning. [If] they entered into the holy place, lo, they are liable to the death penalty.

Tosefta Kelim B.M. 1:11 All enter to build and to repair [the Temple building] and to remove uncleanness. [If] it is the duty for priests [to carry out the dead, and if] there are no priests there, Levites enter. [If] there are no Levites, Israelites enter. [If] it is the duty for clean people [to carry out and if] there are not clean people there, unclean people enter. [If] it is the duty of unblemished [people] [and if] there are no unblemished people, blemished people enter in. And so it says, "And the priests entered the house to purify it and they brought out all the uncleanness."

Tosefta Kelim B.M. 1:12 And just as in the wilderness were three camps, the camp of the Indwelling Presence of God, the camp of the Levites, and the camp of the Israelites, so there were in Jerusalem [three camps]: From the gate of Jerusalem to the gate of the Temple Mount is the camp of Israel. From the gate of the Temple Mount up to Nicanor's gate is the camp of the Levites. From the Nicanor's gate and inward is the camp of the Indwelling Presence of God. And that [corresponded to the place within] the curtains in the wilderness. In the time of journeying, no aspect of sanctity applied lo them, and people were not liable concerning them on account of uncleanness.

The Halakhah with its capacity for not only classification but, consequently, also for hierarchization, does not treat as an all-or-nothing proposition either sanctification or cultic cleanness. That is the advantage of seeing all things as matters of degree, location within a continuum. In the present case, the Halakhah works out in detail the general theory of the gradations of sanctification matched by those of uncleanness. We can understand the Halakhah of Hullin only within the nurturing context of the general theory of sanctification, spatial (locative), temporal, and circumstantial, involving answers to the questions of where, when, and whom. We can grasp what is at stake in Hullin only when we turn for a brief survey to other exercises of hierarchical classification with special reference to sanctification and consequent sanctity. The exercise works itself out by saying the same thing twice in connection with opposites, first, sanctification, then, uncleanness, hierarchizing each, matching the one with the other. The statement is framed in locative terms.

First comes spaces, the one holier than the other. M. Kel. 1:6–9 spells out the hierarchy of sanctification in locative terms, as follows: There are ten degrees of holiness: (1) The land of Israel is holier than all lands. And what is its holiness? For they bring from it the omer, and the firstfruits, and the Two Loaves, which they do not bring (thus) from all lands. (2) The cities surrounded by a wall are more holy than it the land. For they send from them the lepers, and they carry around in their midst a corpse so long as they like. But once it has gone forth, they do not bring it back. (3) Within the wall of Jerusalem is more holy than they For they eat there lesser sanctities and second tithe. (4) The Temple mount is more holy than it. For Zabim, and Zabot, menstruating women, and those that have given birth do not enter there. (5) The rampart is more holy than it. For gentiles and he who is made unclean by a corpse do not enter there. (6) The court of women is more holy than it. For a tebul-yom does not enter there, but they are not liable on its account for a sin offering. (7) The court of Israel is more holy than it. For one who yet lacks atonement offerings made in the completion of his purification rite does not enter there, and they are liable on its account for a sin offering. (8) The court of the priests is more holy than it. For Israelite(s) do not enter there except in the time of their cultic requirements: for laying on of hands, for slaughtering, and for waving. (9) The area between the porch and the altar is more holy than it. For those priests who are blemished or whose hair is unloosed do not enter there. (10) The sanctuary is more holy than it. For a priest whose hands and feet are not washed does not enter there. (11) The Holy of Holies is more holy than they. For only the high priest on the Day of Atonement at the time of the service enters there.

We address the opposite of sanctification, which is, cultic contamination of uncleanness. What is more holy also is more sensitive or susceptible to uncleanness, and what is less holy is less susceptible. So we come next to rites of protecting the holy from the unclean, meaning, degrees of susceptibility to the contraction of uncleanness. Gradations of

3. SPACE: The land of Israel is holier than all lands

sanctification matched by a hierarchy of susceptibility to uncleanness is expressed at M. Hag. 2:5ff.: They wash the hands for eating unconsecrated food, tithe, and heave offering; and for eating food in the status of Holy Things they immerse; and as to the preparation of purification water through the burning of the red cowl, if one's hands are made unclean, his entire body is deemed to be unclean as well. He who immerses for the eating of unconsecrated food and is thereby confirmed as suitable for eating unconsecrated food is prohibited from eating tithe. If he immersed for eating tithe and is thereby confirmed as suitable for eating tithe, he is prohibited from eating heave offering. If he immersed for eating heave offering and is thereby confirmed as suitable for eating heave offering, he is prohibited from eating food in the status of Holy Things. If he immersed for eating food in the status of Holy Things and is thereby confirmed as suitable for eating food in the status of Holy Things, he is prohibited from engaging in the preparation of purification water. If, however, one immersed for the matter requiring the more stringent rule, he is permitted to engage in the matter requiring the less stringent rule. If he immersed but was not confirmed, it is as though he did not immerse.

The counterpart to the hierarchy of sanctification involves a hierarchy of the relative virulence — capacity to impart uncleanness — of the various sources of uncleanness, twenty in all, as at M. Kel. 1:1–4: The Fathers of Uncleannesses are (1) the creeping thing, and (2) semen of an adult Israelite, and (3) one who has contracted corpse uncleanness, and (4) the leper in the days of his counting, and (5) sin offering water of insufficient quantity to be sprinkled. Lo, these render man and vessels unclean by contact, and earthenware vessels by presence within the vessels' contained airspace. But they do not render unclean by carrying. Above them: (6) carrion, and (7) sin offering water of sufficient quantity to be sprinkled. For they render man unclean through carrying, to make his clothing unclean. But clothing is not made unclean through contact. Above them: (8) he who has intercourse with a menstruating woman, for he conveys uncleanness to what lies far beneath him in like degree as he conveys uncleanness to what lies above. Above them: (9) the flux of the Zab, and (10) his spittle and (11) his semen and (12) his urine, and (13) the blood of the menstruating woman, for they render unclean through contact and carrying. Above them: (14) the saddle, F for it the saddle is unclean under a heavy stone. Above the saddle: (15) the couch, for touching it is equivalent to carrying it. Above the couch: (16) the Zab, for the Zab conveys uncleanness to the couch, but the couch does not convey equivalent uncleanness to the couch. Above the Zab: (17) the Zabah, for she renders him that has intercourse with her unclean for seven days. Above the Zabah: (18) the leper, for he renders unclean by his coming into a house. Above the leper: (19) a bone about the size of a barley corn, for it renders unclean for a seven days' uncleanness. Weightiest of them all: (20) the corpse, for it renders unclean by overshadowing a mode of rendering uncleanness by which none of the rest conveys uncleanness.

As to the hierarchization of classifications of space, a single example suffices to make the same point, with reference to both the camps in the wilderness and its counterpart, the division of Jerusalem itself:

1:12 A. And just as in the wilderness were three camps, the camp of the Indwelling Presence of God, the camp of the Levites, and the camp of the Israelites, so there were in Jerusalem [three camps]:
B. From the gate of Jerusalem to the gate of the Temple Mount is the camp of Israel.
C. From the gate of the Temple Mount up to Nicanor's gate is the camp of the Levites.
D. From the Nicanor's gate and inward is the camp of the Indwelling Presence of God.
E. And that [corresponded to the place within] the curtains in the wilderness.

But the species of the genus, the camp of Israel, have also to be differentiated from one another, so:

F. In the time of journeying, no aspect of sanctity applied lo them, and people were not liable concerning them on account of uncleanness.

Tosefta Kelim 1:12

Here, then, we see how the Halakhah undertakes the systematic work of hierarchical classification within the category-formations of which the system is comprised.

With these facts in mind, we return to our Halakhah, now reading it in its larger religious and systemic context. How so? When it comes to the preparation of meat, the Halakhah deals with three settings: [1] the Temple, [2] outside of the Temple and holy city the Land of Israel, and [3] foreign land. And for all three, it insists, the same rules pertain, even despite the considerable differences that apply. Since all territory outside of the Land of Israel is by definition unclean, the premise of the Halakhah is that, despite that fact, Israel is to consume its secular meat in accord with those rules of sanctification that pertain to food produced in the Land and its preparation. The laws of cultic cleanness may apply to the household in the Land of Israel but cannot pertain abroad; nonetheless, the other principal admonitions apply overseas. The existence of the Temple or its destruction makes no difference.

3. SPACE: The land of Israel is holier than all lands

Then with the classifications established, how do we accomplish the work of hierarchization? Affirming the unique holiness of the Temple and the Land of Israel, the Halakhah of Hullin wants to show how the holiness of the people Israel retains its own integrity, wherever the people is located, whatever the condition of the Temple and its altar. And that demonstration accomplished, the Halakhah establishes that the sanctity of Israel the people is higher in the hierarchy than the sanctity of the Land and of the Temple and its altar. How is that shown? It is that Israel remains holy even outside of the Land, even in the age without the Temple. That is why meat prepared for Israel, wherever it has itself been nourished, even on gentile ground, must be prepared as though for the altar in Jerusalem. Then Israel's sanctity persists, even when that continuum in which it stood, the chain of continuity with the Temple altar in Jerusalem (as the formulation of Deuteronomy 12:20–24 framed matters), has been disrupted, and Israel's sanctity endows with sanctity even animals raised in unclean ground, so powerful is the sanctification that transforms Israel. The liturgy, stating in its way what the Halakhah sets forth in its manner, explains why, in the Afternoon Worship for the Sabbath: "You are unique and your name is unique, and who is like your people, Israel, a unique people on earth?"

Why turn in particular to the Halakhah of Hullin (secular slaughter) to make that statement that Israel is holier than the Land and than the Temple and endows with sanctity the animals slaughtered to nourish the people? Because the Written Torah supplies a law that contains the entire message, when it imposes the same requirements that pertain to slaughter of an animal sacrifice for the altar in Jerusalem to killing an animal for the use of Israel at home. That means meat Israel eats is subject to the same regulations that apply to meat God receives on the altar-fires. The same law is explicit that meat for those who are not holy, that is, gentile-idolaters, is not subject to the same rules (Ex. 22:30, Dt. 14:21). So the point cannot be missed: food for God and for Israel must be prepared in comparable manner, which does not apply to food for gentiles.

How does that principle affect animals raised abroad? The laws of Hullin apply to them, because the laws apply to unconsecrated animals as much as consecrated ones. The destiny—nourishing Israel—is what counts, that alone. The beast intended for Israelite consumption at the table even in a foreign country must be prepared as though for God on the altar in Jerusalem, and that can only mean, because the beast is intended (by the act of correct slaughter) for Israel, the use of the beast by Israel sanctifies the beast and necessitates conformity with the rules of slaughter for God in the Temple. Israel, even abroad, renders the food that it eats comparable to food for the altar.

What has food-preparation to do with the consideration of location? The rule that permits slaughter of meat outside of the Temple (Dt. 12:20–24) is explicit that that rule speaks of Israel outside of the Temple in Jerusalem. So even if the act of slaughter does not take place in Jerusalem, the act must conform, because the focus is on Israel, wherever Israel is located — even far from Jerusalem, as Scripture states explicitly. The Halakhah before us simply carries to its logical next step that same conception: even so far from Jerusalem as territory that to begin with is laden with corpse-uncleanness, that is, foreign soil; and even in an age in which Jerusalem is no more, and, it goes without saying, even in connection with a beast that has not been consecrated for the altar.

Since Scripture itself has separated the act of slaughter from the rite of sacrifice in the Temple, the Oral Torah has done little more than explore the consequences of that rule when it states that the requirements of slaughter in the cult pertain also outside of the cult, thus wherever Israelites are located, and whenever the act takes place — even outside of the Land altogether, even during the time that the Temple is no longer standing. If within the logic set forth by the Written Torah at Dt. 12:20–24 is contained an Israel outside of Jerusalem, then the next step, and it is not a giant step, is to contemplate an Israel outside of the Land altogether, not to say a Temple in ruins. The integral connection of slaughter of animals and sacrifice at the altar having been broken when all cultic activity was focused by Deuteronomy within Jerusalem, all that the Oral Torah has done is to address in so many words the extreme consequences of that situation: if the rules apply even to unconsecrated beasts, and even to the Land beyond Jerusalem, and even outside of the Temple, then by the same token, logic dictates a utopian consequence. The same laws apply even when no animals are being consecrated at all, and they apply even when no Temple stood, and they pertain even abroad.

So the Written Torah in any event set the stage when it took up the situation of slaughter not in behalf of the transaction at the altar and not in the setting of the holy place at all. And consequently, the Halakhah worked out in the critical detail of the sustenance of life the conviction that Israel the people forms the locus of sanctification. then all else follows. That is why I claim, it is particularly through their repeated formulation Halakhah of Hullin, — the repetition of the same formula making certain why should not miss the point — and only through those laws, that sages can have made their statement. That allegation about the enduring, ubiquitous sanctification inherent in Israel the people — even outside of the Land, even in the time of the Temple's destruction pervades the exposition of the laws in detail. It is an amazing statement in its insistence upon the priority and permanence of that act of sanctification — the sanctity of Israel — whatever may become of the holiness of the altar and of the Land!

Accordingly, the system hierarchizes space along with the other dimensions of being. The Temple is a holy place, Jerusalem is a holy city, and the Land of Israel is the holy land. Yet the ultimate focus of holiness is not space, not time, but the people, Israel, wherever located, whenever contemplated. Mishnah-tractate Hullin transforms the process of nourishing the individual Israelite into a statement of broad social, historical consequence about the enduring sanctification of Israel, down to the least Israelite individual — wherever living, whenever alive.

To understand why, we begin with the fundamental program of the Mishnah: to make concrete and orderly the encounter of Israel and God. God and corporate Israel, God and the Israelite family, God and the Israelite household — the law of the Mishnah affords concrete occasions for these encounters. But how far into the Israelite interior do these encounters extend? If God also meets the singular, the individual Israelite, we have yet to identify the grounds for intersection. Nor do we know where and when; under what circumstances and in what context the meeting regularly takes place. But we already have ample grounds for forming a theory. Since Israel and God meet in Jerusalem, at God's abode in the Temple, the household table, analogous to the table of the Lord in the Temple, presents itself as a likely meeting-place. For the outcome of meeting God is life eternal, and it is where life is nurtured that Israel and God should come together. But at stake is no abstraction, "life," but the concrete transactions by which life is comprised: the household, the village, the family, corporate society, and what happens to them in history. The issue then concerns the social space in which Israel and God meet.

Mishnah-tractate Hullin addresses the preparation of meat for the domestic table. As I shall show, it encompasses what is private and what is public, what endures and what is transient, in a single coherent statement. In doing so, it draws together the routine and the historical, events at home and events on the stage of world history. The encounter of Israel and God takes place in God's context, in nature and in history, in two disparate settings — one private, the other cosmic. The one that takes place in nature comes about when an Israelite takes life to sustain life. The other, the historical, is scarcely congruent; it emerges in the grand, consequential happenings of history.

These two points of juncture, nature and history, private and public, prove risibly incongruous and disproportionate. How the law of the Mishnah regularizes the slaughter of animals for domestic, secular use—not for Temple offerings—and how it sorts out great public moments of time, on the surface scarcely relate, let alone correspond. But as we shall see, they follow a common pattern, matching a moment in nature to a moment in history. The law of the Mishnah treats them within the same program, calling upon the same pattern to define their uniform context, as we shall see in this chapter and the next. A cosmic construction accommodates them both, and once more it is comprised by space, the Temple and the Land of Israel and the people Israel.

II. TAKING LIFE TO SUSTAIN ISRAEL'S LIFE: HULLIN

At issue, clearly, is the theology of who and what is "Israel," and the issue is worked out in terms of place: is "Israel" a location or a group, and what is the relationship between where one is situated and what one is?

The theory of location—space—that Rabbinic Judaism puts forth comes to concrete expression in the context of laws governing the production of food. *Where* one is situated in producing food matters less than *for whom* the food is produced. The individual Israelite is answerable to God for what he or she eats. That never is treated as a private, wholly secular act in the exercise of merely subjective taste. It is a deed governed by public law, one that carries cosmic significance. The Torah is clear that God is deeply concerned for what priests and other Israelites eat and how food is made ready for their domestic table. That concern pertains to how crops are raised and disposed of, and it also extends to how animals are killed for meat, doing so for the altar providing the model for doing so for the domestic table. Turning nature to man's nurture defines a dimension of Israel's sanctification.

To gain perspective on the particularity of the matter at hand, we recall that public laws govern other aspects of food-preparation. How and where—in the Land or outside—crops are planted and harvested, the rhythm of the cultivation of the fields, the disposition of the produce of the Land—all are subject to rules that embody an entire theory of Israel's social order. That theory centers on the Land, the production and utilization of its produce, thus an account of the proper use of space. The laws of tithing and separating priestly rations, exemplifying the whole, represent dietary rules as much as do those considered in Hullin. The dietary rules

3. SPACE: The land of Israel is holier than all lands

of Hullin are represented by the taboo against mixing milk and meat, the requirement about covering up the blood of a beast that is slaughtered for domestic consumption, and above all, about the proper manner in which to slaughter an animal for the domestic table.

There is, however, an important distinction between the proper slaughter of animals for domestic, secular purposes and all those other concerns. In the preparation of domestic foods, meat is differentiated from vegetables and other produce. Hullin's interest in meat-preparation concerns matters that contain no counterpart in the comparable processes of preparing the crops for the table.

God claims a share of the crops of the Land and God is intensely interest in how they are grown. Once God's interest in produce is accommodated, no further rules govern how the food is prepared or utilized. One may not grow grapes and wheat side by side in the Land of Israel. But one drinks wine and eats bread at the same meal. Produce that grows on its own in the Seventh Year may not be treated as a commercial commodity, but the Israelite at home may prepare grain grown in that year in any number of ways. How the food is produced — land use — matters, but what is done with it (within broad limits) does not — it simply does not matter to God. By contrast, apart from the prohibition of hybridization and the requirement of tithing flocks and herds, few regulations of a holy order pertain to producing meat. But when it comes to the individual's consuming meat, precisely how the living beast is killed and prepared engages God's concern.

So while God does not care what kind of a scythe is used for harvesting grain, God docs take an interest in the condition of the knife that is used for slaughtering a cow. And God does not take account of whether grapes or wheat are ripe and fat or wizened, but God does care about the health of the beast that is slaughtered for meat, rejecting one that is dying as unfit for Israelite consumption.

I refer to the *terefah*-beast, one that could not have survived but is not killed by the act of slaughter, rather that will die of natural causes but is not yet dead. To explain: Since the main point of the act of slaughter is deliberately to take the life of the living beast, rather than allowing the animal to die of natural causes and only then to use its meat, a category between suitable and unsuitable has to take account of an interstitial case. A suitable act of slaughter kills the beast and attends to its blood. An unsuitable act of slaughter does not. But what about a beast that has not died on its own out of the fullness of life, but that also has not been slaughtered in the ordinary manner?

Such an interstitial case is taken up under the category, *terefah*. That word, at Ex. 22:30, refers to a beast clawed by a wild animal: "You shall be men consecrated to me; therefore you shall not eat any flesh that is torn by beasts in the field; you shall cast it to the dogs." *Terefah* then pertains to carrion, a beast that dies without a proper act of slaughter. Ex. 22:30 then refers to a beast that has not yet died but that cannot survive. This yields the notion that beasts that bear some imperfection capable of causing death cannot be eaten by Israelites. Thus both beasts that die on their own, carrion, and those that are going to die by reason of wounds or imperfections, *terefah*-beasts, are prohibited. In these and other ways, meat-preparation for the individual responds to God's presence among the people of Israel.

Blood is what is at issue. First, because harvesting meat, not vegetables, involves the shedding of blood. Second, because shedding blood at the altar engages God's intense concern, and shedding blood for the domestic table is analogous. The Torah repeatedly asserts that "the blood is the life." It is deliberate in making provision for the disposition of the blood produced in slaughtering an animal. If killed for God's meal, that is to say, in the Temple courtyard, the animal yields blood for the altar, to be sprinkled at the corners in an act of expiation. The beast further produces the sacrificial parts to be burned up in smoke on the altar-fires and thence to ascend to God. The beast may also yield meat for the priests and their families to eat. If the animal is killed for the Israelite's meal, the animal yields blood to be covered with dust, which is to say, returned to the earth.

In transactions involving animals serving Heaven's and Israel's purposes, God and Israel therefore stand in alignment with one another. Here is an act, for the benefit of the individual Israelite, that is subjected to acute public scrutiny, by reason of the analogical context: the slaughter of beasts to produce meat for sale to the Israelite market. Here is the outcome of the imperative, "You shall be holy, for I the Lord your God am holy" (Lev. 19:2) — the concretization of holiness through the proper disposition of the blood, which is the life.

III. THE DOMESTIC TABLE COMPARED WITH THE TEMPLE ALTAR

The equation of the spaces — table and altar — tangibly serves only the situation in which the Temple stands, in which Israel itself is located in the Land of Israel, and in which both consecrated and unconsecrated beasts are subject to the rite. Then the analogy between table and altar begins

3. SPACE: The land of Israel is holier than all lands

in the palpable and undeniable facts of time, place, and circumstance. A sequence of questions comes in the wake of the analogy. The first is this: if the analogy depends on the facts of historical, social reality, does it continue to govern when those facts have changed? What is at issue concerns space in the age in which the Temple and its altar lie in ruins and vast segments of the community of Israel reside outside the boundaries of the Land of Israel. So too, since the Temple no longer stands, the very status of the consecration of a beast is subject to complications, and hence, the standing of beasts not consecrated for the altar requires attention. In that time and circumstance, no beasts are so consecrated and there is no locus for receiving them even if they were. The governing analogy of table and altar then proves asymmetrical to workaday reality.

One might be tempted to argue that the facts of history and society make no difference to the logic of the law of the Mishnah. But that contradicts the law's basic character. For, to begin with, the laws of the Mishnah flow from Scripture's narrative; they are conveyed by historical documents. These tell what happened to a particular people, corporate Israel, holy Israel, in relationship to a particular territory, and the sages draw lessons for the design of the social order from these recapitulated events. The laws are portrayed in such a way that they do not take form in an ahistorical vacuum. They respond to a historical context. They are formed if not by circumstance then in response to what Israel has done or what God has done. That represents the affirmation of the Scriptural narratives themselves, which persist in linking social imperatives to actualities in formulas like "You shall...for you were...," "You shall keep the Sabbath, for you were slaves in Egypt...," "For in six days the Lord made heaven and earth...therefore you shall...," and the like. And that propensity for systematically thinking about history—the irregularities of the here and now—produces the question faced when the law of the Mishnah addresses how, in the household, individual Israelites secure and prepare food.

Articulated and answered in Mishnah-tractate Hullin, the specific question is, What happens when the fires have gone out on the Temple altar, when Israel locates itself outside the Land of Israel, and when animals no longer are consecrated for divine service at all? Then the material foundation for the balance of the altar and the table, the analogy between slaughter for God and slaughter for everyday food, is lost. If we read Scripture's requirements in connection with taking the life of an animal for God's use and human use as a set of interdependent, categorical actions—Israel is nourished as God is nourished—then what law persists in this time is not self-evident.

IV. THE PARTICULAR LAWS OF MISHNAH-TRACTATE HULLIN

As usual with the Mishnah's laws, the legal specifics do not easily yield their theological generalizations. The subject of the tractate is the proper modes of killing and dividing the animals that are used for meat at home. The first four chapters of the tractate deal with that subject. Most of the rules for slaughtering an animal for God's table apply also to slaughtering one for the Israelite's household. True, we cannot ignore the infinitely more elevated level of sanctification that applies to the holy space of the Temple and the holy caste of the priests than to the Israelite household and the caste of Israelites. But If we control for the fixed differences, we can account for the few consequential differences.

The story does not end with the legal narrative that requires beasts for ordinary Israel to be slaughtered and evaluated as though for use on the altar. Other food taboos pertinent to preparation of meat meals cover the next eight chapters, in each instance spelling out regulations set forth in the Torah. These cover the law against slaughtering the dam and its young on the same day (Lev. 22:28); the requirement to cover up the blood of the slaughtered beast (Lev. 17:13–14); the taboo against consuming the sciatic nerve (Gen. 32:32); and the taboo against cooking meat with milk (Ex. 23:19, 34:26, Dt. 12:21), food-uncleanness, and then two chapters on what is owing to the priest from the meat of animals slaughtered at home, for secular purposes (Dt. 18:3); then the gift of first fleece to the priest (Dt. 18:4); and finally, the law of letting the dam go from the nest when one takes the eggs (Dt. 22:6–7).

What holds the whole together is the generative issue throughout. That is, predictably, how the domestic table is like the Temple altar. And that draws in its wake the complementary issue, how is it different? Since the table compares with the altar, how and where and why is it subject to a different rule from that pertaining to the altar? So the process is familiar: it is the work of comparison first, then contrast, that animates the Mishnah's intellectual program.

The analogical-contrastive analysis begins at the head of the tractate by stating the difference between an act of slaughter performed solely by a priest for the Lord's altar and one that is performed by an ordinary person. The requirements for the two settings exhibit striking differences, as is to be expected. In the Temple priests ordinarily slaughter the beast and are the only ones who can sprinkle the blood on the altar. In the household any Israelite performs the act of slaughter and, as to the blood, anyone may cover up the blood as well. Temple rites take place in daylight, the

3. SPACE: The land of Israel is holier than all lands

counterpart act of slaughter in the household may be done at night. And so on. The main point is that, for the table unlike the altar, any Israelite (here including a Samaritan or an apostate) may perform the act of slaughter and it may be carried out at any time, day or night. This is how it is stated in the law of the Mishnah:

> (1) All slaughter, (2) and their act of slaughter is valid, Except for a deaf-mute, an imbecile, and a minor lest they impair [the fitness of the carcass] through their act of slaughter). But all of them who performed an act of slaughter, with others watching them — their act of slaughter is valid. The act of slaughter of a gentile [produces] carrion. And it [the meat] imparts uncleanness through being carried. He who slaughters at night — and so too a blind person who slaughtered — his act of slaughter is valid. He who slaughters on the Sabbath or on the Day of Atonement, even though he [thereby] becomes liable for his life — his act of slaughter is valid.
>
> *Mishnah-tractate Hullin 1:1*

Then, how are the two settings comparable? The actual act is the same: a knife is applied to the throat and drawn across the two organs of the throat, windpipe and gullet. But that mode of slaughter applies only to beasts, not to fowl, in the Temple, while in the household or village, it serves for both.

> He who slaughters [cuts] one [organ, either the windpipe or the gullet] in the case of fowl, or two [both the windpipe and the gullet] in the case of a beast — his act of slaughter is valid. And the greater part of one [of the organs] is equivalent to [the whole of] it. [He who cuts through] half of one [organ] in the case of fowl and one and a half [organs] in the case of a beast — his act of slaughter is invalid. [He who cuts through] the greater part of one [organ] in the case of fowl or the greater part of two [organs] in the case of a beast — his act of slaughter is valid.
>
> *Mishnah-tractate Hullin 2:1*

Beasts are slaughtered in exactly the same way for the altar and for the household. The rule joining household to altar goes a step further. The act of slaughter for domestic use must be intentional and carried out intentionally by an individual, just as in the case of the altar: "If the knife fell and effected the act of slaughter, even if it effected the act of slaughter properly, it is invalid. As it is said, 'And you will slaughter... and you will eat...' (Deut. 12:21)" — just as *you* effect the act of slaughter, so do *you* eat."

That exegesis carries us back to the metaphor that compares the domestic table with God's altar in the Temple. The introduction of the issue of correct intentionality underscores that the altar and the table form a single genus, the operative traits being dictated by the altar. Just as in the

Temple offerings may be presented on behalf of gentiles, so an Israelite may slaughter a gentile's beast on behalf of the gentile. But if the intent is improper, the act is null, just as it would be if the officiating priest declared an improper intentionality in connection with a critical component of the rite, for instance by tossing the blood with the wrong purpose in mind. So the law states:

> He who slaughters [a gentile's beast] on behalf of a gentile — his act of slaughter is valid.
>
> *Mishnah-tractate Hullin 2:7*

The Mishnah's law does not address the issue of the gentile's intentionality, only the naked facts of the transaction: one may slaughter a gentile's beast on his behalf. But what about the intention involved? If the person who slaughters the beast at the moment of doing so forms and expresses the intention that the beast serve for Zeus, the act is an act of idolatry and the meat is forbidden for Israelite — not only cultic — use or benefit:

> He who slaughters (1) for the sake of mountains, (2) for the sake of valleys, (3) for the sake of seas, (4) for the sake of rivers, (5) for the sake of deserts — his act of slaughter is invalid. [If] two take hold of a knife and perform an act of slaughter, one for the sake of any of the forenamed, and one for the sake of a valid purpose, their act of slaughter is invalid.
>
> *Mishnah-tractate Hullin 2:8*

The critical point is that improper intentionality invalidates the act of slaughter for the altar and for the table alike. It produces meat of an idolatrous character. But that does not extend to a post facto disposition of the blood with an improper attitude. Further, slaughtering an unconsecrated beast outside of the Temple with the intent of offering up a sacrifice produces carrion. So a clear distinction differentiates slaughtering in the household and for its purposes from slaughtering in the Temple for its appropriate considerations.

But what links the two venues proves equally striking: what renders an animal unfit for the altar invalidates it for the table as well. And conversely, what the altar will not accept the household table cannot receive either. Simply put, when Israel eats meat, it eats the meat of the same classification and character as the meat that God consumes at the altar. Accordingly, beasts (but not fowl) are slaughtered for the altar and the domestic table in accord with one and the same protocol, and the critical consideration that pertains to the altar — the attitude of the officiating priest — pertains

3. SPACE: The land of Israel is holier than all lands

to the table. What counts is the attitude of the person who carries out or supervises the act of slaughter (as the case requires).

But there is yet another striking difference between the household and the Temple. The law of the Mishnah encompasses the Israelite household both in the Holy Land and abroad, and systematically states that prohibitions set forth in the Torah concerning preparation of meat and poultry apply in both settings, and pertain whether or not the Temple is standing, as well as to both unconsecrated and consecrated beasts. The recurrent formula, "(1) in the Land and outside the Land, (2) in the time of the Temple and not in the time of the Temple, (3) in the case of unconsecrated beasts and in the case of consecrated beasts," insists that these rules transcend boundaries of space, time, and circumstance. That leaves Israel the community as the focus of sanctification.

That carries us to the centerpiece of Mishnah-tractate Hullin, and it is here that spatial considerations enter in. It is the explicit statement that meat for Israelites is subject to sanctification even when the governing analogy no longer pertains: *outside of the Land*, and it follows, also when the Temple is in ruins, and for beasts that to begin with have not been sanctified for the altar. Then the eternity of Israel transcends the ephemerality of the Temple; Israel's table remains sanctified and therefore subject to the rules of cultic slaughter, even after God's table has been desecrated.

First, what justifies the distinction between ephemeral and enduring within the legal system of the Mishnah? The principle is well established, that, as between the enduring and the ephemeral, the enduring takes precedence, thus:

> Whatever is [offered] more often than its fellow takes precedence over its fellow: (1) Daily whole offerings take precedence over additional offerings.
>
> And whatever is more holy than its fellow takes precedence over its fellow: (1) The blood of the sin offering takes precedence over the blood of the burnt offering, because it makes atonement [for a sin]...
>
> *Mishnah-tractate Menahot 10:1–4*

Where is the theology in all this? It lies right at the surface. By that same principle of hierarchical classification, then, the Israelite's table takes precedence over "the Lord's table," and Israel is holier than the Temple. That is because *Israel wherever located is God's abode even when there is no Temple.* The Mishnah makes that statement in so many words when it says that the laws that apply to the altar and the table apply to the table even when the altar is destroyed. We shall rapidly survey the principal statements of that view, together with the details of the law governing slaughter for secular purposes that the law of the Mishnah encompasses.

Only when we encounter the laws in the language in which the Mishnah portrays those laws does the full power of the system come to expression. That is in its nearly-liturgical repetition of the same sacred formula, replicated in topic after topic. Then, working our way through the details, we are shown the regularities and order that yield theological truth. That is why I cite the entire set of topics as the opening statement of each formulates them. Then alone the power of patterned language and thought takes effect. I state very simply that I find this tractate, at these passages, the single most affecting theological writing in the formative canon of Judaism.

> [The prohibition against slaughtering on the same day] "it and its young" (Lev. 22:28) applies (1) in the Land and outside the Land, (2) in the time of the Temple and not in the time of the Temple, (3) in the case of unconsecrated beasts and in the case of consecrated beasts. How so? He who slaughters it and its offspring, (1) which are unconsecrated, (2) outside [the Temple courtyard] — both of them are valid. And [for slaughtering] the second he incurs forty stripes. [He who slaughters] (1) Holy Things (2) outside — [for] the first is he liable to extirpation, and both of them are invalid, and [for] both of them he incurs forty stripes. [He who slaughters] (1) unconsecrated beasts (2) inside [the Temple courtyard] — both of them are invalid, and [for] the second he incurs forty stripes. [He who slaughters] (1) Holy Things (2) inside — the first is valid, and he is exempt [from any punishment], and [for] the second he incurs forty stripes, and it is invalid.
>
> Mishnah-tractate Hullin 5:1

The pattern is established by speaking specifically of the holiness of the Land, the time of the Temple, and consecrated beasts, and insisting that the Israelite table at home takes priority in the level of sanctification over the Land, Temple-times, and beasts sanctified for the altar.

> [The requirement to] cover up the blood (Lev. 17:13–14) applies in the Land and abroad, (2) in the time of the Temple and not in the time of the Temple, (3) in the case of unconsecrated beasts, but not in the case of Holy Things. And it applies (4) to a wild beast and a bird, (5) to that which is captive and to that which is not captive. And it applies (6) to a *koy*, because it is a matter of doubt [whether it is wild or domesticated]. And they do not slaughter it [a *koy*] on the festival. But if one has slaughtered it, they do not cover up its blood.
>
> Mishnah-tractate Hullin 6:1

Now the issue is covering up the blood, and the outcome is the same. The other items are self-evident.

3. SPACE: The land of Israel is holier than all lands

M. 7:1 [The prohibition of] the sinew of the hip [sciatic nerve, Gen. 32:32] applies (1) in the Land [of Israel] and outside of the Land, (2) in the time of the Temple and not in the time of the Temple, (3) to unconsecrated animals and to Holy Things. It applies (1) to domesticated cattle and to wild beasts, (2) to the right hip and to the left hip. But it does not apply (3) to a bird, because it has no hollow [of the thigh or spoon-shaped hip And its fat is permitted. Butchers are believed (1) concerning it and (2) concerning the [forbidden] fat (Lev. 3:17, 7:23).

M. 8:1 [As to the separation of milk and meat (Ex. 23:19, 34:26, Dt. 12:21)]: Every [kind of] flesh [i.e., meat, of cattle, wild beast, and fowl] is it prohibited to cook in milk, except for the flesh of fish and locusts. And it is prohibited to serve it up onto the table with cheese, except for the flesh of fish and locusts. He who vows [to abstain] from flesh is permitted [to make use of] the flesh of fish and locusts.

M. 10:1 [The requirement to give to the priests] the shoulder, the two cheeks, and the maw (Deut. 18:3) applies (1) in the Land and outside of the Land, (2) in the time of the Temple and not in the time of the Temple, (3) to unconsecrated beasts, but not to consecrated beasts. For it [the contrary] might have appeared logical: Now, if unconsecrated animals, which are not liable for the breast and thigh [which are taken from peace offerings for the priests, (Lev. 7:31)], are liable for the [priestly] gifts [of the shoulder, cheeks, and maw], Holy Things, which *are* liable for the breast and thigh, logically should be liable to the priestly gifts. Scripture therefore states, "And I have given them to Aaron the priest and to his sons as a due for ever" (Lev. 7:34) — he has a right [in consecrated beasts] only to that which is explicitly stated [namely, the breast and thigh].

M. 11:1–2 [The laws concerning the obligation to donate to the priest] the first shearings [of wool from the sheep of one's flock (Deut. 18:4)] apply both inside the Land of Israel and outside the Land of Israel, in the time the Temple [in Jerusalem stands] and in the time the Temple does not [stand]. [And the laws apply] to [the fleece of] unconsecrated [animals] but not to [the fleece of animals that were] consecrated [to the Temple]. A stricter rule applies to [the obligation to give to the priest] the shoulder, the two cheeks and the maw [of one's animals] than to [the obligation to give to the priest] the first shearings [of wool from the sheep of one's flock]. For [the obligation to give to the priest] the shoulder, the two cheeks and the maw [of one's animals] applies both to the [large] animals of one's herd and to the [small] animals of one's flock.

M. 12:1 [The requirement to] let [the dam] go from the nest [Deut. 22:6–7] applies (1) in the Land and outside of the Land, (2) in the time of the Temple and not in the time of the Temple, (3) to unconsecrated [birds] but not to consecrated ones. A more strict rule applies to covering up the blood than to letting [the dam] go from the nest: For the requirement of covering up the blood applies (1) to a wild beast and to fowl, (2) to that which is captive and to that which is not captive. But letting [the dam] go from the nest applies only (1) to fowl and applies only (2) to that which is not captive. What is that which is not captive? For example, geese and fowl which make their nest in an orchard. But if they make their nest in the house (and so Herodian doves), one is free of the requirement of letting the dam go.

Mishnah-tractate Hullin 7:1, 8:1, 10:1–2, 11:1, 12:1

With all this evidence before us, the law of the Mishnah is fully exposed: the analogy to the altar governs — but only within explicit limits. Preparation of meat whether for the Temple altar or for the home table is subject to the same rules, which is why those rules extend the sanctity of the altar to the home. Since the law of the Mishnah treats the altar and the table as forming a single entity as far as sanctification is concerned, differentiated only in that the one is holier than the other, its task is to compare, then contrast, the two realms of the holy when it comes to meat-preparation. That logical requirement — showing where and how two entities that are alike differ — accounts for the problematics of the law. Thus for example, Hullin (M. 5:2) sets up a grid: [1] unconsecrated versus consecrated beasts, [2] inside and outside the Temple courtyard — the grid yields a variety of results as the possible cases are systematically considered. Then, another distinction is introduced (M. 6:1): Blood of a consecrated beast is to be tossed on the altar; that of a secular one is to be buried. But that distinction only underscores the main point, which is to compare and contrast the two realms of sanctification in connection with the consumption of meat.

The topical program of the law of the Mishnah is in two parts, first what pertains to preparation of meat, covering up the blood, the prohibition of the sciatic nerve, separation of meat from dairy products ("cooking meat in milk"), and the cultic uncleanness of food; and second, what involves gifts of meat or animal by-products to the priests. Letting the dam go from the nest when taking the young is placed at the end, because it has no bearing on the altar at all ("to unconsecrated birds but not to consecrated ones"). That the concern for general uncleanness should enter the picture presents no surprise; the law of the Mishnah takes for granted that Israelites will eat their meat not only in accord with the requirements of the Torah, such as are specified, but also in accord with the rules of cultic cleanness that govern, to begin with, in the Temple itself.

What about cultic cleanness in the household? The law of the Mishnah does not state that meat consumed at home is to be eaten in the state of cultic cleanness as it is in the Temple (whether by the altar, whether by the priests). But, as a matter of fact, the exposition at Chapter Nine rests on that premise. It begins:

> The (1) hide, and (2) grease, and (3) sediment, and (4) flayed-off meat, and (5) bones, and (6) sinews, and (7) horns and (8) hooves join together [with the meat to which they are attached to form the requisite volume] to impart food uncleanness, but [they do] not [join together to impart] uncleanness of carrion. Similarly: He who slaughters unclean cattle for a gentile — while it yet is writhing, it imparts food

3. SPACE: The land of Israel is holier than all lands

uncleanness, but [it does] not [impart] uncleanness of carrion — (1) until it dies, or (2) until one cuts off its head. [Scripture thus] has [prescribed] more [conditions] to impart food uncleanness than uncleanness of carrion.

Mishnah-tractate Hullin 9:1

These principles form the foundations of the rules. The law of the Mishnah compares and contrasts two categories of uncleanness that affect meat: food-uncleanness and carrion. Food contracts uncleanness from various specified sources, including a corpse or a dead creeping thing. Meat untouched by a corpse or dead creeping thing falls into one category, meat classified as unclean as carrion into another. The consequences of the one kind of uncleanness differ from those of the other. The law of the Mishnah is generated by the labor of hierarchical classification — that is characteristic of the Mishnah. It exhibits a systematic concern for asking how different species of the same genus (two different sources of uncleanness affecting meat) join together or function together to produce the same result — if they do.

As usual, we find particulars at the core of the Mishnah's discussion. A minimum volume of food is required for contracting uncleanness — a negligible volume is deemed null and outside of the system altogether. Therefore, in estimating whether that requisite volume of food has been formed, do we differentiate food that has become unclean by reason of a corpse from food that has become unclean by reason of being declared carrion? It is the volume of food that is in question.

Another way of asking the same question is, do we regard the semi-attached or distinct components of the carcass to form part of the carcass for purposes of assessing whether or not the requisite volume for receiving uncleanness has been reached? Thus, the issue is framed in terms of "connection," meaning, treating as a single entity distinct parts of the beast, that is, the hide (which separates from the flesh), the grease or sediment or bones or sinews or horns or hooves. If we do treat these as part of the beast, they contribute to the formation of the requisite volume to contract uncleanness. Otherwise, they do not.

The governing distinction is stated at the outset, namely, the specified, distinct components of the carcass do join together, when attached, to form the requisite volume to impart food uncleanness; for that purpose they are deemed integral to the carcass. But they do not join together to impart uncleanness by reason of carrion, meaning, in a beast that has died of natural causes, the specified components of the carcass are not assigned an integral part in the carcass. Clearly, the entire discussion presupposes a domestic venue and not a setting in the Temple, where, for example, no one is going to slaughter unclean cattle for a gentile. And what follows is that the law of the Mishnah everywhere takes for granted that considerations of uncleanness, not only those of suitability (proper slaughter and the like) pertain. So the law of the Mishnah makes sense only if its fundamental premise — comparing the altar to the table — extends even to imposing the cleanness-taboos of the former upon the latter.

V. GRADATIONS OF SANCTIFICATION

Let us return now to the gradations of sanctification, our starting point, gradations of sanctification and uncleanness, and these are expressed in three dimensions, genetically, spatially and temporally. The sanctity that encompasses Israelites one by one by their families is distinct from the sanctity that permeates the Land of Israel. And the sanctity of the Land of Israel itself is distinct from the sanctity that is embodied in the Temple and on upward to its altar — and beyond. For the law of the Mishnah, the hierarchy is expressed in three realms or levels of sanctification: [1] the Land, [2] the Temple, extending to cover the period when the Temple stood and the period of its ruin, and [3] Israel, each with its own place on the ladder of holiness that rises from earth to heaven.

The law of the Mishnah here states in so many words what it wants to know. That is whether [1] the destruction of the Temple and cessation of the offerings, [2] the degradation of the Land of Israel — its loss of its Israelite residents — and [3] the exile of the holy people, Israel, from the Holy Land, affect the rules of sustenance in the model of the nourishment of God, The question pertains to three venues: [1] in the Temple, [2] in the Land, [3] among the holy people. But the venue of the Temple encompasses periodization. The answer to the question of spatial as well as genetic and temporal hierarchization is, whatever the condition of the Temple and its altar, whatever the source — the Holy Land or unclean gentile lands — of animals, and whatever the location of the people Israel — whether in the Holy Land or not — one thing persists. And that is the sanctification of Israel, the people.

That status of holiness imputed to the social entity (Israel) and to each individual (Israelite) therein — endures [1] in the absence of the cult and [2] in alien, unclean territory and [3] whatever the source of the food that Israel eats. Israel's sanctity is eternal, unconditional, absolute. The sanctification that inheres in Israel, the people, transcends the Land and outlives the Temple and its cult.

3. SPACE: The land of Israel is holier than all lands

Since the sanctity of Israel, the people, persists beyond the Temple and outside of the Land, that sanctity stands at a higher point in the hierarchy of domains of the holy that ascend from earth to heaven and from humanity to God. The result of our inquiry concerning corporate Israel and the individual Israelite and their relationship, now comes into play. The social given is corporate Israel. That fact is now recapitulated in the issues before us: the status of Israel — in the Land or abroad, possessed of the Temple or excluded therefrom — in preparing meat, whether for God or for Israel itself. These issues address the condition of corporate Israel. But they play themselves out on the domestic table of the individual Israelite man, woman, and child, whether formed into families or not, whether constituting households or not and wherever they are located.

The law of the Mishnah, to make its statement about the eternal sanctification of the people, Israel, explicitly responds to three facts: [1] Israelites live not only in the holy land but abroad, in unclean lands; [2] the Temple has been destroyed and not yet rebuilt; [3] and, consequently, animals are slaughtered not only in the Temple in the Land but in unconsecrated space and abroad, and the meat is eaten not only in a cultic but in a profane circumstance.

Holy, corporate Israel's sanctification endures beyond the Land, outside the Temple, and after the age in which the active source of sanctification, the altar, functions. It continues when the others do not. How then do we hierarchize Temple, Land, and corporate Israel? The desuetude of the one, the abandonment of the other — neither ultimately affects the standing of the Israel. The Land and the Temple have lost that sanctity that infused them when Israel dwelt on the Land and the Temple altar was nourished by Israel's priesthood and produce. But the sanctification of Israel itself endures through history, eternal and untouched by time and change. And when Israel returns to the Land and rebuilds the Temple, the sanctification of the Land and the Temple will once more be realized.

That returns to the agendum the question of history. Anyone who wonders whether the law of the Mishnah that applied to the Temple and the home when the Temple was standing and Israel was in the Land of Israel continues to apply with the Temple in ruins and Israel in exile here finds the answer. And every meal at which the Israelite eats meat embodies that answer in a most active form: the menu itself. Although the sanctity of the Temple stands in abeyance, the sanctity of the Israelite table persists. Although Israel is in exile from the Holy Land, Israel remains holy. Although in the Temple rules of uncleanness are not now kept, they continue in force wherever Israelites may be. Birds and animals that flourish outside of the

Land, when prepared for the Israelite table, are regulated by the same rules that apply in the Land and even (where relevant) at the altar. So Israel, the people, not only retains sanctity but preserves it outside of the Land, and the sanctity of Israel transcends that of the Temple and its altar. Corporate Israel is endowed with a higher degree of sanctity than the Temple and the Land — and, in the hierarchy of the sacred, stands at the apex, closest to God.

The law of the Mishnah does not treat as an all-or-nothing proposition either sanctification or cultic cleanness. That is the advantage of seeing all things as matters of degree, location within a continuum. In the present case, the law of the Mishnah works out in detail the general theory of the gradations of sanctification matched by those of uncleanness. We can understand the law of Mishnah-tractate Hullin only within the nurturing context of the general theory of sanctification, spatial (locative), temporal, and circumstantial, involving answers to the questions of where, when, and whom. The outcome is that when it comes to the preparation of meat, the law of the Mishnah deals with three locative settings: [1] the Temple, [2] the Land of Israel, and [3] foreign land. These correspond to two temporal periods: [1] when the Temple stood and [2] now, when the Temple lies in ruins.

And for all three settings and for both periods, the Mishnah insists, the same rules pertain, even despite the considerable differences that apply. Since all territory outside of the Land of Israel is by definition unclean, the premise of the law is that, in spite of that fact, Israel is to consume its secular meat in accord with those rules of sanctification that pertain to food and its preparation. The laws of cultic cleanness may apply to the household in the Land of Israel but cannot pertain abroad; nonetheless, the other principal admonitions apply everywhere. The metaphor is persistent: the existence of the Temple or its destruction makes no difference. And the same is so for the possession of the Land.

VI. WHY HULLIN IN PARTICULAR?

Why is it particularly the law of Mishnah-tractate Hullin that makes the statement at hand? Israel — the Israelite person, the people of Israel — is holier than the Land and holier even than the Temple, endowing with sanctity the animals slaughtered to nourish the people? That theological proposition comes to the fore here in particular because the written Torah supplies the law that contains the entire message. It does so when it imposes the same requirements that pertain to slaughter of an animal sacrifice for the altar in Jerusalem and to killing an animal for the use of

3. SPACE: The land of Israel is holier than all lands

Israel at home, specifically, burying the blood or draining it. That means that the meat Israel eats is subject to the same regulations that apply to the meat that God receives on the altar-fires. That very law states that meat for those who are not holy, that is, for gentiles or idolaters, is not subject to the same rules (Ex. 22:30, Dt. 14:21). So, it is unmistakable: food for God and for Israel must be prepared in comparable manner, which rule does not apply to food for gentiles.

History enters in when we ask how that principle affects animals raised abroad. The laws of Hullin apply to them, because the laws apply to unconsecrated animals as much as consecrated ones. The purpose in nature — nourishing Israel — is alone what counts. The beast intended for Israelite consumption at the domestic table even in a foreign country must be prepared as though for God on the altar in Jerusalem, and that can only mean, since the beast is intended (by the act of correct slaughter) for Israel, the use of the beast by Israel sanctifies the beast and necessitates conformity with the rules of slaughter for God in the Temple. Israel, even abroad, renders the food that it eats comparable to food for the altar.

Then comes the matter of the Temple and its condition. We ask, What has food-preparation to do with the consideration of location? The rule that permits slaughter of meat outside of the Temple (Dt. 12:20–24) explicitly states that it speaks of corporate Israel outside of the Temple in Jerusalem. So, even if the act of slaughter does not take place in Jerusalem, the act must conform, because the focus is on Israel, wherever Israel is located — even far from Jerusalem (for so the law is formulated in Scripture). The law of the Mishnah before us simply carries the same conception forward in a logical way: the same considerations govern even so far from Jerusalem as territory that to begin with is laden with corpse-uncleanness, that is, foreign soil; and even in an age in which Jerusalem is no more; and, it goes without saying, even in connection with a beast that has not been consecrated for the altar.

Since Scripture itself has separated the act of slaughter from the rite of sacrifice in the Temple, the law of the Mishnah has done little more than explore the consequences of that rule. This it does when it states that the requirements of slaughter in the cult pertain also outside of the cult, thus wherever Israelites are located, and whenever the act takes place — even outside of the Land altogether, even during the time that the Temple is no longer standing. If an Israel outside of Jerusalem is contained within the logic set forth by the Torah at Deuteronomy 12:20–24, then the next step, and it is not a giant step, is to contemplate an Israel outside of the Land altogether, not to say a Temple in ruins.

The integral connection of slaughter of animals and sacrifice at the altar having been broken when all cultic activity was focused by Deuteronomy within Jerusalem, all that the law of the Mishnah has done is to address in so many words the extreme consequences of that situation. If the rules apply even to unconsecrated beasts, and even to the Land beyond Jerusalem, and even outside of the Temple, then by the same token, logic dictates a utopian consequence. The same laws apply even when no animals are being consecrated at all, and they apply even once the Temple no longer stands, and they pertain even abroad.

So the Torah sets the stage by addressing the situation of slaughter not in behalf of the transaction at the altar and not in the setting of the holy place. And, consequently, the law of the Mishnah worked out in the critical details of the sustenance of life, the conviction that Israel the people forms the locus of sanctification. What follows is that this allegation about the enduring, ubiquitous sanctification inherent in Israel the people — even outside of the Land, even in the time of the Temple's destruction — pervades the exposition of the laws in detail. It is an amazing statement in its insistence upon the priority and permanence of the sanctity of Israel — whatever may become of the holiness of the altar and of the Land.

VII. LOCATION, OCCASION, THE CHARACTER OF THE ENCOUNTER, IN GOD'S CONTEXT, OF GOD AND THE ISRAELITE

Affirming the unique holiness of the Temple and the Land of Israel, Mishnah-tractate Hullin still wants to show how the holiness of the people, Israel, retains its own integrity even when out of touch with the holiness of the Temple and the land. Israel's enduring sanctification transcends location and occasion because it is realized at the moment at which life-blood is spilled in the preservation of life. That takes place anywhere Israelites are located and any time the act of slaughter takes place. Thus, the law of the Mishnah establishes in practical ways that Israel remains holy even outside of the Land, even in the age without the Temple. Meat prepared for Israel, wherever the meat has itself been nourished, even on gentile ground, must be prepared as though for the altar in Jerusalem. Then Israel's sanctity persists, even when that continuum in which it stood, the chain of continuity with the Temple altar in Jerusalem (as the formulation of Deuteronomy 12:20–24 framed matters), has been disrupted. Israel's sanctity endows with sanctity even animals raised in unclean ground, so

3. SPACE: The land of Israel is holier than all lands

powerful is the sanctification that transforms Israel. God is present not only at the table of the Israelite but wherever animals are killed to provide meat for the Israelite's table. And that is a presence not in response to what is said but what is done: God responds when blood is shed.

Then God's presence is not only locative but temporal and occasional. God is present when the slaughterer takes up the knife and cuts the vital organs of the throat. And that occasion is defined by an Israelite, not a priest alone, not a male alone, not an adult alone:

> All slaughter except for a deaf-mute, an imbecile, and a minor lest they impair the fitness of the carcass through their act of slaughter. All are valid to carry out an act of slaughter even a Samaritan, even an uncircumcised man, and even an Israelite apostate.
>
> *Mishnah-tractate Hullin 1:1*

In light of that startling fact, much becomes clear. The act of any Israelite capable of deliberate action in slaughtering an animal for meat suffices to win God's attention. The character of the encounter is defined by the action, not by the person, and the transaction resembling the blood-rite is possible solely by reason of the status of all individual Israelites: God responds to every one of them engaged in an action of the specified sort. The encounter of God and the individual Israelite, not defined by caste-status, gender, or age, then comes about because, at this particular action, the Israelite matters by reason of what he or she validly does, which is take a life for Israelite benefit, as the priest at the altar takes a life for God's.

So we must ask, Is the act of slaughter for the domestic table comparable to the act of slaughter for the altar? As we have seen, formally that is explicitly the fact. But, categorically, we cannot maintain that food-preparation for the altar always is comparable to food-preparation for the domestic table. Grain, oil, and wine, not only meat, comprise God's meals. As a matter of fact, other topics concerning dietary laws, for example, removing from grain and produce, including olives and grapes, the share that belongs to God and is assigned to God's protected castes — including the priests and the poor — each is treated in its own terms and none is not comparable to any other.

What we see is that through one aspect of dietary laws, the law of the Mishnah makes a statement of one sort, through another aspect, a statement of another sort. In the division pertaining to Agriculture, the dietary rules recapitulate the overarching statement that division of the law makes about the standing and sanctity of the Land. In the division pertaining to Holy Things, the rules pertinent to the Israelite's food recapitulate a statement that can be made only in the context of Holy Things and nowhere else. The division of Agriculture speaks of the interplay of the realms of sanctification of the Land and of the people, Israel, in relationship to God as co-proprietor of the Land with Israel. There we find the sharing of the gifts of the Land with its proprietors, God and Israel. The division of Holy Things in speaks of the interplay of the realms of sanctification of the altar of God and the table of Israel. Here we find the issue of location made specific in the matter of enlandisement — precisely the opposite issue from the one that animates the division of Agriculture.

Both deal with the generic category, sanctification, but do so distinctively: it is sanctification that is enlandised or locative (Agriculture) versus utopian (Holy Things). But what joins the two statements together should not be missed, since both concern the same generative principle, the inherent sanctification of Israel and the consequent requirement that Israel sustain itself in accord with the rules of sanctification of food that is offered to God. In brief, Israel is holy and God is holy and where pertinent, the same rules dictate the appropriate source and correct preparation of food for both. But the conception — Israel's sanctification in a continuum with God's holiness and with the Land's holiness — provokes reflection on one set of issues here and another set in connection with the division of Agriculture.

For the law of Mishnah-tractate Hullin the sanctification of Israel, corporate and personal, pertains, as it states time and again, in the Land and outside, in the time of the Temple and afterward, in connection with consecrated and secular beasts. And so, at an infinitely higher point in the hierarchy, does God's — wherever, whenever God is present — even in history, especially in history.

THE PHILOSOPHICAL PREMISE
OF JUDAISM

4.
ANALYSIS:
Hierarchical classification and the Law's Philosophical Demonstration of Monotheism

I. HIERARCHICAL CLASSIFICATION

The law of the Mishnah, seen whole, presents a profoundly philosophical system, one that employs numerous, diverse cases to make a single general point. It is that hierarchical classification yields a demonstration of the truth of monotheism. All things reach upward to the One. This system involves philosophical method to deal with issues important in philosophy about the order and unity of being.

The Mishnah's philosophical method derives from the natural history of Aristotle and aims at the hierarchical classification of all things. It follows that the Mishnah's systemic statement, its philosophy of Judaism, demonstrates that all things in place, in proper rank and position in the hierarchy of being, point to, stand for, one thing. The system and structure ask the questions philosophers ask, concerning the nature of things, and answer them in the way the philosophers answer them, through orderly sifting of data in the process of natural philosophy. The only point of difference is subject-matter, but, after all, philosophers in the great tradition took up multiple questions; some worked on this, some on that, some on the other thing, and no single corpus of data predominated.

To identify the telos of thought in the Mishnah, I state the generative proposition of the Mishnah very simply: in the Mishnah, many things are made to say one thing, which concerns the nature of being, all teleologically hierarchized, to state matters in simple terms. The system of the Mishnah registers these two contrary propositions: many things yield one, one thing encompasses many. These propositions of course complement each other, because, in forming matched opposites, the two provide a complete and final judgment of the whole. The philosophy of Judaism must be deemed ontological, for it is a statement of an ontological order that the system makes when it claims that all things are not only orderly, but ordered in such wise that many things fall into one classification, and one thing may hold together many things in a single classification.

For this philosophy rationality consists in hierarchy of the order of things. That rationality is revealed by the possibility always of effecting the hierarchical classification of all things: each thing in its taxon, all taxa in correct sequence, from least to greatest. And showing that all things can be ordered, and that all orders can be set into relationship with one another, we transform method into message. The message of hierarchical classification is that many things really form a single thing, the many species a single genus, the many genera an encompassing and well-crafted, cogent whole. Every time we speciate, we affirm that position; each successful labor of forming relationships among species, e.g., making them into a genus, or identifying the hierarchy of the species, proves it again. Not only so, but when we can show that many things are really one, or that one thing yields many (the reverse and confirmation of the former), we state in a fresh way a single immutable truth concerning the ultimate unity of all being in an orderly composition of all things within a single taxon. The method of the Mishnah as well as its message come to us only in cases, and in asking about the Judaism behind the texts, we have to learn how to derive from cases an account of premises and presuppositions. This we shall now do with attention to the Mishnah's method, on the one side, and an important part of its message, on the other.

I turn to a very brief sample of the Mishnah's authorship's sustained effort to demonstrate how many classes of things — actions, relationships, circumstances, persons, places — really form one class. This supererogatory work of classification then works its way through the potentialities of chaos to explicit order. It is classification transformed from the how of intellection to the why and the what for and, above all, the what does it all mean. Recognition that one thing may fall into several categories and many things into a single one comes to expression, for the authorship of the Mishnah, in diverse ways. One of the interesting ones is the analysis of the several taxa into which a single action may fall, with an account of the multiple consequences, e.g., as to sanctions that are called into play, for a single action. The right taxonomy of persons, actions, and things will show the unity of all being by finding many things in one thing, and that forms the first of the two components of what I take to be the philosophy's teleology.

- A. There is one who ploughs a single furrow and is liable on eight counts of violating a negative commandment:
- B. [specifically, it is] he who (1) ploughs with an ox and an ass [Deut. 22:10], which are (2,3) both Holy Things, in the case of (4) [ploughing] Mixed Seeds in a vineyard [Deut. 22:9], (5) in the Seventh Year [Lev. 25:4], (6) on a festival

4. ANALYSIS: Hierarchical classification and the Law's Philosophical Demonstration of Monotheism

[Lev. 23:7] and who was both a (7) priest [Lev. 21:1] and (8) a Nazirite [Num. 6:6] [ploughing] in a grave-yard.

C. Hanania b. Hakhinai says, "Also: He is [ploughing while] wearing a garment of diverse kinds" [Lev. 19:19, Deut. 22:11).

D. They said to him, "This is not within the same class."

E. He said to them, "Also the Nazir [B8] is not within the same class [as the other transgressions]."

Mishnah-tractate Keritot 3:9

Here is a case in which more than a single set of flogging is called for. B's felon is liable to 312 stripes, on the listed counts. The ox is sanctified to the altar, the ass to the upkeep of the house (B2,3). Hanania's contribution is rejected since it has nothing to do with ploughing, and sages' position is equally flawed. The main point, for our inquiry, is simple. The one action draws in its wake multiple consequences. Classifying a single thing as a mixture of many things then forms a part of the larger intellectual address to the nature of mixtures. But it yields a result that, in the analysis of an action, far transcends the metaphysical problem of mixtures, because it moves us toward the ontological solution of the unity of being.

The real interest in demonstrating the unity of being lies not in things but in abstractions, and among abstractions *types* of actions take the center-stage. Mishnah-tractate Keritot works out how many things are really one thing. This is accomplished by showing the end or consequence of diverse actions to be always one and the same. The issue of the tractate is the definition of occasions on which one is obligated to bring a sin-offering and a suspensive guilt-offering. The tractate lists those sins that are classified together by the differentiating criterion of intention. If one deliberately commits those sins, he is punished through extirpation. If it is done inadvertently, he brings a sin-offering. In case of doubt as to whether or not a sin has been committed (hence: inadvertently), he brings a suspensive guilt offering. Lev. 5:17–19 specifies that if one sins but does not know it, he brings a sin-offering or a guilt offering. Then if he does, a different penalty is invoked, with the suspensive guilt offering at stake as well. While we have a sustained exposition of implications of facts that Scripture has provided, the tractate also covers problems of classification of many things as one thing, in the form of a single-sin-offering for multiple sins, and that problem fills the bulk of the tractate.

1:1 A. Thirty-six transgressions subject to extirpation are in the Torah...

1:2 A. For those [transgressions] are people liable, for deliberately doing them, to the punishment of extirpation,

B. and for accidentally doing them, to the bringing of a sin offering,

- C. and for not being certain of whether or not one has done them, to a suspensive guilt offering [Lev. 5:17] —
- D. "except for the one who imparts uncleanness to the sanctuary and its Holy Things,
- E. "because he is subject to bringing a sliding scale offering (Lev. 5:6–7, 11)," the words of R. Meir.
- F. And sages say, "Also: [except for] the one who blasphemes, as it is said, 'You shall have one law for him that does anything unwittingly' (Num. 15:29) — excluding the blasphemer, who does no concrete deed."

1:7
- A. The woman who is subject to a doubt concerning [the appearance of] five fluxes,
- B. or the one who is subject to a doubt concerning five miscarriages
- C. brings a single offering.
- D. And she [then is deemed clean so that she] eats animal sacrifices.
- E. And the remainder [of the offerings, A, B] are not an obligation for her.
- F. [If she is subject to] five confirmed miscarriages,
- G. or five confirmed fluxes,
- H. she brings a single offering.
- I. And she eats animal sacrifices.
- J. But the rest [of the offerings, the other four] remain as an obligation for her [to bring at some later time] —
- K. M'SH S: A pair of birds in Jerusalem went up in price to a golden denar.
- L. Said Rabban Simeon B. Gamaliel, "By this sanctuary! I shall not rest tonight until they shall be at [silver] denars."
- M. He entered the court and taught [the following law]:
- N. "The woman who is subject to five confirmed miscarriages [or] five confirmed fluxes brings a single offering.
- O. "And she eats animal sacrifices.
- P. "And the rest [of the offerings] do not remain as an obligation for her."
- O. And pairs of birds stood on that very day at a quarter-denar each [one one-hundredth of the former price].

3:2
- A. [If] he ate [forbidden] fat and [again ate] fat in a single spell of inadvertence, he is liable only for a single sin offering,
- B. [If] he ate forbidden fat and blood and remnant and refuse [of an offering] in a single spell of inadvertence, he is liable for each and every one of them.
- C. This rule is more strict in the case of many kinds [of forbidden food] than of one kind.
- D. And more strict is the rule in [the case of] one kind than in many kinds:
- E. For if he ate a half-olive's bulk and went and ate a half-olive's bulk of a single kind, he is liable.
- F. [But if he ate two half-olive's bulks] of two [different] kinds, he is exempt.

3:4
- A. There is he who carries out a single act of eating and is liable on its account for four sin offerings and one guilt offering:
- B. An unclean [lay] person who ate (1) forbidden fat, and it was (2) remnant (3) of Holy Things, and (4) it was on the Day of Atonement.
- C. R. Meir says, "If it was the Sabbath and he took it out [from one domain to another] in his mouth, he is liable [for another sin offering]."

4. ANALYSIS: Hierarchical classification and the Law's Philosophical Demonstration of Monotheism

D. They said to him, "That is not of the same sort [of transgression of which we have spoken heretofore since it is not caused by eating (A)]."

Mishnah-tractate Keritot 1:1, 2, 7, 3:2, 4

M. Ker. 1:7 introduces the case of classifying several incidents within a single taxon, so that one incident encompasses a variety of cases and therefore one penalty or sanction covers a variety of instances. At M. 3:1–3 we deal with diverse situations in which a man is accused of having eaten forbidden fat and therefore of owing a sin-offering. At M. 3:1 the issue is one of disjoined testimony. Do we treat as one the evidence of two witnesses? The debate concerns whether two cases form a single category. Sages hold that the case are hardly the same, because there are differentiating traits. M. 3:2–3 show us how we differentiate or unify several acts. We have several acts of transgression in a single spell of inadvertence; we classify them all as one action for purposes of the penalty. That what is at stake is the problem of classification and how we invoke diverse taxic indicators is shown vividly at M. 3:2 in particular. Along these same lines are the issues of M. Ker. 3:3, 4–6: "There is he who carries out a single act of eating and is liable on its account for four sin-offerings and one guilt-offering; there is he who carries out a single act of sexual intercourse and becomes liable on its account for six sin-offerings," with the first shown at M. 3:4.

The recognition that one thing becomes many does not challenge the philosophy of the unity of all being, but confirms the main point. If we can show that differentiation flows from within what is differentiated—that is, from the intrinsic or inherent traits of things—then we confirm that at the heart of things is a fundamental ontological being, single, cogent, simple, that is capable of diversification, yielding complexity and diversity. The upshot is to be stated with emphasis.

That diversity in species or diversification in actions follows orderly lines confirms the claim that there is that single point from which many lines come forth.

Carried out in proper order—[1] the many form one thing, and [2] one thing yields many—the demonstration then leaves no doubt as to the truth of the matter. Ideally, therefore, we shall argue from the simple to the complex, showing that the one yields the many, one thing, many things, two, four.

1:1 A. [Acts of] transporting objects from one domain to another, [which violate] the Sabbath, (1) are two, which [indeed] are four [for one who is] inside, (2) and two which are four [for one who is] outside,
B. How so?

C. [If on the Sabbath] the beggar stands outside and the householder inside,
D. [and] the beggar stuck his hand inside and put [a beggar's bowl] into the hand of the householder,
E. or if he took [something] from inside it and brought it out,
F. the beggar is liable, the householder is exempt.
G. [If] the householder stuck his hand outside and put [something] into the hand of the beggar,
H. or if he took [something] from it and brought it inside,
I. the householder is liable, and the beggar is exempt.
J. [If] the beggar stuck his hand inside, and the householder took [something] from it,
K. or if [the householder] put something in it and he [the beggar] removed
L. both of them are exempt.
M. [If] the householder put his hand outside and the beggar took [something] from it,
N. or if [the beggar] put something into it and [the householder] brought it back inside,
O. both of them are exempt.

Mishnah-tractate Shabbat 1:1

M. Shab. 1:1 classifies diverse circumstances of transporting objects from private to public domain. The purpose is to assess the rules that classify as culpable or exempt from culpability diverse arrangements. The operative point is that a prohibited action is culpable only if one and the same person commits the whole of the violation of the law. If two or more people share in the single action, neither of them is subject to punishment. At stake therefore is the conception that one thing may be many things, and if that is the case, then culpability is not incurred by any one actor. The Sabbath-exposition appears so apt and perfect for the present proposition that readers may wonder whether the authorship of the Mishnah could accomplish that same wonder of concision of complex thought more than a single time. Joining rhetoric, logic, and specific proposition transforms thought into not merely expository prose but poetry.

My final demonstration of the power of speciation in demonstrating the opposite, namely, the generic unity of species and the hierarchy that orders them, derives from the treatment of oaths, to which we now turn. The basic topical program of Mishnah-tractate Shebuot responds systematically to the potpourri of subjects covered by Leviticus Chapters Five and Six within the (to the priestly author) unifying rubric of those who bring a guilt-offering. Lev. 5:1–6 concerns oaths, an oath of testimony, and one who touches something unclean in connection with the Temple cult, and finally, one who utters a rash oath.

4. ANALYSIS: Hierarchical classification and the Law's Philosophical Demonstration of Monotheism

1:1 A. Oaths are of two sorts, which yield four subdivisions.
 B. Awareness of [having sinned through] uncleanness is of two sorts, which yield four subdivisions.
 C. Transportation [of objects from one domain to the other] on the Sabbath is of two sorts, which yield four subdivisions.
 D. The symptoms of negas are of two sorts, which yield four subdivisions.
1:2 A. In any case in which there is awareness of uncleanness at the outset and awareness [of uncleanness] at the end but unawareness in the meantime — lo, this one is subject to bringing an offering of variable value.
 B. [If] there is awareness [of uncleanness] at the outset but no apprehension [of uncleanness] at the end, a goat which [yields blood to be sprinkled] within [in the Holy of Holies], and the Day of Atonement suspend [the punishment],
 C. until it will be made known to the person, so that he may bring an offering of variable value.
2:1 A. Awareness of uncleanness is of two sorts, which yield four subdivisions [M. 1 IB].
 B. (1) [If] one was made unclean and knew about it, then the uncleanness left his mind, but he knew [that the food he had eaten was] Holy Things,
 C. (2) the fact that the food he had eaten was Holy Things left his mind, but he knew about [his having contracted] uncleanness,
 D. (3) both this and that left his mind, but he ate Holy Things without knowing it and after he ate them, he realized it —
 E. lo, this one is liable to bring an offering of variable value.
 F. (1) [If] he was made unclean and knew about it, and the uncleanness left his mind, but he remembered that he was in the sanctuary;
 G. (2) the fact that he was in the sanctuary left his mind, but he remembered that he was unclean,
 H. (3) both this and that left his mind, and he entered the sanctuary without realizing it, and then when he had left the sanctuary, he realized it — lo, this one is liable to bring an offering of variable value.

Mishnah-tractate Shebuot 1:1–2, 2:1

M. Shebuot 1:1–7, 2:1–5 accomplish the speciation of oaths, on the one side, and uncleanness in regard to the cult, on the other. That single work of speciation then joins two utterly disparate subjects, oaths and uncleanness, so showing a unity of structure that forms a metaphysical argument for the systemic proposition on the unity of being. We do so in a way that is now to be predicted. It is by showing that many things are one thing, now, as I said, oaths, uncleanness. When the priestly author joined the same subjects, it was because a single offering was involved for diverse and distinct sins or crimes. When the Mishnaic author does, it is because a single inner structure sustains these same diverse and distinct sins or crimes. Comparing the priestly with the Mishnah's strategy of exposition underlines the remarkable shift accomplished by our philosophers. Their power of formulation — rhetoric, logic together — of course, works to demonstrate through the medium the message that these enormously diverse subjects in fact can be classified within a simple taxonomic principle. It is that there are two species to a genus, and two sub-species to each species, and these are readily determined by appeal to fixed taxic indicators. An abstract statement of the rule of classification (and, it must follow, also hierarchization) will have yielded less useful intellectual experience than the remarkably well balanced concrete exemplification of the rule, and that is precisely what we have in Mishnah-tractate Shebuot Chapters One and Two.

The main point of differentiation — the taxic indicator — derives from the intersecting issues of a divided sequence of time-frames and of awareness. If one knows something at one point in a differentiated process ("the outset," "the meantime," "the end") but does not know that thing at some other point, then we have a grid in two dimensions: sequence of time, sequence of spells of awareness or unawareness. And then the taxic indicators are in place, so the process of speciation and sub-speciation is routine. At stake is the power of the taxic indicator. What is stunning is that the same process of speciation and sub-speciation is explicitly applied to utterly unrelated matters, which demonstrates for all to see that the foundations of knowledge lie in method, which makes sense of chaos, and method means correct knowledge of the classification of things and the ability to identify the taxic indicators that make classification possible. All of this prepares the way for the treatment of oaths, Mishnah-tractate Shebuot 3:1–8:6, that is, the entire tractate.

The upshot may be stated very simply. The species point to the genus, all classes to one class, all taxa properly hierarchized then rise to the top of the structure and the system forming one taxon. So all things ascend to, reach one thing. All that remains is for the theologian to define that one thing: God. But that is a step that the philosophers of the Mishnah did not take. Perhaps it was because they did not think they had to. But I think there is a different reason altogether. It is because, as a matter of fact, they were philosophers. And to philosophers God serves as premise and principle (and whether or not it is one God or many gods, a unique being or a being that finds a place in a class of similar beings hardly is germane!), and philosophy serves not to demonstrate principles or to explore premises, but to analyze the unknown, to answer important questions.

The methodological premises of the Mishnah are Aristotelian. A brief account, based upon the standard textbook picture, of the taxonomic method of Aristotle permits us to compare the philosophical method of the

4. ANALYSIS: Hierarchical classification and the Law's Philosophical Demonstration of Monotheism

philosophy of Judaism with that of the methodologically-paramount natural philosophy of the Greco-Roman world. We begin with the simple observation that the distinction between genus and species lies at the foundation of all knowledge. Adkins states the matter in the most accessible way, "Aristotle, a systematic biologist, uses his method of classification by genera and species, itself developed from the classificatory interests of the later Plato, to place man among other animals... The classification must be based on the final development of the creature..."[1] But to classify, we have to take as our premise that things are subject to classification, and that means that they have traits that are essential and indicative, on the one side, but also shared with other things, on the other. The point of direct contact and intersection between the Mishnah's philosophy of hierarchical classification and the natural philosophy of Aristotle lies in the critical conviction concerning the true nature or character of things. Both parties concur that there *is* such a true definition—a commonplace for philosophers, generative of interesting problems, e.g., about Ideas, or Form and Substance, Actual and Potential, and the like—of what things really are.[2]

But how are we to know the essential traits that allow us to define the true character of, e.g., to classify, things? And this is the point at which our comparison becomes particular, since what we need to find out is whether there are between Aristotle's and Judaism's philosophies only shared convictions about the genus and the species or particular conceptions as to how these are to be identified and organized. The basic conviction on both sides is this: objects are not random but fall into classes and so may be described, analyzed, and explained by appeal to general traits or rules.

II. ARISTOTLE AND THE MISHNAH'S DEDUCTIVE REASONING

The component of Aristotelianism that pertains here is "the use of deductive reasoning proceeding from self-evident principles or discovered general truths to conclusions of a more limited import; and syllogistic forms of

---

[1] A. W. H. Adkins, *From the Many to the One. A Study of Personality and Views of Human Nature in the Context of Ancient Greek Society, Values, and Beliefs* (Ithaca, 1970: Cornell University Press)., pp. 170–171.

[2] But only Aristotle and the Mishnah carry into the material details of economics that conviction about the true character or essence of definition of things. The economics of the Mishnah and the economics of Aristotle begin in the conception of "true value," and the distributive economics proposed by each philosophy then develops that fundamental notion. The principle is so fundamental to each system that comparison of one system to the other in those terms alone is justified.

demonstrative or persuasive arguments."³ The goal is the classification of things, which is to say, the discovery of general rules that apply to discrete data or instances. Minio-Paluello states,

> "In epistemology...Aristotelianism includes a concentration on knowledge accessible by natural means or accountable for by reason; an inductive, analytical empiricism, or stress on experience in the study of nature...leading from the perception of contingent individual occurrences to the discovery of permanent, universal patterns; and the primacy of the universal, that which is expressed by common or general terms. In metaphysics, or the theory of Being, Aristotelianism involves belief in the primacy of the individual in the realm of existence; in correlated conceptions allowing an articulate account of reality (e.g., 10 categories; genus-species-individual, matter-form, potentiality-actuality, essential-accidental; the four material elements and their basic qualities; and the four causes-formal, material, efficient and final); in the soul as the inseparable form of each living body in the vegetable and animals kingdoms; in activity as the essence of things; and in the primacy of speculative over practical activity."

The manner in which we accomplish this work is to establish categories of traits, and these will yield the besought rules or generalizations that make possible both classification, and, in the nature of things, therefore also hierarchization.

Clearly, when we review some of the more obvious characteristics of Aristotle's logical and taxonomic principles, in specific terms we find only occasional points of contact with the principles we uncover in the Mishnah's philosophical structure. Only in general does the manner in which Aristotle does the work of definition through classification also characterize the way in which sages do the same work. But there are points of intersection. For instance, while the actual and the potential form critical taxic categories for Aristotle, they prove subsidiary, though pertinent, in the Mishnah. While for the Mishnah, the matter of mixtures defines a central and generative problematic, for Aristotle, the same matter is subsumed into other compositions altogether. It constitutes a chapter in the story of change, which is explained by the passage of elements into one another. (We take up the matter of mixtures in a later chapter.)

That will help us to account for the destruction of one element and the creation of another. In this connection Allan says:

> Aristotle does not mean by 'mixture' a mere shuffling of primary particles, as if the seeds of wheat and barley were mixed in a heap, but genuine change of

---

3   Minio-Paluello, Lorenzo, "Aristotelianism," *Encyclopedia Britannica* 1:1155–1161., p. 1155.

quality resulting in a new 'form,' towards which each component has made a contribution.[4]

The consideration of the classes of mixtures plays its role in Aristotle's account of the sublunary region; it is not—as represented by Allan—a point at which Aristotle repeatedly uncovers problems that require solution, in the way in which the issue of mixtures forms the source for the Mishnah's solution of urgent problems.

Enough has been said to justify comparing Aristotle's and the Halakhah's philosophies, but I have yet to specify what I conceive to be the generative point of comparison. It lies in two matters, first, the paramount one of the shared principles of formal logic, which I find blatant in the Mishnah and which all presentations of Aristotle's philosophy identify as emblematic. The second, as is clear, is the taxonomic method, viewed from afar. Let us turn only briefly to the former. When we follow a simple account of the way in which we attain new truth, we find ourselves quite at home. Allan's account follows:[5]

> Induction...is the advance from the particular to the general. By the inspection of examples...in which one characteristic appears conjoined with another, we are led to propound a general rule which we suppose to be valid for cases not yet examined. Since the rule is of higher generality than the instances, this is an advance from a truth 'prior for us' toward a truth 'prior in nature.'

My representation of the Mishnaic mode of presentation of cases that, with our participation, yield a general rule, accords with this logic, which is inductive.

The more important of the two principles of sound intellectual method, is the taxonomic interest in defining through classification. This definitive trait of natural philosophy is what we find in common between Aristotle's and the Mishnah's philosophical method, and the points in common prove far more than those yielded by the general observation that both systems appeal to the identification of genera out of species. In fact, what philosophers call the dialectical approach in Aristotle proves the same approach to the discovery or demonstration of truth as that we find in the Mishnah. Owens sets the matter forth in the following language:[6]

---

[4] Allan, D. J., *The Philosophy of Aristotle* (London, New York, Toronto, 1952: Oxford University Press/Geoffrey Cumberlege), p. 60.
[5] Op. cit., pp. 126ff.
[6] Joseph Owens, *A History of Ancient Western Philosophy*, pp. 309ff.

> Since a theoretical science proceeds from first principles that are found within the thing under investigation, the initial task of the philosophy of nature will be to discover its primary principles in the sensible thing themselves.

I cannot imagine a formulation more suited to the method of the Mishnah than that simple statement. For the Mishnah's philosophers compose their taxonomy by appeal to the indicative traits of things, rather than to extrinsic considerations of imposed classification, e.g., by reference to Scripture. The philosophers whose system is set forth in the Mishnah appeal to the traits of things, deriving their genera from the comparison and contrast of those inherent or intrinsic traits. This I take to be precisely what is stated here.

> In accordance with the general directives of the Aristotelian logic, the process of their discovery will be dialectical, not demonstrative.

This distinction is between genuine reasoning and demonstration. If the parallels in method are clear, where do we find the difference between Aristotle's system and the Mishnah's? It is that the goal of Aristotle's system, the teleological argument in favor of the unmoved mover, and the goal of Judaism's system, the demonstration of the unity of being, are essentially contradictory, marking utterly opposed positions on the fundamental character of God and the traits of the created world that carries us upward to God. So we establish the philosophical character of the method of the Mishnah's system, only at the cost of uncovering a major contradiction: the proposition that animates the one system stands in direct opposition, as to its premises, implications, and explicit results, with the results of the other. Aristotle's God attained through teleological demonstration accomplished through the right classification of all things, and the Mishnah's God, whose workings in the world derive from the demonstration of the ontological unity of all things, cannot recognize one another. And that is the case even though they are assuredly one.

III. MESSAGE: THE TAXONOMIC POWER OF HUMAN INTENTIONALITY

Now that we have considered the premises, in philosophy, of the Mishnah's method, let us turn to a specific presupposition that operates throughout. A principal philosophical premise of the Mishnah is that intentionality governs. A subdivision of the larger analysis of the character and effects

4. ANALYSIS: Hierarchical classification and the Law's Philosophical Demonstration of Monotheism

of responsibility[7] the matter of intentionality bears theological messages. In fact, it is at the point of intentionality that God and the human being meet. We encountered that meeting in the opening chapter of this book, in our consideration of the power of God to hear and remember what man says and does. For one fundamental principle of the system of Judaism attested in the Mishnah is that God and the human being share traits of attitude and emotion. And they communicate all the time. They want the same thing. For example, it is made clear in Mishnah-tractate Maaserot, man and God respond in the same way to the same events, since they share not only ownership of the Land but also the same viewpoint on the value of its produce. When the farmer wants the crop, so too does God. When the householder takes the view that the crop is worthwhile, God responds to the attitude of the farmer by forming the same opinion.

Through its analysis of intentionality, in quite abstract terms as a matter of fact, the Mishnah's theological anthropology brings God and the householder into the same continuum and indeed prepares the way for understanding what makes the entire Halakhic system work. We return to intentionality in a later chapter.) But in what kind of language, and precisely through what sort of discourse, does the authorship of the Mishnah set forth principles that motivate the entire system of the Mishnah and the Halakhah? Here I shall show that through little that authorship says much, and in discourse on matters of no consequence at all, indeed, matters that, in the setting of the writers of the document, had no practical bearing at all, principal conceptions emerge.

The Mishnah's discussion on intention works out several theories concerning not God and God's relationship to humanity but the nature of the human will, a decidedly philosophical topic. The human being is defined as not only sentient but also a volitional being, who can will with effect, unlike beasts and, as a matter of fact, angels (which do not, in fact, figure in the Mishnah at all). On the one side, there is no consideration or will or attitude of animals, for these are null. On the other side, will and attitude of angels, where these are represented in later documents, are totally subservient to God's wishes. Only the human being, in the person of the farmer, possesses and also exercises the power of intentionality. And it is the power that intentionality possesses that defines the central consideration. Because a human being forms an intention, consequences follow, whether or not given material expression in gesture or even in speech. An account of the

---

[7] For the philosophical issues set forth in the context of Aristotle's thought, see Richard Sorabji, *Necessity, Cause and Blame. Perspectives on Aristotle's Theory* (London, 1980: Duckworth).

Mishnah's sages' philosophical anthropology—theory of the character and structure of the human being—must begin with the extraordinary power imputed by the Mishnah's system to the will and intentionality of the human being.

But that view comes to expression with regard to human beings of a particular sort. The householder-farmer (invariably represented as male) is a principal figure, just as the (invariably male) priest in the Temple is another. The attitude of the one toward the crop, like that of the other toward the offering that he carries out, affects the status of the crop. It classifies an otherwise-unclassified substance. It changes the standing of an already-classified beast. It shifts the status of a pile of grain, without any physical action whatsoever, from one category to another. Not only so, but as we shall now see, the attitude or will of a farmer can override the effects of the natural world, e.g., keeping in the status of what is dry and so insusceptible to cultic uncleanness a pile of grain that in fact has been rained upon and wet down. An immaterial reality, shaped and reformed by the householder's attitude and plan, overrides the material effect of a rain-storm. And that example brings us to the way in which these profound philosophical issues are explored. It is in the remarkable essay on theories of the relationship between action and intention worked out in Mishnah-tractate Makhshirin and exemplified by Chapter Four of that tractate.[8]

The subject-matter that serves as medium for sages' theories of human will and intention hardly appears very promising. Indeed, the topic of the tractate before us on its own hardly will have led us to anticipate what, in fact, will interest sages. The subject matter of tractate Makhshirin, to which we now turn, is the affect of liquid upon produce. The topic derives from the statement of Lev. 11:37: "And if any part of their carcass [a dead creeping thing] falls upon any seed for sowing that is to be sown, it is clean; but if water is put on the seed and any part of their carcass falls on it, it is unclean for you." Sages understand this statement to mean that seed that is dry is insusceptible to uncleanness, while seed that has been wet down is susceptible.[9]

They further take the view—and this is the point at which intention or human will enters in—that if seed, or any sort of grain, is wet down *without*

---

[8] It goes without saying, however, that numerous other chapters of the Mishnah yield the same fundamental concern with the matter of how intentionality relates to action, much as Sorabji's discussion shows Aristotle's interest in assigning blame through a consideration of responsibility and causation.

[9] Dry grain is inert. Only when it is wet down will the flour and yeast come to life. When the dough forms a crust in the oven the yeast dies, and the bread becomes liable to the dough offering. Tractate Hallah is incomprehensible without tractate Makhshirin and vice versa.

4. ANALYSIS: Hierarchical classification and the Law's Philosophical Demonstration of Monotheism

the assent of the farmer who owns the grain, then the grain remains insusceptible, while if seed or grain is wet down with the farmer's assent, then the grain is susceptible to uncleanness. The upshot is that that grain that a farmer wets down and that is touched by a source of uncleanness, e.g., a dead creeping thing, is then deemed unclean and may not be eaten by those who eat their food in a state of cultic cleanness in accord with the laws of the book of Leviticus pertaining to the priests' food in the Temple. Intentionality thus overrides the natural condition of the grain, and the householder becomes primary actor through his act of will.

Once we agree that what is deliberately wet down is susceptible and what is wet down not with the farmer's assent or by his intention is insusceptible, then we work out diverse theories of the interplay between intention and action. And that is the point, over all, at which the authorship of Mishnah-tractate Makhshirin enters in and sets forth its ideas. Tractate Makhshirin is shown to be formed of five successive layers of generative principles, in sequence:

1. Dry produce is insusceptible, a notion which begins in the plain meaning of Lev. 11:34, 37.

2. Wet produce is susceptible only when *intentionally* wet down, a view expressed in gross terms by Abba Yosé as cited by Joshua.

3. Then follow the refinements of the meaning and effects of *intention*, beginning in 'Aqiba's and Tarfon's dispute, in which the secondary matter of what is tangential to one's primary motive is investigated.

4. This yields the contrary views, assuredly belonging to second-century masters, that what is essential imparts susceptibility and what is peripheral to one's primary purpose does not; and that both what is essential and what is peripheral impart susceptibility to uncleanness. (A corollary to this matter is the refinement that what is wet down under constraint is not deemed wet down by deliberation.)

5. The disputes on the interpretation of intention — Is it solely defined by what one actually does or modified also by what one has wanted to do as well as by what one has done? — belonging to Yosé and Judah and his son Yosé.

We see from this catalogue of successive positions, assigned to authorities who lived in successive generations, that the paramount theme of the tractate is the determination of the capacity of the eligible liquids to impart susceptibility to uncleanness. The operative criterion, whether or not the liquids are applied intentionally, obviously is going to emerge in every pericope pertinent to the theme. If I now summarize the central and generative theme of our tractate, we may state matter as follows.

THE PHILOSOPHICAL PREMISE OF JUDAISM

First, liquids are capable of imparting susceptibility to uncleanness only if they are useful to men, e.g., drawn with approval, or otherwise subject to human deliberation and intention. The contrary view is that however something is wet down, once it is wet, if falls within the rule of Lev. 11:34, 38, and is subject to uncleanness.

Second, if we begin with the fundamental principle behind the tractate, thus: it is

(1) that which is given in the name of Abba Yosé-Joshua (M. Makhshirin 1:3M): Water imparts susceptibility to uncleanness only when it is applied to produce intentionally or deliberately. This yields a secondary and derivative rule:

(2) 'Aqiba's distinction at M. Makhshirin 4:9 and M. Makhshirin 5:4: Water intrinsic to one's purpose is detached with approval, but that which is not essential in accomplishing one's primary purpose is not under the law, If water be put. What 'Aqiba has done is to carry to its logical next stage the generative principle. If water applied with approval can impart susceptibility to uncleanness, then, it follows, only *that part* of the detached and applied water is essential to one's intention is subject to the law, If water be put. Items in the name of second-century authorities that develop 'Aqiba's improvement of Abba Yosé's principle raise an interesting question:

(3) What is the relationship between intention and action? Does intention to do something govern the decision in a case, even though one's action has produced a different effect? For example, if I intend to wet down only part of an object, or make use of only part of a body of water, but then wet down the whole or dispose of the whole, is the whole deemed susceptible? Does my consequent action revise the original effects of my intention?

Aristotle will not have taken much interest in such issues of enchantment and cult; but reframed as a consideration of the relationship between intentionality and act, cause and result, intent and responsibility, he will have found himself at home. For the deep thought on the relationship between what one does and what one wants to see happen explores the several possible positions. Judah and his son, Yosé, take up the position that ultimate deed or result is definitive of intention. What happens is retrospectively deemed to decide what I wanted to happen (M. Makhshirin 3:5–7). Others of the same period, Yosé in particular (M. Makhshirin 1:5), maintain the view that, while consequence plays a role in the determination of intention, it is not exclusive and definitive. What I wanted to make happen affects the assessment of what actually has happened. Now the positions on the interplay of action and intention are these:

4. ANALYSIS: Hierarchical classification and the Law's Philosophical Demonstration of Monotheism

1. Judah has the realistic notion that a person changes his mind, and therefore we adjudge a case solely by what he does and not by what he says he will do, intends, or has intended, to do. If we turn Judah's statement around, we come up with the conception predominant throughout his rulings: *A case is judged in terms solely of what the person does.* If he puts on water, that water in particular that he has deliberately applied imparts susceptibility to uncleanness. If he removes water, only that water he actually removes imparts susceptibility to uncleanness, but water that he intends to remove but that is not actually removed is not deemed subject to the person's original intention. And, it is fair to add, we know it is not subject to the original intention, because the person's action has not accomplished the original intention or has placed limits upon the original intention. What is done is wholly determinative of what is originally intended, and that is the case whether the result is that the water is deemed capable or incapable of imparting susceptibility to uncleanness. We move from effect to cause to intentionality: responsibility is the obvious outcome.

2. Yosé at M. Makhshirin 1:5 expresses the contrary view. Water that has been wiped off is detached with approval. But water that has remained on the leek has not conformed to the man's intention, and that intention is shown by what the man has actually done. Accordingly, the water remaining on the leek is not subject to the law, If water be put. The upshot is to reject the view that what is done is wholly determinative of what is originally intended. We sort things out by appeal to nuances of effect. Once, in assessing blame, we invoke the consideration of intentionality, then matters become more complicated.

3. Simeon's point at M. Makhshirin 1:6 is that the liquid left on the palm of the hand is not wanted and not necessary to the accomplishment of one's purpose. Simeon's main point is that liquid not essential in accomplishing one's purpose is not taken into account and does not come under the law, If water be put. Why not? Because water is held to be applied with approval *only* when it serves a specific purpose. That water which is incidental has not been subjected to the man's wishes and therefore does not impart susceptibility to uncleanness. Only that water that is necessary to carry out the farmer's purpose imparts susceptibility to uncleanness. If a pile of grain has been wet down, then water that the farmer has deliberately applies effects susceptibility to uncleanness to that part of the grain-pile that it has touched. But water that is incidental and not subject to the farmer's initial plan has no effect upon the grain, even though, as a matter of fact, grain at some other point in the pile may be just as wet as grain the farmer has deliberately watered.

Simeon and Yosé deem water to have been detached and applied with approval only when it serves a person's essential purpose, and water that is not necessary in accomplishing that purpose is not deemed subject to the law, If water be put. That is why Simeon rules as he does. Yosé states a different aspect of the same conception. Water that actually has dripped of the leek in no way has fallen under the person's approval. This is indicated by the facts of the matter, the results of the person's actual deed. And this brings us to the concrete exposition of the chapter at hand. With the positions and principles just now outlined, the reader can follow the discussion with little difficulty. We begin with the simple distinction between water that I want for the accomplishment of my purpose, and water that I do not want, and that category of water does not have the power to impart susceptibility to uncleanness.

The recurrent formula, "If water be put," alludes to Lev. 11:34, 37, and refers to the deliberate watering down of seed or produce. But at stake is the classification of the water. The kind of water to which allusion is made is in the category of "If water be put," meaning that that water, having served the farmer's purpose, has the power to impart susceptibility to uncleanness should it fall on grain. Water that is not in the category of "If water be put," should it fall on grain by some sort of accident, does not impart susceptibility to uncleanness to grain that is otherwise kept dry. It remains to observe that the reason the farmer wets down grain is that the grain is going to be milled, and milling grain requires some dampening of the seed. Accordingly, we have the counterpart to the issue of tithing. When the farmer plans to make use of the (now-tithed) grain, and indicates the plan by wetting down the grain, then the issue of cultic cleanness, that is, preserving the grain from the sources of cultic uncleanness listed in Leviticus Chapters Eleven through Fifteen, is raised. Before the farmer wants to use the produce, the produce is null. The will and intentionality of the farmer, owner of the grain, are what draws the produce within the orbit of the immaterial world of uncleanness and cleanness.

Now to the actual texts I have chosen for illustrating not only the issues but the way in which the issues are set forth and analyzed: arguments about very picayune questions indeed, and, furthermore, questions lacking all concrete relevance in the world in the second century in which the Mishnah's philosophers actually lived.

A. He who kneels down to drink —
B. the water that comes up on his mouth and on his moustache is under the law, If water be put. [That water imparts susceptibility to uncleanness should it drip

4. ANALYSIS: Hierarchical classification and the Law's Philosophical Demonstration of Monotheism

      on a pile of grain, since the farmer has accomplished his purpose — getting a drink — by stirring up that water and getting it into his mouth or on his moustache.]

C. [The water that comes up] on his nose and on [the hair of] his head and on his beard is not under the law, "If water be put." [That water does not have the power to impart susceptibility to uncleanness should it fall on a pile of dry produce.]

D. He who draws [water] with a jug —

E. the water that comes up on its outer parts and on the rope wound round its neck and on the rope that is needed [in dipping it] — lo, this is under the law, If water be put on.

F. And how much [rope] is needed [in handling it]?

G. R. Simeon b. Eleazar says, "A handbreadth."

H. [If] one put it under the water-spout, [the water on its out parts and on the rope, now not needed in drawing water] is not under the law, If water be put.

M. Makhshirin 4:1

What must get wet in order to accomplish one's purpose if deemed wet down by approval. But water not needed in one's primary goal is not subject to approval. The pericope consists of A–C and D–H, the latter in two parts, D–E + F–G, and H. The point of A–C is clear. Since, D–E, in dipping the jug into the water, it is not possible to draw water without wetting the outer parts and the rope, water on the rope and the outer pats is deemed affected by one's wishes. Simeon b. Eleazar glosses. At H one does not make use of the rope and does not care to have the water on the outer parts, since he can draw the water without recourse to either. Accordingly, water on the rope and on the outer parts does not impart susceptibility to uncleanness.

A. He on whom rains fell,

B. even [if he is] a Father [principal source] of uncleanness —

C. it [the water] is not under the law, If water be put [since even in the case of B, the rainfall was not wanted].

D. But if he shook off [the rain], it [the water that is shaken off] is under the law, If water be put.

E. [If] he stood under the water-spout to cool off,

F. or to rinse off,

G. in the case of an unclean person [the water] is unclean.

H. And in the case of a clean person, [the water] is under the law, If water be put.

M. Makhshirin 4:2

The pericope is in two parts, A–D and E–H, each in two units. The point of A + C is that the rain does not come under the person's approval.

Therefore the rain is not capable of imparting susceptibility to uncleanness. If by some action, however, the person responds to the rain, for example, if he shook off his garments, then it falls under his approval. B is certainly a gloss, and not an important one. The principal source of uncleanness, e.g., the *Zab* of Leviticus, Chapter Fifteen, derives no benefit from the rain and therefore need not be explicitly excluded. At E, however, the person obviously does want to make use of the water. Therefore it is rendered both susceptible to uncleanness and capable of imparting susceptibility to other tings. G makes the former point, H, the latter. Perhaps it is G that has generated B, since the distinction between unclean and clean is important at G–H and then invites the contrast between A + B and E + G, that is, falling rain *versus* rain-water pouring through the waterspout and deliberately utilized.

> A. He who puts a dish on end against the wall so that it will rinse off, lo, this [water that flows across the plate] is under the law, If water be put.
> B. If [he put it there] so that it [rain] should not harm the wall, it [the water] is not under the law, If water be put
>
> M. Makhshirin 4:3

The established distinction is repeated one more, with reference to an inanimate object. Now we make use of the water for rinsing off the plate. Accordingly, the water is detached with approval. But if the plate is so located as to protect the wall, then the water clearly is not wanted and therefore does not have the capacity to impart susceptibility to uncleanness.

> I. A. A jug into which water leaking from the roof came down —
> B. The House of Shammai say, "It is broken."
> C. The House of Hillel say, "It is emptied out."
> D. And they agree that he puts in his hand and takes pieces of fruit from its inside, and they [the drops of water, the pieces of fruit] are insusceptible to uncleanness.
>
> M. Makhshirin 4:4

> II. F. A trough into which the rain dripping from the roof flowed [without approval] —
> G. [water in the trough and] the drops [of water] that splashed out and those that overflowed are not under the law, If water be put.
> H. [If] one took it to pour it out —
> I. The House of Shammai say, "It is under the law, If water be put."
> [Since he poured the water away only when the tub was moved to another place, it may be said that he did not object to the water when the tub was in its original place.]

4. ANALYSIS: Hierarchical classification and the Law's Philosophical Demonstration of Monotheism

    J.   The House of Hillel say, "It is not under the law, If water be put."
          [His pouring away showed that he did not want the water even in the tub's original place.]

III. K.   [If] one [intentionally] left it out so that the rain dripping from the roof would flow into it —
    L.   the drops [of water] that splashed out and those that overflowed —
    M.   The House of Shammai say, "They are under the law, If water be put" [all the more so what is in the trough].
    N.   The House of Hillel say, "They [the drops that splashed or overflowed] are not under the law, If water be put.
    O.   [If] one took it in order to pour it out, these and those agree that [both kinds of water] are under the law, If water be put. [For since the owner did not empty it where it stood, the water is deemed to be detached with his approval.]
    P.   He who dunks the utensils,
          and he who washes his clothing in a cave [pond] —
    Q.   the water that comes up on his hands is under the law, If water be put.
    R.   [And the water that comes up] on his feet is not under the law, If water be put.
    S.   R. Eleazar says, "If it is impossible for him to go down [into the water] unless his feet become muddy, even [the drops of water] that come up on his feet are under the law, If water be put [since he wants to clean his feet]."

M. Makhshirin 4:5

The composite is in the following parts: A–D, a complete and well balanced Houses' dispute, in which the apodosis exhibits exact balance in the number of syllables, F–G, which set the stage for the second Houses' dispute, at H–J; K–L, the protasis for the third dispute, which depends upon F (+ G = L) — a trough that happens to receive rain *versus* one deliberately left out to collect rain, and the standard apodosis, M–N; and a final agreement, O, parallel to D. R–S form a separate pericope entirely. The issue of A–D is this: We have left a jug containing fruit in such a position that water leaking from the roof fills it. We want to empty the fruit out of the jug. But we want to do so in such a way that the water in the jug does not received the capacity to impart susceptibility to uncleanness to the fruit contained in the jug. There are these considerations.

(1) Clearly, in is present location, the water is insusceptible. Why? Because it did not fall into the jug with approval.

(2) If then we break the jug, we accomplish the purpose of treating the water as unwanted and this is what the Shammaites say we should to (B).

(3) But if we merely empty out the fruit, we stir the water with approval; the fruit in the jug forthwith is wet down by the water, with approval, and becomes susceptible.

The Hillelites (C) say that if we pour out the fruit, that suffices. Why? Because the man wants the fruit, not the water. So the water does not have the capacity to impart susceptibility to uncleanness. In its original location it is not subject to approval. The Shammaites and Hillelites agree that, so long as the fruit in the jug is unaffected by the water, the fruit is insusceptible to uncleanness. It is not made susceptible even by the water which is removed with the fruit.

The second Houses' dispute, F–J, goes over the ground of the first. There is no significant difference between water that has leaked into the jug and water that has fallen into the trough, A/F. But the issue, G, is different. Now we ask about water that overflows. Does this water flow with approval? Certainly not, both parties agree. None of this water is wanted. What if the man then takes up the trough with the intention of pouring the water out? We already know the Hillelite position. It is the same as at C. There is no reason to be concerned about moving the trough in order to empty it. The man pours out the water. By his deed he therefore indicates that he does not want it. The Shammaites are equally consistent. The man has raised the trough to pour out the water. In moving the water, he (retrospectively) imparts the stamp of approval on the original location of the water. The reference at G is only to set the stage for K–L, since the water in the trough of F itself is insusceptible.

At K the problem is that the man deliberately dose collect the water. Accordingly, he certainly has imparted his approval to it. The problem of L is that part of the water splashes out or overflows. Clearly, the man wanted the water and therefore, what overflowed or splashed out has not conformed to his original wishes. That is, if he shook the tree to bring down the water, all parties agree that the water that falls is subject to the man's approval. But the water that does not fall is a problem. Here too the Shammaites say that what has been in the trough and overflowed has been subject to the man's intention. Therefore, like the water in the trough, the drops that splash out or overflow are under the law, If water be put. But the House of Hillel maintain that the water not in the location where the man has desired it is not subject to this wishes, and therefore does not impart susceptibility to uncleanness.

O completes the elegant construction by bringing the Hillelites over to the Shammaite position. If the man lifted up a trough of water that he *himself* has collected, then his is water that at one point in its history has surely conformed to the man's wishes and therefore has the capacity to impart insusceptibility to uncleanness. The Hillelites of N clearly will agree that the water in the trough is subject to the law, If water be put, just as the Shammaites at L–M will maintain the same. The dispute of M–N concerns only the liquid referred to at L. P–R go over the ground of M. 4:1. That is,

4. ANALYSIS: Hierarchical classification and the Law's Philosophical Demonstration of Monotheism

water necessary to accomplish the man's purpose is subject to the law, If water be put. That which is not important in the accomplishment of his purpose is not subject to the law. Eleazar's gloss, S, adds that if the man's feet grow muddy in the process of getting the water, then he will want to clean his feet, and even the water on his feet therefore is subject to the law, If water be put. There is nothing surprising in this unit, but the exposition is elegant indeed.

- A. A basket that is full of lupines and [that happens to be] placed into an immersion-pool —
- B. one puts out his hand and takes lupines from is midst, and they are insusceptible to uncleanness.
- C. [If] one took them out of the water [while still in the basket] —
- D. the ones that touch the [water on the sides of the] basket are susceptible to uncleanness.
- E. And all the rest of the lupines are insusceptible to uncleanness.
- F. A radish that is in the cave-[water] —
- G. a menstruant rinses it off, and it is insusceptible to uncleanness.
- H. [If] she brought it out of the water in any measure at all, [having been made susceptible to uncleanness in the water], it is unclean.

M. Makhshirin 4:6

We go over the point at which the Houses agree at M. Makhshirin 4:4D. The lupines in the basket are wet on account of the water in the pool, but that does not render them susceptible to uncleanness. Accordingly, since the water is not detached with approval, when one takes the lupines out of the basket, they remain insusceptible. The water on the basket, however, is detached with approval, since presumably the basket has been immersed to render it clean from uncleanness. (The lupines — being food — in any event cannot be cleaned in the pool.) Accordingly, at C, the ones in the basket that touch the sides of the basket are in contact with water capable of imparting susceptibility to uncleanness, having been used with approval. The others, however, although wet, remain clean. Why? Because they have not touched water that has been detached with approval. The sentence-structure is slightly strange, since A sets the stage for a thought, but the thought begins afresh at B. This is then extreme apocopation at A–B, less clear-cut apocopation at C–D.

The same form is followed at F–H. The radish in the water is insusceptible to uncleanness. The menstruant rinses it off. While the radish is in the water, it remains insusceptible. But the woman has rinsed her hands and the radish. Accordingly, the water on the radish is detached with approval. It renders the radish susceptible to uncleanness, and as soon as the radish is taken out of the water, the woman's touch imparts uncleanness.

    A. Pieces of fruit that fell into a water-channel —
    B. he whose hands were unclean reached out and took them —
    C. his hands are clean, and the pieces of fruit are insusceptible to uncleanness.
    D. But if he gave thought that his hands should be rinsed off [in the water], his hands are clean, and the [water on the] pieces of fruit is under the law, If water be put.

M. Makhshirin 4:7

The pericope is in the severe apocopation characteristic of the present set, A, B, and C being out of clear syntactical relationship to one another. We should have to add, at A *as to pieces...*, then at B, *if he whose hands...*, and C would follow as a complete sentence. But A is not continued at B–C. Rather, we have apocopation. We have a further illustration of the principle of the foregoing. The owner wants to retrieve the fruit. Even though his hands are unclean, he reaches out and takes the fruit. What is the result? The hands are made clean by the water-flow. But the fruit remains insusceptible to uncleanness. Why? Because it was not the man's intent to rinse off his hands in the water channel and so to clean them. If, D adds, that was his intent, then his hands of course are clean, but the fruit now has been rendered susceptible to uncleanness.

    A. A [clay] dish that is full of water and placed in an immersion-pool,
    B. and into [the airspace of] which a Father of uncleanness put his hand,
    C. is unclean [but the water remains clean].
    D. [If he was unclean only by reason of] contact with unclean things, it is clean.
    E. And as to all other liquids — they are unclean.
    F. For water does not effect cleanness for other liquids.

M. Makhshirin 4:8

The present pericope is not phrased in the expected apocopation, for C refers to the dish and so completes the thought of A. We have an exercise in several distinct rules. First, a clay pot is made unclean only by a Father of uncleanness. Second, it is not cleaned by immersion in the pool but only by breaking. But the sides of the pot are porous, as at M. Makhshirin 3:2. Therefore, third, the water in the pot is deemed in contact with the immersion-pool. The dish is touched by a Father of uncleanness and is therefore made unclean. But, D, someone in the first remove of uncleanness is not able to contaminate the pot. The liquid in the pot is not referred to at A–D, but E demands that we understand

4. ANALYSIS: Hierarchical classification and the Law's Philosophical Demonstration of Monotheism

the liquid in A–C and D to be clean. Why? Because the water referred to at A certainly is cleaned and kept clean in the pool, along the lines of M. Makhshirin 4:6–7. E then simply registers the fact that liquids apart from those enumerated at M. Makhshirin 6:4 are not cleaned in an immersion-pool. E–F should also tell us that if other liquids are in the pot, the pot also is unclean, because liquids in the first remove of uncleanness do impart uncleanness to clay or earthenware utensils. Accordingly, E–F form either a slightly awry gloss, taking for granted that A–C have said *the water is clean, even though it* [the pot] *is unclean,* or they belong to a pericope other than the present one, which is highly unlikely.

> A. He who draws water with a swape-pipe [or bucket] [and pieces of fruit later fell into the moisture or water remaining in the pipe or bucket],
> B. up to three days [the water] imparts susceptibility to uncleanness. [Afterward it is deemed to be unwanted (Maimonides).]
> C. R. 'Aqiba says, "If it has dried off, it is forthwith incapable of imparting susceptibility to uncleanness, and if it has not dried off, up to thirty days it [continues to] impart susceptibility to uncleanness."
>
> M. Makhshirin 4:9

The dispute poses A–B against C. We deal now with a wooden pipe or bucket. Do we deem the bucket to be dried off as soon as it is empty? No, B says, the water in the bucket, detached with approval (by definition) remains able to impart susceptibility for three days. 'Aqiba qualifies the matter. If the water drawn with approval was dried out of the bucket, whatever moisture then is found in the bucket is not wanted; the man has shown, by drying out the bucket or pipe, that he does not want moisture there. If it is not dried out, then whatever liquid is there is deemed to be detached from the pool with approval and therefore able to impart uncleanness for a very long time. Only after thirty days do we assume that the wood is completely dry of the original water detached with approval.

> A. Pieces of wood on which liquids fell and on which rains fell —
> B. if [the rains] were more [than the liquids], [the pieces of wood] are insusceptible to uncleanness.
> C. [If] he took them outside so that the rains might fall on them, even though they [the rains] were more [than the liquids], they [the pieces of wood] are [susceptible to uncleanness and] unclean.
> D. [If] they absorbed unclean liquids, even though he took them outside so that the rains would fall on them, they are clean [for the clean rain has not had contact with the unclean absorbed liquid].
> E. But he should kindle them only with clean hands alone [to avoid contaminating the rain-water of D].

F. R. Simeon says, "If they were wet [freshly cut] and he kindled them, and the liquids [sap] that exude from them were more than the liquids that they had absorbed, they are clean"

M. Makhshirin 4:10

The pericope is in the following parts: A–B balanced by C; and D, qualified by E. F is an important gloss of D–E. The point of A–B is familiar from M. Makhshirin 2:3. If we have a mixture of unclean and clean liquids, we determine matters in accord with the relative quantity of each. If the clean liquids are the greater part, the whole is deemed clean. Accordingly, since the rain, which is insusceptible and does not impart susceptibility to uncleanness unless it falls with approval, forms the greater part, B, the liquids on the pieces of wood are deemed clean. But if, C, the man deliberately arranged for the rain to fall on the pieces of wood, then the rain falls on the wood with approval, is susceptible to uncleanness, and is made unclean by the unclean liquids already on the wood.

D raises a separate question. What if pieces of wood have absorbed unclean liquids? The answer is that what is absorbed does not have contact with what is on the surface—that is the meaning of absorption. Therefore if rain falls on wood that has absorbed unclean liquids, the rain does not impart susceptibility to uncleanness if it has not fallen with approval. D does not treat that matter; it wishes to say something additional. Even if the rain falls with approval, the wood remains clean. Why? Because nothing has made the rain unclean. That secondary point then invites E — or E imposes the detail, *even if*, on D: Even though he took them outside, so the rain falls with approval, E adds, since the rain *has* fallen with approval, it is susceptible to uncleanness. Accordingly, the man should kindle the wood only with clean hands, lest he make the rain-water unclean.

Simeon deals then with a still further point. If the wood is freshly cut when kindled, then the unclean absorbed liquids are deemed neutralized by the sap. If the exuded liquid caused by the heat is more than the still-absorbed liquid, then the clean, exuded liquid forms the greater part, and the whole is clean, just as at A–B. Simeon, Maimonides says, differs from D (+ E). We hold, as at A–D, that if unclean liquids are absorbed by the wood, they are deemed clean and do not impart uncleanness to the oven, *only* in the case in which the wood is wet. Then, when it is heated, it produces sap in greater quantity than the unclean liquids that it absorbed. But if not, the wood imparts uncleanness to the oven when it is heated because of the unclean liquid that has been absorbed.

Now if we reflect on the detailed rules we have observed, one thing will have struck the reader very forcefully. What Scripture treats as un-

4. ANALYSIS: Hierarchical classification and the Law's Philosophical Demonstration of Monotheism

conditional the authorship of the Mishnah has made contingent upon the human will. Specifically, when Scripture refers at Lev. 11:34, 37, to grain's being made wet, it makes no provision for the attitude of the owner of the grain, his intention in having wet the grain, or his will as to its disposition. What is wet is susceptible, what is dry is insusceptible. The effect of the water is *ex opere operato*. Yet, as we see, that very matter of the attitude of the householder toward the grain's being made wet forms the centerpiece of interest. The issue of intentionality thus forms the precipitating consideration behind every dispute we have reviewed, and, it is clear, the Priestly authors of Leviticus could not have conceived such a consideration. The introduction of that same concern can be shown to characterize the Mishnah's treatment of a variety of biblical rules and to form a systemic principle of profound and far-reaching character. We may draw a simple and striking contract, for instance, between the following bald statements:

1. "Whatever touches the altar shall become holy" (Ex. 29:37)

It would be difficult to find a less ambiguous statement. But here is the rule of the Mishnah's sages:

2. "The altar sanctifies *that which is appropriate to it*" (M. Zebahim 9:1)…"And what are those things which, even if they have gone up, should go down [since they are not offered at all and therefore are not appropriate to the altar]? "The flesh for the priests of Most Holy Things and the flesh of Lesser Holy Things [which is designated for priestly consumption]" (M. Zeb. 9:5).

To understand the conflict between statement No. 1 and statement No. 2 we have to understand how an animal enters the category of Most Holy Things or Lesser Holy Things. It is by the action of the farmer, who owns the beast and designates it for a purpose, within the cult, that imparts to the beast that status of Most Holy Things or Lesser Holy Things. In both cases, the rule is that such a beast yields parts that are burned up on the alter, and other parts that are given to the priests to eat or to the farmer, as the case may be.

Now the point is that it is the farmer who has designated a beast owned by him for sacrifice in the status of Most Holy Things or Lesser Holy Things. His disposition of the offering then places that offering into the classification that yields meat for the officiating priest out of the carcass of the sacrificial beast. Here is, in principle, something that is *surely* appropriate to the altar. But because of the designation, that is, the realization of the act of intentionality, of the householder, the owner of the beast, the beast has fallen into a classification that must yield meat to be eaten, and that meat of the carcass that is to be eaten is taken off the altar, though it is fit for being burnt up as an offering to God, and given to the owner or to the priest, as the rule may require.

It would be difficult to find a more profound difference, brought about by a keen appreciation for the power of the human will, between the Scripture's unnuanced and uncontingent rule and the Mishnah's clear revision of it. It would carry us far afield to catalogue all of the innumerable rules of the Mishnah in which intentionality forms the central concern. The rather arcane rules of Mishnah-tractate Makhshirin show us how sages thought deeply and framed comprehensive principles concerning will and intentionality and then applied these principles to exceedingly picayune cases, as we should, by now, expect. A simple conclusion seems well justified by the chapter we have examined in its broader conceptual context.

IV. THE JUDAISM BEHIND...

From the cases at hand, we may formulate the following presuppositions — "the Judaism behind" these particular rulings: will and deed constitute those actors of creation which work upon neutral realms, subject to either sanctification or uncleanness: the Temple and table, the field and family, the altar and hearth, woman, time, space, transactions in the material world and in the world above as well. An object, a substance, a transaction, even a phrase or a sentence is inert but may be made holy, when the interplay of the will and deed of the human being arouses or generates its potential to be sanctified. Each may be treated as ordinary or (where relevant) made unclean by the neglect of the will and inattentive act of the human being. Just as the entire system of uncleanness and holiness awaits the intervention of the human being, which imparts the capacity to become unclean upon what was formerly inert, or which removes the capacity to impart cleanness from what was formerly in its natural and puissant condition, so in the other ranges of reality, the human being is at the center on earth, just as is God in heaven. And all of this comes to us in arguments about the status of some drops of water.

5.
MIXTURES

I. THE THREE TYPES OF MIXTURES

A standard issue of natural philosophy involves the nature of mixtures. That is a recurrent issue in the Halakhah. In the Halakhic system of Judaism mixtures take three forms. First is the mixture in which two formerly distinct substances are fully blended, second is the one in which they are partially joined, and finally is the one in which the components remain essentially distinct. Mixtures therefore present cases of confusion, where we do not know the classification to which the components of the mixture, or the entire mixture, belong. A variety of principles come into play, depending on the circumstance.

Among the many exegetical expositions of the principles of mixtures, one stands out. It is shows what we accomplish by joining together two or more distinct sets of taxic indicators and demonstrating the interplay of all of them together. The three types of mixtures, complete, partial, and the one of mere juxtaposition, find instantiation here. One grid concerns the traits of solids as against those of liquids, and of what is wet as against what is dry. A second deals with levels of sanctification, that is, Most Holy Things, pertaining to the Temple altar, priestly rations, pertaining to the Temple but not to the altar, secular food, pertaining to the home and not sanctified at all. A third deals with removes from the original source of uncleanness, from the Father of Uncleanness out to something that has touched something that has touched a Father of Uncleanness, which is to say, something in several removes away. Not only are these distinct classifications brought together and superimposed upon one another, but they serve to make a single point, which is that whatever is more holy than something else is also more susceptible to uncleanness than something else. The matter of removes of uncleanness, which is worked out here, provides a fine introduction to the classification of mixtures, which defines a component of the Halakhah's generic hermeneutics:

THE PHILOSOPHICAL PREMISE OF JUDAISM

Mishnah-tractate Tohorot 1:9–3:1

1:9 A. Loaves of Holy Things, in the hollows of which is water preserved in cleanness fitting for Holy Things —
 B. [if] one of them was made unclean by a creeping thing, they all are unclean.
 C. In the case of heave offering, it [the creeping thing] renders unclean at two removes and renders unfit at one [third remove].
 D. If there is between them dripping liquid, even in the case of heave offering, the whole is unclean.

2:1 A. The woman who was pickling vegetables in the pot —
 and touched a leaf — outside of the pot, on a dry spot —
 B. even though it is an egg's bulk in size,
 C. it is unclean. But the whole is clean.
 D. [If] she touched a place on which there is liquid,
 E. if there is in it an egg's bulk, the whole is unclean.
 F. [If] there is not an egg's bulk in it, it is unclean. But the whole is clean.
 G. [If the wet leaf] returned to the pot, the whole is unclean.
 H. [If] she was [unclean because of] contact with [something unclean with] corpse uncleanness and touched,
 I. whether a place which is wet or a place which is dry,
 J. if there is in it an egg's bulk, the whole is unclean.
 K. [If] there is not an egg's bulk, it is unclean, but the whole is clean,
 L. [If] one who had immersed on the self — same day was emptying the pot with unclean hands, and she saw liquid on her hands —
 M. there being doubt whether it [the liquid] had splashed from the pot, or whether the stalk had touched her hands —
 N. the vegetable is unfit, but the pot is clean.

2:2 A. R. Eliezer says, "(1) He who eats food unclean in the first remove is unclean in the first remove; (2) [he who eats] food unclean in the second remove is unclean in the second remove; (3) [he who eats) food unclean in the third remove is unclean in the third remove."
 B. R. Joshua says, "(1) He who eats food unclean in the first remove and food unclean in the second remove is unclean in the second remove. He who eats food] unclean in the third remove is unclean in the second remove so far as Holy Things are concerned, and is not unclean in the second remove so far as heave offering is concerned —
 C. "in the case of unconsecrated food
 D. "which is prepared in conditions of cleanness appropriate to heave offering."

2:3 A. Unconsecrated food: in the first remove is unclean and renders [heave offering] unclean.
 B. [Unconsecrated food] in the second remove is unfit but does not convey uncleanness.
 C. And [unconsecrated food] in the third remove is eaten in pottage of heave offering.

2:4 A. Heave offering: in the first and in the second removes is unclean and renders [Holy Things] unclean.

5. MIXTURES

- B. [Heave offering] in the third remove is unfit and does not convey uncleanness.
- C. And [heave offering] at the fourth remove is eaten in a pottage of Holy Things.

2:5
- A. Holy Things: in the first and the second and the third removes are susceptible to uncleanness and convey uncleanness.
- B. And [Holy Things] in the fourth remove are unfit and do not convey uncleanness.
- C. And [Holy Things] in the fifth remove are eaten in a pottage of Holy Things.

2:6
- A. Unconsecrated food: in the second remove renders unconsecrated liquid unclean and renders unfit foods of heave offering.
- B. Heave offering: at the third remove renders unclean liquid of Holy Things and renders unfit foods of Holy Things,
- C. if it [the heave offering] was prepared in conditions of cleanness pertaining to Holy Things.
- D. But if it was prepared in conditions pertaining to heave offering, it renders unclean at two removes and renders unfit at one remove in reference to Holy Things.

2:7
- A. R. Eleazar says, "The three of them are equal:
- B. "Holy Things and heave offering and unconsecrated food: which are at the first remove of uncleanness render unclean at two removes and unfit at one [further] remove in respect to Holy Things,
- C. "render unclean at one remove and spoil at one [further] remove in respect to heave offering,
- D. "and spoil unconsecrated food.
- E. "That which is unclean in the second remove in respect to all of them renders unclean at one remove and unfit at one [further] remove in respect to Holy Things,
- F. "and renders liquid of unconsecrated food unclean,
- G. "and spoils foods of heave offering.
- H. "The third remove of uncleanness in respect to all of them renders liquids of Holy Things unclean,
- I. "and spoils foods of Holy Things."

2:8
- A. He who eats food unclean in the second remove should not work in the olive press.
- B. And unconsecrated food which is prepared in accord with the rules pertaining to Holy Things — lo, this is like unconsecrated food.
- C. R. Eleazar b. R. Sadoq says, "Lo, it is like heave offering,
- D. "conveying uncleanness at two removes and rendering unfit at one [further] remove."

3:1
- A. Grease, bean mash and milk,
- B. when they are [in the form of] running liquid,
- C. lo, they are in the first remove of uncleanness.
- D. [If] they congealed, lo, they are in the second remove of uncleanness.
- E. [If] they became liquid [again], [if they are of the volume of] an egg, exactly — it is clean.
- F. [If they are of the volume of] more than an egg, it is unclean, for as soon as the first drop [of moisture] exuded, it was made unclean, [by the remainder which is] the bulk of an egg.

The amazing composition, running on through M. Toh. 1:9, 2:1–8, and 3:1(–4), goes over [1] the classification of foods as to levels of sanctification, on the one side, and [2] their (consequent) susceptibility at removes of uncleanness, on the other. That is what I mean by a mixed grid. For each item — sanctification, uncleanness — forms a discrete classificatory exercise on its own. But only by bringing them together and showing their profound complementarity does the author make his point.

The basic taxonomic principle — with which we are already familiar — is that what is more holy also is more susceptible to uncleanness, and what is less holy is less susceptible. But it is possible to make that point only by the fabrication of a mixed grid, that is to say, by the imposition of one grid upon the other. What happens, therefore is that the system of classification makes its own further points through the reclassification of already-classified taxa. And that fact, which we shall now grasp in detail, reinforces with enormous power the philosophy's basic insistence upon the generative force of order over chaos. For just as the classification-system generates new classes of things and works its way to and from Scripture, so here we see how the philosophy of a well-ordered world generates new principles as it works its way through the ordering of already-accomplished taxonomic structures.

From these general methodological observations we turn to the somewhat abstruse case before us, even though the author has so framed his conceptions that little clarification is needed, so orderly is the form and so neat the exposition. "Susceptible to uncleanness" in fact forms a taxonomic judgment, for it means susceptible to uncleanness *at further removes from the original source of uncleanness*, from the Father of Uncleanness to the fourth remove therefrom. That is to say, the Father of uncleanness (e.g., the corpse), touches something; that is in the first remove; then what that touches is in the second remove; what that touches is in the third remove; and on to the fourth — so much for the grid of uncleanness.

The second grid is that of sanctification. Unconsecrated food lies at the bottom of the structure; it will be unaffected beyond the first remove of uncleanness; food in the status of heave offering will be made unclean by what is unclean in the second remove; Holy Things will be made unclean by what is unclean in the third remove from the original source; and so on. The main point then is that Holy Things are affected or produce affects at several removes of uncleanness, heave offering at fewer, unconsecrated food at fewest of all.

5. MIXTURES

The upshot of the dual taxonomy is simple. And a dispute introduces the third level of classification, the one that sustains dispute and so confirms the unquestioned validity of the initial two levels. For without a variable, there is no dispute, without dispute, no discourse, and without discourse, no reaffirmation by indirection of the basic philosophical truth that the system at every point and in any manner of speech proposes to affirm. At the level of dispute therefore is the admissible variable, and that concerns how we impose our taxic indicators: to what they apply. Do we gauge the case by reference to what receives or to what imparts uncleanness. To spell this out: two competing conceptions are in play. One is that we gauge contamination in accord with the status of what *receives* the contamination; the other is that we gauge contamination in accord with that which *imparts* contamination. Where do we see the dispute? The authorship leaves us no doubt. M. 2:3–6 focus upon that which imparts contamination. M. 2:7 stresses the capacity of food to receive uncleanness, that is, in accord with its level of sanctification.

Then we come to yet another grid, the third. This one is pertinent but essentially distinct from the first two: solids versus liquids. M. 3:1–4 make the distinction between solid or congealed food and liquid state of the same food. When food is solid, it imparts uncleanness in accord with the rules of solid food; when in liquid form, in accord with those of liquid. What about food of exactly an egg's bulk? When congealed, it imparts uncleanness. But when it begins to liquefy, then a drop of liquid which exudes has diminished the solid food, formerly exactly of the bulk of an egg, to less than the bulk of an egg that is requisite for imparting uncleanness. Is the drop of liquid unclean? No, it is not. This entire exercise in taxonomy, holding together a variety of rules and considerations, must be cited as (in my opinion) the Mishnah's single finest taxonomic composition, extending from M. 1:1 through M. 3:4.

The Halakhah in its own terms thus goes over the same conceptions as those of the Stoic theory of mixture, stated by S. Sambursky in the following terms:

> As far as classification is concerned, the Stoic theory is much clearer. It distinguished between three types of mixture. One of them, mingling or mechanical mixture, is identical with what Aristotle defines by 'composition' (as in the case of the mixture of barley and wheat), and it applies essentially to bodies of a granular structure where a mosaic-like mixture results, each particle of one component being surrounded by particles of the other. The other extreme is fusion, which leads to the creation of a new substance whereby the individual properties of each of the components are lost... Between these two types lies a third case of 'mixture' proper (krasis for

liquids, mixis for non-liquids), which, from the Stoic point of view, represents the most important category of blending. Here a complete interpenetration of all the components takes place, and any volume of the mixture, down to the smallest parts, is jointly occupied by all the components in the same proportion, each component preserving its own properties under any circumstances, irrespective of the ratio of its share in the mixture. The properties are preserved in all cases where, as opposed to the case of fusion, the components can be separated out by putting a sponge into the mixture...

Certainly an example of fusion is the contamination of liquids. Once unclean, they are unclean always at a single remove; the uncleanness affects the whole equally and profoundly. An example of mingling is connection which takes place after uncleanness has affected one part of what is connected. And an example of the middle sort of mixing is the blending of solids unclean in various removes.

The same taxonomy of mixtures that the Halakhah works out is replicated in Greek scientific thinking about the same matter. This is shown by Alexander Aphrodisiensis, cited by Samuel Sambursky, who writes:

Certain mixtures... result in a total interpenetration of substances and their qualities, the original substances and qualities being preserved in this mixture; this he calls specifically krasis of the mixed components. It is characteristic of the mixed substances that they can again be separated, which is only possible if the components preserve their properties in the mixture... This interpenetration of the components he assumes to happen in that the substances mixed together interpenetrate each other such that there is not a particle among them that does not contain a share of all the rest. If this were not the case, the result would not be krasis but juxtaposition.[1]

This same view is presented in concrete terms by the Halakhah, as we should anticipate. That is to say, when we hold that a substance at the first remove and one at the second remove interpenetrate and are regarded as entirely unclean at the first remove, we say much the same thing. Can they now be separated? And if they are separated, what is the result? The Halakhic category-formations at appropriate points raise precisely that issue, in terms of removes of uncleanness to be sure. The matter of connection is of the same order of theoretical interest. Uncleanness affecting all parts of material after they have been connected affects them all when they are separated. But if something is made unclean, then connected to something else, that latter substance is unclean just as is

---

[1] Samuel Sambursky, *Physics of the Stoics* (London, 1959), p. 13.

5. MIXTURES

the former. But when it is separated, it is unclean in a lower remove, only by virtue of its contact with that which was originally contaminated. So now we have a mosaic-like mixture, in which each element in the whole preserves its own individuality.

II. ZEBAHIM

We now turn to concrete expressions of the theory of mixtures that the Halakhah realizes in concrete cases.

M. 8:1   All [animals that had been designated for the purpose of] offerings that were mixed up with (1) sin offerings that had been left to die [M. Tem. 2:2] or (2) an ox sentenced to be stoned — even one [sin offering left to die] in ten thousand [suitable animal offerings] — let all of them be left to die. [If] they [animals designated for use as offerings] were mixed up with (1) an ox upon which a sin was committed, or [71A] (2) [an ox] which had been found guilty of killing a man on the evidence of a single witness or on the evidence of the owner, (1) with an ox which had sexual relations with a human, or (2) with an ox with which a human had sexual relations, or (3) with an ox which had been set aside [for idolatry (M. Tem. 6:1)], or (4) with an ox which had been worshipped, or (5) with an ox which had served as a harlot's hire, or (6) with an ox which had served as the price of a dog, or (7) with an ox which was crossbred, [71B] or (8) with an ox which was terefah, or (9) with an ox born from the side — let them [any of those beasts that had been confused in this way] pasture until they suffer a blemish [since one of them is a valid consecrated beast], and [then] be sold, and let [the owner] bring [another sacrifice, purchased] with the proceeds of the best of them of that kind [that had been mixed up with the invalid beasts]. [If] they were mixed up with unblemished unconsecrated beasts, the unconsecrated beasts are to be sold to those who require that particular kind [of sacrifice].

M. 8:2   Consecrated beasts [belonging to several owners, which were mixed up] with [other] consecrated beasts of the same kind [of offering, so that while all the beasts in the lot have been designated for the same purpose, we still do not know to whom in particular the several beasts belong] — this one is offered for the sake of one [among the owners] and that one is offered for the sake of one [among the owners]. Consecrated beasts [which were mixed up] with other consecrated beasts [e.g., burnt offerings and peace offerings], not of the same kind [of offerings] [and which therefore are offered with different rites, e.g., different numbers of acts of sprinkling blood, rules of consuming the flesh, and the like] — let them pasture until they suffer a blemish, and [then] be sold [separately], and let [the owner] bring with the proceeds of the best of them [a sacrifice] [e.g., peace offerings] of that kind, and let him lose [make up] the [added] difference from his own property. [If] they were mixed up with a firstling or with tithe [of cattle] — let them pasture until they suffer a blemish, and be eaten as a firstling [by priests] and as tithe [by ordinary folk] [but not slaughtered in the public market or sold by weight]. All can be mixed up [without the possibility of discerning an animal for one sacrifice from that for another], except a sin offering, [which is female or which is a male goat], with a guilt offering, [which is a male sheep or ram].

We have to assume that any item in the mixture bears the traits of Most Holy Things and hence treat all components of the mixture in accord with the pertinent regulations.

M. 8:6   Blood which was mixed with water, if it [the mixture] has the appearance of blood, is valid. [If] it was mixed in wine, they regard it as if it were water [and if the mixture is blood-color, it is valid]. [If] it [blood of Holy Things] was mixed with the blood of a beast or with the blood of fowl [which were unconsecrated], they regard it as if it were water. R. Judah says, "Blood [under any circumstances] does not annul blood."

That which imposes its traits upon the entirety of the mixture dictates the classification of the mixture.

M. 11:8   [If] one cooked in it Holy Things and unconsecrated food, or Most Holy Things and Lesser Holy Things, if they were [sufficient] to impart flavor, lo, that [the rule of which is] less [stringent] is eaten in accord with [that the rule of which] is the more stringent [thus applying to the more holy things]. And [if they do not impart flavor] they do [not] require scouring and rinsing, and [if the invalid proportion of the mixture does not impart flavor], they do not invalidate merely by having made contact. An [unfit] wafer which touched [another] wafer, or a piece of meat [which touched] another piece of meat — not the whole of the wafer or the whole of the piece(s) [of meat] is prohibited. Prohibited is only the place which absorbed [that which is forbidden].

T. 10:14   [If] one cooked in it [a pot] Most Holy Things, one scours and rinses [at the time at which it no longer is permitted to eat] Most Holy Things [M. Zeb. 11:8B]. [If one cooked in it] Lesser Holy Things, one scours and rinses [the pot at the time at which it no longer is permitted to eat] Lesser Holy Things. [If] one cooked in it Most Holy Things and Lesser Holy Things, one scours and rinses [the pot at the time at which it no longer is permitted to eat] the more strict of the two. [If] one rinsed but did not scour, scoured but did not rinse, one should eat [what is left in the pot] in accord with the rule governing the more stringent of the two of them.

What imparts its distinctive trait to the entirety of the mixture dictates the classification of the mixture.

5. MIXTURES

III. HULLIN

M. 6:5 Blood that was mixed with water, if it has the appearance of blood, one is liable to cover it up. [If] it was mixed with wine, they regard it as if it were water. [If] it was mixed up with blood of a [domesticated] beast or with blood of a wild beast, they regard it as if it were water.

M. 8:3 A drop of milk which fell on a piece [of meat], if it is sufficient to impart flavor to that piece [of meat] — it is prohibited. [If] one stirred the pot, if there is in it sufficient [milk] to impart flavor to that [entire] pot['s contents], it [the contents of the pot] is prohibited. The udder: one cuts it open and takes out its milk. [If] he did not cut it open, he does not transgress on that account. The heart: One cuts it open and takes out its blood. [If] he did not cut it open, he does not transgress on that account. He who serves up fowl with cheese on the table does not transgress a prohibition.

The principle is familiar. M. 9:1, cited in the context of connection, also impinges on the matter of mixtures; there it is difficult to distinguish the one from the other.

IV. TEMURAH

M. 6:1 All [animals] which are prohibited for the altar prohibit in any number at all [the utilization for sacred purposes of animals among which they are confused, and these are as follows]: (1) the one which has sexual relations with a human being; (2) and the one with whom a human being has sexual relations; (3) and the one which is set aside [for idolatrous worship]; (4) and the one which has actually been worshiped; (5) and the [harlot's] hire; (6) and the price of a dog [one given in payment for a dog]; (7) and the hybrid; (8) and the terefah; (9) and the one which is born from the side. What is the one which is set aside [A3]? The one which is set aside for idolatrous worship. It is prohibited, but what is on it is permitted. What is the one which is actually worshiped [A4]? Any which people serve. [Both] it and what is on it are prohibited. This and that [however] are permitted for eating.

Here we have a mixture of beasts of various classifications and require a rule on how to dispose of them. All the animals among which they are confused are affected and subject to the pertinent prohibitions.

V. MIQVAOT

M. 3:1 Two immersion pools which [respectively] do not contain forty seahs — and into this one fell a log and a half [of drawn water], and into that one [fell] a log and a half and [then] they were mingled together are fit, since the

THE PHILOSOPHICAL PREMISE OF JUDAISM

category of unfitness never applied to them. But: an immersion pool which does not contain forty seahs [of fit water]—and three logs of drawn water fell into it—and it was divided into two [parts]—is unfit, since the category of unfitness applied to it. It always remains in its unfitness, until there will go forth from it its fullness and more.

M. 3:2 How so? The cistern which is in the courtyard—and three logs [of drawn water] fell into it—it always remains in its state of unfitness, until there will go forth from it its fullness and more. Or: until one will set up in the courtyard [another pool containing] forty seahs, and the upper [water] will be cleaned by the lower one.

M. 3:4 [If three logs of drawn water fell or are poured into a pool] from one utensil, from two, and from three, they join together. [If three logs of drawn water fell into a pool] from four utensils, they do not join together. A person who had an emission of semen who was sick, upon whom nine qabs of water fell—and a clean person on whose head and the greater part of whose body three logs of drawn water fell—from one utensil, from two, and from three—they join together. From four—they do not join together. Under what circumstances? When the second began before the first ceased. And under what circumstances? When he did not intend to add more [drawn water]. But if he intended to add more, even one qartob in the entire year they join together to form three logs [of drawn water].

M. 4:4 Drawn water and rainwater which mingled in the courtyard, or in a hollow, or on the steps of a cave—if the greater part is formed by fit [water], it is fit, and if the greater part is [formed by] unfit [water], it is unfit. Half and half—it is unfit. When? At the time that they mingled together before they reached the immersion pool. [If] they [each] were flowing in an unbroken stream into the water—if it is known that forty seahs of fit water fell into it before three logs of drawn water fell into it, it is fit. And if not, it is unfit.

M. 6:1 Any [pool of water] which is mingled with [water of] an immersion pool is [deemed to be as valid] as the immersion pool. Holes of the cave and clefts of the cave—one dunks in them as they are. A pit of the cavern—they do not dunk in it unless it [the hole between the pit and the immersion pool] is as large as the spout of a water-skin. Said R. Judah, "When is that the case? At the time that it stands by itself. But if it does not stand by itself, they dunk in it just as it is."

M. 6:3 Three immersion pools—in this one are twenty seahs [of fit water], and in this one are twenty seahs [of fit water], and in this one are twenty seahs of drawn water—and [the one containing] drawn [water] is at the side—and three people went down and dipped in them, and it [the water in the three pools] was mingled together—the immersion pools are clean. And the people who immersed are clean. [If] the one containing drawn [water] was in the middle, and three people went down and immersed in them, and they were mingled together—the immersion pools are as they were. And those who immersed are as they were.

5. MIXTURES

T. 3:7 Two immersion-pools, each containing twenty *se'ahs*, one with drawn water, and one with fit water—two went down and brought the two into contact and immersed in them—even if it [water] was red and turned white, or white and turned red—the immersion-pools remain as they were, and the ones who immersed remain as they were.

M. 6:7 The intermingling of immersion pools is through a hole the size of the spout of a water-skin, in the thickness and capacity—two fingers turned around in full. [If there is] doubt whether it is the size of the spout of a water-skin or not the size of the spout of a water-skin, it is unfit, because it derives from the Torah. And so: the olive's bulk of a corpse, and the olive's bulk of carrion, and the lentil's bulk of a [dead] creeping thing. Whatever stops up the spout of the water-skin diminishes it.

M. 6:8 They clean immersion pools: a higher pool by the lower pool, and a distant by a nearby [pool]. How so? One brings a pipe of earthenware or lead, and puts his hand under it until it is filled with water, and draws it along and makes it touch. Even by as much as a hair's breadth suffices. [If] the upper one contains forty seahs [of fit water], and in the lower pool there is nothing—one draws [water and carries it] on the shoulder and puts it into the upper one, until there will descend into the lower one forty seahs.

Once one mingles the valid water of an immersion pool with another body of water, the whole is deemed completely mixed, with the result that the entire volume is valid.

VI. MAKHSHIRIN

M. 2:1 The sweat [of damp walls] of houses, pits, cisterns, and caves is clean. The sweat of man is clean. [If] one drank unclean water and sweated, his sweat is clean. [If] one entered drawn water and sweated, his sweat is unclean. [If] he dried himself off and afterward sweated, his sweat is clean.

M. 2:2 [If the water of] a bathhouse is unclean, its sweat is unclean. And [if the water of a bathhouse] is clean, it[s sweat] is subject to the law, "If water be put." The pool which is in the house—the [wall of the] house sweats on its account—if it [the pool] was unclean, the sweat of [the walls of] the entire house which is [produced] on account of the pool is unclean.

M. 2:3 Two pools—one clean, and one unclean—that [wall which sweats] nearer to the unclean one is unclean, and that [which sweats] near the clean one is clean. Half and half-it is unclean. Unclean iron which one smelted with clean iron, if the greater part is from the unclean, [the metal] is unclean, and if the greater part is from the clean, it is clean. Half and half-it is unclean. Pots into which Israelites and gentiles urinate—if the greater part is from the unclean [gentile source], it [the urine in the pot] is unclean, and if the greater part is from the clean [Israelite source], [the urine in the pot] is clean. Half and half-it is unclean. Dirty water on which rainwater fell—if the greater part [of the consequent mixture of water] is from the unclean [water], it is unclean. And if the greater part is from the clean, it is clean. Half and half-it is clean, When [does the foregoing rule apply]? When the dirty water came first. But if the rainwater, in whatever volume preceded the dirty water, [the consequent mixture] is unclean.

T. 1:7   They follow [the status of] the majority.

The disposition of mixtures presents no surprises. The character of the larger part of the mixture is determinative.

VII. MIXTURES IN THE FIRST DIVISION OF THE HALAKHAH: BIKKURIM

Let us now consider the role that problems of mixtures play in the exposition of the Halakhah of an entire division, Zeraim/agriculture. We shall see that the division spins out its topical exposition by framing problems of mixtures. Reference is made throughout to the exposition of Mishnah-Tosefta Zeraim set forth in *The Law of Agriculture in the Mishnah and the Tosefta*. Leiden, 2005: E. J. Brill. I–III. These are as follows: *A History of the Mishnaic Law of Agriculture. Berakhot, Peah (Roger Brooks). II. Demai (Richard S. Sarason), Kilayim (Irving Mandelbaum), Shebii (Louis Newman) III. Terumot (Alan J. Avery-Peck), Maaserot (Martin Jaffee), Maaser Sheni Peter Haas), Hallah (Avi Havivi), Orlah (Howard Essner), Bikkurim (Margaret Wenig and David Weiner).*

Bikkurim

The concern of M. Bik. 1:1–2 is to set up a taxonomic grid to cover four possibilities as specified, do not bring first fruits at all, bring but do not recite, bring and recite. The criterion is ownership of the land on which the firstfruits have grown. Status and circumstance are held together. The farmer must own the land, and those who do not bring firstfruits do not own the land. If someone owns the land but is not entitled to inherit a portion of the land, if someone buys trees without buying the ground on which they grow, and the like, they do not recite. All of these amplifications of the base-verse of Scripture in fact hold together diverse indicators in a single well framed grid of classification. Mishnah-tractate Bikkurim Chapter Two presents a hierarchical comparison of diverse kinds of agricultural gifts and tithes, of human blood and the blood of a domesticated animal or reptile, and between the interstitial beast called a koy, which is neither domesticated nor wild, and a wild or a domesticated animal. This entire representation of information carries forward the interest of Chapter One in the comparison and contrast of various classifications of person within the grid of various classifications of landownership. Now we organize the rules governing various other species of a single genus (the genus in Chapter One being the firstfruits' governing rules). Essentially what we see at M. 2:1–11 is the workings of polythetic taxonomy. M. 2:1 addresses the comparison of heave offering and firstfruits, yielding the conception of rules that apply to both, to one but not the other, to the other but not the one—a first class exercise in comparison and contrast for what is essentially a hierarchical taxonomy.

Dema'i

The issue at M. Dem. 5:3–11 is connection or joining together. Ordinarily tithes may be taken from one item or batch of produce for another (Sarason, p. 165). People do not have to give tithe separately from each item or batch individually. But, Sarason explains, "In the case of produce purchased from an am ha ares, we may do so only if we are certain that all of the produce derives from a single source, e.g., a single baker or farmer," and therefore is entirely in a single classification or category. For one cannot separate tithes from an item of produce that owes tithes in behalf of an item that is exempt and vice versa (just as we saw, mutatis mutandis, in connection with the theory of obligation as defining categories or classifications in connection with prayers!). We ask here about bread purchased from a variety of types of bread dealers, the individual, the store, the monopolist, then we deal with different portions of food gathered by a poor man (M. 5:4, 5) and finally food purchased by a wholesaler from various provision dealers. In all cases the issue is "whether or not all of the bread or produce derives from a single source and thus is of equivalent status with respect to tithing obligations" (Sarason, p. 166). That is to say, the problem throughout is the classification of things that are alike in some ways and different in others, and we want, in the present case, to keep things as much uniform as we possibly can, that is to say, to treat as the principle point of differentiation the issue of obligation to tithing. M. 5:10–11 go over an interstitial category, the perforated pot, which in some ways is in the classification of the ground and in some ways is not.

The issue of M. Dem. 6:1–2 concerns the status of crop grown on property which has mixed ownership, or crop that itself is subject to shared ownership. This is a different sort of mixture. To what extent is one man held to be owner of the whole of the crop, such that he is responsible for tithing the whole crop if he is scrupulous about tithing and the other is not? This question of the mixture of ownership or the sorting out of issues of responsibility for a property where the ownership is suffused throughout then addresses the principle of mixtures: whole, partial, null. At M. Dem. 6:1–2 does the man who works someone else's field for a share of the crop have to tithe that portion of produce that goes to the landowner? If the landowner is held to own the produce, the sharecropper need not tithe it. Where ownership is diffused or mixed, then the result is not the same. We proceed at M. Dem. 6:3–5 to the disposition of heave offering and first tithe between landlord and sharecropper when one is a priest or Levite and the other not. May the priest or Levite claim the Israelite's portion of the appropriate due for himself, or does the Israelite give it to any priest of his choice? And the answer depends again on who owns the field (Sarason, pp. 202–3). At M. 6:7–10 we have joint ownership of produce or property held by persons of differing status. Sarason: "Do both have an equal share in every part of the whole, or may we apply the principle of retrospective designation and claim that the particular portion which each one takes, in whatever part of the property, was his from the outset? So the issue throughout the chapter (6:1–12) is one of mixtures.

The main concern at M. Dem. 7:6, 7, 8 is the prohibition against separating tithes for produce which has not yet been tithed for produce which has been tithed. These form distinct categories and must be kept apart form one another. M. 7:7 explains how to separate heave-offering of the tithe from a mixture of tithed and untithed produce or of first tithe and untithed produce. The main concern is not to separate tithe for untithed produce from that portion of the mixture that already has been tithed. The philosophical problem, then, is one of classification and separation of what should be kept distinct.

Hallah

M. Hal. 1:1 addresses the issuing of whether or not five species of grain join together to produce dough of sufficient volume to incur liability to the dough-offering. Since they share in common the trait that they rise on account of yeast, they do. So the genus encompasses all of the species, with the result that the classification-process is neatly illustrated. These

5. MIXTURES

are interstitial cases at M. Hal. 1:3. All of these classifications of grain are subject to ownership other than that of the farmer. But that fact does not change their status as to dough offering. We take no account of the status with regard to ownership, past or present use as another type of offering, or the stage of growth of the grain whence the dough derives. This then forms the other side of the taxonomic labor: indicators that do not register as against those that do at M. 1:1–2. M. Hal. 1:5 asks about dough in diverse categories, e.g., dough prepared like sponge cake from beginning to end of the processing. The point now is that dough is liable to dough offering only if prepared in the manner that is normal for bread. This dough is prepared as bread normally is, but not entirely so. M. 1:6 goes on to a special case. When we are not sure of the classification of something, we then appeal to human attitude of will, as at M. Hal. 1:8. Dogs' dough (dough biscuits) may or may not serve for human use. If human beings regard it as edible, then it falls into the category of ordinary food, and if not, it does not. The classification of dough-offering in the context of other portions of food that have been designated as holy is stated at M. Hal. 1:9. Dough-offering is in the classification of heave-offering and the same rules apply to both, a point that is laboriously stated through examples. How do we classify produce? The taxic indicator is whether or not it was grown in the Land. If it was, it is liable to dough offering, if not, not. What about the affect of location upon produce? If it is grown abroad but brought to the Land, is it exempt? How do we assess liability to dough offering vis à vis the Land? Whatever produce is eaten in the Land, whether or not grown there, is subject to dough offering. So M. Hal. 2:1, with an interstitial case tacked on at M. 2:1. The issue of M. Hal. 2:4 is connection and separation. If one makes the dough in portions too small to incur liability but they toughed one another, they remain exempt; if they stick together, they form a mass of sufficient size and are so liability. The issue then is the character of the contact: touching or connection. M. 2:5 treats the same question. Does the condition of uncleanness or cleanness form a taxic indicator? Not with reference to dough-offering, so M. Hal. 2:8. One may remove dough offering from a batch of unclean dough in behalf of a batch of clean dough, effecting a connection between the two batches so that for that purpose they form a single batch, but not transmitting uncleanness from the unclean to the clean through that connection. This is a subtle and interesting exercise in the interplay of connection and mixture. In assessing the status of a mixture, we invoke the character of the whole in assessing the condition of the parts. If one part of the mixture has imposed its character on the whole mixture, then the status of the mixture is defined by that part, so M. Hal. 3:7, 10. M. Hal. 3:8–9 make the point that where we have a mixture of materials each in its own status, we may or may not treat the mixture as unified. If we can avoid doing so and hence accomplish our goal in one way, we do so; if not, then we treat the mixtures as unified. This is said with two different cases, a fine instance in which a principle is expressed through examples.

Kila'yim

Mishnah-tractate Kila'yim from 1:1 through 7:8 considers plants and the rule governing cultivating together different species of plants. The first consideration is resemblance. But it is not decisive when there are other traits of speciation. These items resemble one another and are not considered diverse kinds with one another, M. Kil. 1:1–4C. Other items, M. Kil. 1:4C–6 even though they resemble each other, are considered diverse kinds. M. Kil. 1:7–9 proceed to the matter of grafts, which is forbidden. M. 1:9 through M. 3:7 proceed to sowing together different kinds of crops in the same space, in adjacent spaces, crops among vines. We proceed, M. Kil. 4:1–7:8 to the issue of sowing crops in a vineyard. This is permitted if within or around a vineyard is an open space of the specified dimensions. If there is ample space between the vines, that space may be used. But if the appearance is such that the vines appeared mixed with grain, then the grain must be uprooted. The basic consideration is that grain or vegetables not create the appearance of confusion in the vineyard. Everything in the long sequence of rules derives from that single concern. At M. Kil. 8:1 we have a hierarchical classification, in terms of the stringency of the rule, of the several species of the genus, diverse kinds. We start at the top, with the most severe prohibition: diverse kinds of the vineyard; then come seeds, garments, animals, in descending order of stringency. This is an absolutely first-class example of the working of hierarchical classification; the passage in context serves as a bridge from the top items to the next in line and imposes upon the tractate as a whole large scale order as a systematic account, in descending order of severity, of the rules against hybridization. Then, M. Kil. 8:2, the basic rule is set forth. Now the classes of animals — domesticated, wild, clean, unclean — are sorted out as to the basic prohibition. The prohibition of mingling fibers, with particular attention to wool and linen, occupies M. Kil. 9:1–10. Scripture's basic rule is amplified with special attention to mixtures, e.g., camel's hair and sheep's wool hackled together. Here we assign the traits of the dominant component of the mix to the entire mixture. Items that resemble wool and linen but are not of wool and linen, or that are not intended to serve as garments, are not subject to the prohibition. The issue of intention is explicitly excluded. Even if one does not intend permanently to use a piece of cloth as a garment, it still may not be used at all if it is a mixture of diverse kinds, and so too at M. 9:2F.

Ma'aser Sheni

M. M.S. 1:1–2 address the issue of preserving in the classification of the sacred what has been sanctified, whether produce or an animal. In both cases these things may not be disposed of the way secular produce or beasts are. They may not be used as common property, e.g., handed to a woman as a token of betrothal. Coins that are exchanged for produce in the status of second tithe must be valid ones, and full value must be received, just as would be the case in the exchange of money for property belonging to the Temple. In all these ways, the farmer preserves the distinction of the consecrated produce or animal and marks its sanctification, a fundamental conception in the consideration of classification. M. 1:3–7 go on to the issue of the transfer in Jerusalem to food of coins that have been substituted for produce in the status of second tithe. Here too we have to maintain the initial classification of these coins, as holy, by doing with them only what is permitted. That is the exchange for food. Hence one may not purchase with that money what cannot be eaten, unless they form an intrinsic part of the food that they accompany; one may not use the money to buy water and salt, which are not food; one obviously may not use the money to buy food outside of Jerusalem or to buy things which one cannot eat, drink, or use as a lotion. In all these ways, the coins are preserved in that classification for which they have been designated. While these rules certainly amplify the conception of Scripture, what Scripture has contributed is the fact, and the way in which that fact is turned into a rule requiring exemplification depends upon the a priori interests of the Mishnah's framers. These, as I said, I identify as a concern, in the present matter, for doing those things that will impose a fixed classification upon matter that can be classified in two opposed ways. Since the principal focus of the tractate is classification, we cannot find surprising the interest in problems of mixture. Here we have coins designated as substitutes for produce and intended for transport to Jerusalem mixed with secular coins. The sanctification does not inhere in the particular coins, but is a matter of true value. Hence which coins one retrieves and designates as second tithe is a matter of indifference. The important point, then, is that the classification of tithe concerns value, not the object itself. Sanctification is relative and not absolute; it is what the farmer conceives to be holy that is holy, and the attitude is determinative, not the physical object, so M. M. S. 2:5. This is shown also at M. M. S. 2:6. When consecrated and unconsecrated coins are mixed together, the status of the consecrated coins is transferred to a fresh batch of coins. The issue proceeds to through M. 2:8–9. But the status of second tithe may be transferred from one person's coins to another person's produce, and the status of second tithe may be transferred from a farmer's coins to his own produce, so M. 2:10–3:4. M. M. S. 4:1–8 address the transfer of holiness from produce to coins, that is, the designation of money to bear the value of the produce from the farm to Jerusalem, where the money is exchanged for produce and the food then eaten. Here, the consideration of the sanctification of the produce does not impose upon the farmer the burden of getting the highest possible price. True value is not the same thing as the best market price. At M. M. S. 4:1 that is made explicit. The exchange takes place under the normally prevailing conditions. That is so both for the transfer of value from produce to coins, M. 4:1 and for the transfer of value from coins back to produce, M. 4:2.

Ma'aserot

The main problem of M. Ma. 1:1ff. is taxonomic. At what point does a crop enter the status of being subject to the removal of tithes and offerings? Prior to that point, it is classified as not liable, afterward, liable. This is subdivided into two categories, as Jaffee says (p. 1): "when in the course of a crop's growth may it be used to satisfy the obligation to tithe? When, further, in the course of the harvest of the crop, must the tithes actually be paid? The answer is that the produce may be tithed as soon as it ripens; it then becomes valuable. But only when the householder by an action claims his harvested produce as personal property must the crop be tithed; that is in general when untithed produce is brought from the field into the home. Hence when the farmer, by an act that expresses his attitude, lays claim on the crop, then God responds by demanding his share of that same crop, owing to him as owner of the Land of Israel. In general, therefore, at stake is the interplay of classification and intentionality. At stake at M. Ma. 2:1 is the point at which some takes possession of produce as a gift. If a person is given produce in the market, he can eat it without tithing; but if he takes it home, he has to tithe it. M. 2:2–4 pursue this matter. M. 2:5–6 go on to the issue of purchase, barter, and finding lost produce.

5. MIXTURES

M. 3:5–10 turn to the imposition of the requirement to tithe by bringing produce from the field into the courtyard, with attention to the definition of the courtyard. All of these materials amplify the basic conception that when one takes possession of produce and deems it of value, then God's share is owing. All of the specified actions of M. Ma. 4:1A involve processing produce. Even if this is done in the field, not in the courtyard, it means that the farmer is taking possession of the produce for his own use and benefit. If, by contrast, one processes the food in a manner not intended to make it fit for eating, that act is null. We turn to the disposition of interstitial cases, e.g., unmet conditions and incomplete procedures, ambiguities in application of the law (Jaffee, p. 11). If one sows coriander for seed, the leaves are exempt from the law, since the intentionality of the farmer classifies the coriander is not-food. If it is sown for the leaves, the seeds and leaves are subject to the law, for the farmer has through his attitude classified the whole as food. The same considerations are worked out at M. 4:6. We turn next, M. 5:1–2, to incomplete procedures, e.g., the status of produce taken from the field prior to the harvest of the crop as a whole. Such produce is not regard as liable to tithing. We ignore the potentiality of the harvest of the whole and deal only with the actuality in hand. We turn next, M. 5:3–5, to produce that is sold or purchased while inedible. Then come incomplete procedures involving produce which is insufficiently processed or the processing of which is in doubt, M. 5:6–7, and finally, produce not grown in the land of Israel. All of these items address ambiguities. The natural conditions of ripeness must exist before human procedures or appropriation can render produce liable. Then we investigate cases in which edibility is of no concern; we ask about acts of appropriation of the produce that fall out of the normal range. In each case we must decide (Jaffee, p. 12) how the farmer's obligation to tithe is modified by the fact that one or another set of necessary conditions is lacking—once more an exercise in classification of the produce in line with several distinct indicative rules.

'Orlah

The issue of taxonomy is present at M. 'Orl. 1:1, where we distinguish parts of a tree by reference to the function or use to which each part is put. Hence the indicator for taxonomic purposes is the plan of the farmer for the tree or for parts of the tree. M. 'Orl. 1:6 works out the proportion at which two distinct bodies of material, one prohibited, one permitted, are deemed such that the permitted overwhelms the prohibited by its greater volume.

It is at a proportion of two hundred to one that we deem the prohibited to be nullified and wholly absorbed into the traits of the permitted. This can take place even when the intention is to accomplish exactly that purpose. M. 'Orl. 1:7 further takes up the question of mixtures. If one curdles milk with the sap of an 'Orlah-tree, the milk is forbidden; so the sap imparts its status to the entire mixture. The issue is the classification of the sap. What is like fruit is fruit; what is not like fruit is not. The like follows the rule of the like, so M. 'Orl. 1:7–8. At stake here is whether sap is like fruit, that is, falls into the classification thereof. The same principle of classification of like under the like rule is expressed at M. 'Orl. 1:9.

Chapter Two as a whole is devoted to the issue of how prohibited produce affects mixtures (Essner, p. 123). The basic point throughout is fundamental to mixtures of the first of the three kinds: complete and undifferentiated, so that a single rule applies to the whole. It is, as I said in context, that it is possible to absorb a quantity of a substance of one kind within the body of a quantity of a substance of another classification, so that the mixture is complete, and the traits of the larger quantity of the substance are imparted to the mixture as a whole. This is made explicit at M. 'Orl. 2:1–3. The issue is "joining together," which is to say, accomplishing a complete and unadulterated mixture, so that the traits attaching to the substance that is the greater in volume now apply to the whole. If the prohibited, however, serves to flavor or leaven the food, it has then imparted its character to the whole, and hence also its status. Also: M. 'Orl. 2:4, 5, 6, 7, 8, 9, 10, 11, 12, 13, 14, 15, 16, 17. M. 'Orl. 2:10 adds that spices join together to render forbidden that which they flavor. Here we treat as a single classification diverse spices, each subject to its own prohibition; they form a common mixture because of two traits: all are subject to a prohibition, and all impart something of a flavor to the whole. M. 'Orl. 2:11–12+13 assess the status of the components of leaven. Eliezer maintains that prohibited and permitted leaven are deemed to fall into the same category as that attaching to the portion of the leaven that completed the volume required to raise the bread; sages take the view that only if the prohibited leaven by itself is sufficient do we deem that leaven to impart its status to the whole. So Eliezer takes account of a process of mixing, the leaven mixing together, then mixing with the dough as a whole. He further asks which portion of the mixed leaven has made it possible for the whole portion to do its job, that is to say, he takes account of the result of the mixture, not merely the traits, as to volume, thereof. The same issue is at M. 'Orl. 2:15–17, but expressed in different terms. So the entire chapter works out the rules governing mixtures.

5. MIXTURES

M. 'Orl. 3:1, 2, 3, 4, 5, 6, 7, 8 go over the same principle of neutralization. The details need not detain us, since the same point is made throughout and simply applied over again. The main point of interest is Meir's view that what is distinct cannot be deemed part of a mixture, and sages hold that everything can form a mixture with everything else, except for six specified items. All have something in their nature that makes them distinct (Essner, p. 138). Merely because human beings treat an items as distinct is no reason to hold it cannot form a mixture in the requisite proportion.

Pe'ah

M. Pe. 1:1–2 classify a variety of distinct items to make the point that all follow a single rule as to a specified volume or quantity. At stake at M. 1:4–6 is the classification of crops within the category of Pe'ah. How does this come about? The answers derive first from taxonomic definition, then from secondary application of the principle implicit in the definition. M. Pe. 1:4–5 classifies the produce that is liable for Pe'ah as that which is agricultural and in the Land of Israel. As at M. Ma. 1:1, when the farmer claims the produce as his own and grows food on it, he must pay for using the earth and leave God's portion for the poor. The evaluation by the farmer of the crop as useful and the act of acquiring the crop mark the point at which Pe'ah is to be designated, just as at M. Ma. 1:1 and for the reasons specified there. In general, therefore, at stake is the interplay of classification and intentionality. God acts and wills in response to human intentions, God's invisible action can be discerned by carefully studying the actions of human beings (Jaffee, p. 5). This is made explicit at M. Pe. 1:6: "Produce becomes subject to tithing as soon as the farmer processes it, the critical moment when he takes possession of the food" (Brooks, p. 51). Thus: "At any time [after the harvest, the farmer] may designate [produce] as Pe'ah, [with the result that the produce he designates] is exempt from [the separation of] tithes, until [the grain pile] is smoothed oven [At this point, the produce becomes liable to the separation of tithes.]"

When is a field a field, and when is it two or ten fields? That taxonomic problem of how many are one, or how one is deemed many, is addressed once more at M. Pe. 2:1–8. The principle of division rests upon the farmer's attitude and actions toward a field. If the farmer harvests an area as a single entity, that action indicates his attitude or intentionality in regard to that area and serves to mark it as a field. For each patch of grain the householder reaps separately a Pe'ah-share must be designated; the action indicates the intentionality to treat the area as a single field. But natural barriers intervene; rivers or hills also may mark off a fields boundaries, whatever the farmer's action and therefore a priori intentionality or attitude. So in classifying an area of ground as a field, there is an interplay between the givens of the physical traits and the attitude, confirmed by action, of the farmer. M. 2:5–8 provide excellent cases for the application of these operative principles. A farmer might harvest a single field delimited by physical barriers, or how may harvest two fields in one lot (Brooks, p. 53). In both cases we ask: do the physical barriers define matters? Or does the attitude of the farmer confirmed by his action dictate the field's boundary? And a further issue is whether or not a field produces a single crop. If it does, then a single portion is designated, even if the produce is harvested on a number of different occasions. Brooks: "Because the householder has ignored the boundaries clearly established by the field's physical characteristics, his actions have no effect. A parallel problem has a tract of land planted with different species of a single genus. Here the farmer's actions are decisive, and, consequently, his intentionality enjoys full play. The applied reason involving issues of classification is fully exposed here.

If food in the status of gleanings becomes confused with ordinary produce, how do we assign the stalks for the poor? M. 5:1–2 give to the poor all produce the status of which is in doubt. By giving the poor all such grain, householders take care not to misappropriate for themselves food that has been set aside for the poor (Brooks, p. 86). The issue here is the classification of gleanings. If it is in the taxon of priestly food, then it is sanctified for the poor alone. The alternative view is that the farmer may substitute food of equal value. Gleanings then are not governed by the analogy of priestly food but by that of second tithe. Then at stake is the issue of classification by analogy, rather than resolving matters of doubt. The issue of M. Pe. 5:7ff. is what constitutes forgetting and what defines a sheaf. The classification here appeals to considerations of intentionality or forgetfulness. Each constitutes a taxonomic indicator. The point is that if anyone involved in harvesting and binding the grain remembers that a sheaf remains in the field, by definition that sheaf cannot enter the category of the forgotten sheaf (Brooks, p. 87). The utter absence of intentionality on the part of the farmer, his workers, and also the poor, who may not practice deception, defines forgetting. So here we are given a fine exercise in the definition of the opposites, forgetting and intentionality. Forgetting on the part of man is deemed the act of intentionality on the part of God. Chapter Six pursues the issue of the role of human intention in determining which sheaves must be left as forgotten produce (Brooks, p. 101). What is the status of a sheaf that the farmer leaves behind with the clear intention of collecting the sheaf later on? What is the farmer binds an unusually large quantity of produce into a single sheaf or places an ordinary sheaf in a special location? The intention is revealed through such an act and the sheaf does not enter the status of forgotten sheaves. Or the fact that the farmer has left the sheaves behind is decisive. We cannot be certain that the householder will ever retrieve the sheaf, so the intentionality is defined by the action, with the result that this is classified as forgotten sheaves.

The interesting taxonomic issue taken up at M. Pe. 7:6 is whether classes that fall within a single category in one respect follow the same rules in all other respects, that is, the validity of polythetic taxonomy. Brooks explains, "Both the fruit of a four-year-old vine and produce in the status of second tithe must be consumed in Jerusalem...at issue is whether or not these two types of produce are subject to precisely the same rules in all other respects. That is to say, since they share one law, do they share all other laws as well?" (Brooks, p. 130). The House of Hillel treat them as wholly analogous. The laws that apply to the one govern the status of the other. The House of Shammai differentiate and have the two sets of food subject to precisely opposing rules. The laws that govern second tithe do not apply to the produce of a vine in its fourth year of growth except for the same detail at hand.

M. Pe. 7:7 asks whether the classification of defective clusters depends upon objective facts or subjective attitudes. The taxonomic question is worked out by our definition of the meaning of "defective," parallel to the sense of the word "forgetting." Is there an objective standard for the shape of a well-formed cluster? In that case, the farmer must give all clusters that do not conform. Then the whole of the vineyard may go to the poor. Eliezer holds that the category of defective cluster applies because of the farmer's evaluation or attitude. If in his view there will be no crop at all, then whatever the condition of the grapeclusters, they cannot be rejected. The farmer cannot anticipate leaving the entire crop to the poor; his intentionality will then be taken into account.

M. Pe. 8:1 asks about the status of produce that has been set aside for the poor but not taken by them. Is the poor offering in the classification of priestly rations? Then it is intrinsically sanctified. If it is not analogous to the priestly rations, then no sanctification inheres. The same problem of comparison and contrast occupies M. 8:2–4. It concerns poor offerings that the poor has taken and now wish to sell? If they are like common produce the food may be sold. But poor offerings are not like common produce, because they are exempt from the separation of tithes. The poor may claim that the produce they sell is in the status of poor offerings and so is exempt from tithing, and so command a higher price. But what of the householder who buys the food? And how can the householder determine whether or not the claim of the poor person as to the status of the food is valid? The entire question arises, therefore, because of the appeal to analogies for the classification of the poor offerings and the consequent identification of the applicable rules.

Shebi'it

The restrictions of the Sabbatical Year take effect prior to the beginning of that year, so M. Sheb. 1:1. This is because, as Newman says (p. 18), "Activities that a farmer performs during one year will be felt only during the year following." Since work done in the sixth year affects the field in the seventh, we therefore deal with an interstitial period of time, in which some work may be done, some not, depending upon its effect. This then forms a problem of classification. How shall I identify the taxic indicators that assign a given type of work to one class of time and actions — the permitted, the sixth year — and how to the other — the forbidden, the seventh year. People may not plow fields toward the end of the sixth year, for this would improve the crow that will grow in the seventh, a concept introduced here and at M. Sheb. 2:1. A farmer may not plant a new tree during the last month of the sixth year, since the sapling will take root only after the New Year that marks the beginning of the seventh (M. Sheb. 2:6). What this means is that the actions of the farmer form a part of the taxonomic problem. Some things that they do provoke the restrictions that will apply, in general, only later on. The classification of acts of labor by appeal to the stated taxic indicators predominates through Chapters One and Two. M. 1:1 is followed up by a series of necessary definitions, then the case of gray areas. We then take up, M. 1:6–8, plowing orchards of saplings, which may be done until the Near Year of the Sabbatical Year. Grain fields may be plowed up to that point at which people cease to plow fields of gourds, M. 2:1. Permitted labor is then set forth at M. 2:2–5: agricultural activities the effects of which apply principally in the sixth year. This is succeeded, M. 2:6–10, by the catalogue of ambiguous cases: agricultural work the effects of which may or may not be felt in the sixth year or the seventh year. The indicator then is clear: the interstitial period of time prior to the Seventh Year and the classification of diverse acts of agricultural labor during that time. The taxonomic problem is precipitated by the unclarity of that span of time, and it is solved by appeal to the taxic indicators beautifully articulated: a classic example of the power of classification to solve problems of order.

5. MIXTURES

M. Sheb. 3:1–4:1 turns to the problem of cultivating the land during the Seventh Year, with special attention to the difference between actually doing so and appearing to do so. There are acts of labor that will not necessarily benefit the field in the Seventh Year, but which may appear to others to do so. For example, one may store manure in the field. But what if this actually enriches the soil during the Seventh Year? Then doing so is prohibited. So how are we to do the work in such a way that we do not appear to be manuring the field? One brings out three dung heaps per seah of land, each of considerable size; then people will not think that it is to manure the field, the heaps being too few and too scattered, so M. Sheb. 3:2. Along these same lines, one may not appear to clear the field for planting (M. Sheb. 3:5–4:1). One can open a stone quarry, so long as it does not appear that the farmer is clearing the land of stones and so preparing it for cultivation. One who tears down a stone fence in his field may remove only the large stones, to indicate that he is not clearing the land, so M. 3:6–7. Newman states, "The sanctity of the Seventh Year depends in the last analysis upon the actions and will of the people of Israel." From a philosophical perspective, what is important is the power of intentionality (here: will) in solving taxonomic problems, assigning to the class of forbidden or prohibited actions things that the attitude of the community at large deems to be work associated with the Seventh Year or not." What grows in the Sabbatical Year is classified as holy. God owns the crop. Everyone has a right to an equal share. Individuals may not dispose of crops of the Seventh Year as they do of their own produce. That is the fact that generates the interesting problems of M. Sheb. 8:1–6, 7–11. The problem of M. 8:1–2 addresses interstitial classes of produce, which may serve either animals or human beings. How do we know its classification? The matter depends upon human intentionality. If someone gathered it with the intention of using the produce for both human beings and cattle, it is classified by that intention; if someone gathered it only for use as wood, it is so classified, and so throughout. Here is a classic case in which, in an ambiguous case, it is the human attitude or intentionality that defines matters. These same considerations are expressed in the notion of "ordinary mode of utilization," M. Sheb. 8:2. We assume that the prevailing attitude applies in any individual case. Therefore we do not take account of an individual's asymptotic attitude or intentionality; we classify by the prevailing attitude. M. 8:3ff. then set forth rules for the disposition of crops within the stated rules. The main point concerns the treatment of crops in a manner different from that characteristic of other years of the Sabbatical cycle.

At M. Sheb. 5:1–5 we address interstitial issues, again sorting out items that fall into two or more classifications by locating the correct taxic indicator. Specifically, we deal with produce that grows over a span of two successive years, e.g., the sixth to the seventh, or the seventh into the eighth. How do we classify that food? The upshot is whether the crop is subject to tithes that are separated during the first six years of the Sabbatical cycle or whether they are governed by the special restrictions that apply to the sanctified produce of the seventh? M 5:1 has the crop classified within the year in which the extended growing season begins the cycle. Crops that begin in the sixth year are not subject to the taboo of the seventh. A second taxic indicator concerns the time in which the greater part of the growth takes place. If more than half of a vegetable's development takes place during the Seventh Year, it is classified within that year. Arum is a special problem, because it is stored underground; precautions have to be taken to assure that the tubers are stored so that they will not produce new leaves. We classify not only crops but also the territories in which Israelites live. These have to be classed, in particular, as to their sanctification, and the taxic indicator derives from the period of time on which Israelites have lived on that land. As Newman says (p. 121), "The longer the period of Israelite occupation, the greater is the sanctify which inheres in that reason, and, concomitantly, the more stringent are the restrictions that apply to the land and its produce." Syria and surrounding areas form an interstitial problem, because it is not within the boundaries of the Land, but many Israelites settled there after the Babylonian exile.

Several grids of rules are joined together in a complex program of taxonomy. Restrictions govern the use and transfer of produce of the Sabbatical Year; restrictions govern retaining crops. Specifically, people may not retain private possession, in their silos, of crops that have ceased to be cultivated in the field on the eve of the Seventh Year and into the Seventh Year. These must be set forth for all to take, just as much as all the things that grow in the Seventh Year itself are deemed ownerless and equally, freely available to everybody. Edible produce that grows during the Seventh Year belongs to everybody, and individuals may not use the food for their own benefit or sell it in the ordinary way. They also may not stockpile produce, and that means, they must remove it. These two sets of considerations then are brought into play at M. Shebi'it Chapters Seven through Nine. M. Sheb. 7:1–2 classify produce by the taxic indicator of use: human consumption, animal consumption, dyeing matter. These matter because they are traded. In the Sabbatical Year they are treated as free for all. A taxic indicator concerns the growing cycle, annual or perennial. Annuals have to be removed from the homes because they disappear from the fields. Perennials grow from season to season and therefore do not fall under that taxic indicator. How this work is carried on is shown at M. Sheb. 7:6.

The law of removal of crops in the house at the point at which crops of the same classification cease to grow in the fields presents its set of taxic problems. Specifically, we address the interstitial issues involved in cases in which it is unclear when the law of removal takes effect. These cases derive from a situation in which the entire species of produce may or may not be subject to removal at a single time—just the sort of problem of sorting matters out that the philosophy of classification is meant to solve. Here the solution derives from a variety of taxic indicators. First, as we see, farmers in various regions harvest one crop at different times. So one thing becomes many things and is so classified. Sometimes part of the crop has been removed from the field, while part of the same species is growing in a private courtyard or is not yet ripe. Since part of the crop is not yet harvested, the rule of removal should not take effect. But since the species is not now available to everybody all at once, perhaps the law does apply. The taxic indicator is whether the inability of certain classes of persons to gather and eat produce can affect the point at which the law of removal applies (Newman, p. 179). Or perhaps the law is not invoked until the last of that species disappears, without regard to whether particular classes of persons can or cannot gather it. These are the opposed principles that set forth the problems of M. Sheb. 9:1–6. As Newman says, "The first theory is that man through his actions and capacities determines when the law of removal takes cffcct. If Israelite farmers harvest a single species of produce in two or more separate lots, each crop is deemed a separate entity. Similarly, the ability of Israelites to harvest and use crops of the Sabbatical Year is decisive. As soon as produce of a given species is no longer available...the householder must remove that same species from the home. Finally, the way in which man stores produce after he has harvested it likewise is probative. If a householder stores several distinct species of produce in a single jar, the whole is treated as a single entity. The principle underlying these rules is that man is the center of his world. Through their actions...farmers and householders order the world in accordance with their wishes... The opposing theory is that the law applies separately to each species of produce, no matter how Israelite farmers may handle them...These rules express the notion that it is God's action, not man's [attitude], which determines the point at which the law takes effect."

M. Sheb. 10:7 provides a classic example of the power of classification. We here demonstrate that once we have classified an object, then everything that pertains to that class of objects pertains to the particular object we have classified. The manner in which one carries out that principle, and the implications thereof, cannot be more adequately portrayed than they are in this simple case.

Terumot

At stake at M. Ter. 1:1–2, 3 is how produce is classified so that part of it falls into the category of heave-offering, that is to say, is sanctified. The Israelite is central to the process of classification, that is, sanctification. So Avery-Peck (p. 3): "The holy heave offering comes into being only if man properly formulates the intention to sanctify part of his produce and indicates that intention through corresponding words and actions. The centrality of human intention in this process is illustrated by the fact that individuals deemed to have no understanding, e.g., imbeciles and minors, and therefore no power of intention, may not validly designate heave-offering." No produce is intrinsically holy. All depends upon the intentionality, as to classification, of the householder. That accounts for the interest at M. 1:1–2 in an act of classification accomplished through full intentionality of someone with the power of intentionality. The indicative traits of those excluded from the process then bear the generalization. The process of classification of produce is subjected to a fundamental rule at M. Ter. 1:4–5. It is that the classification must be unambiguous, so that what is separated for produce of one taxon cannot serve as heave offering for produce of a different taxon. That conception may be expressed in more familiar, philosophical terms: each species must be kept distinct among a genus. Wine and grapes form a common genus: liquid and solid form of the same thing, so too olives and olive oil. One cannot separate olives as heave offering for oil hence is a way of saying one must preserve the distinct taxa of species within a common genus. This may be expressed any number of ways, but it is always that single principle of taxonomy. But this then raises the complex question addressed here and beyond: what if one has done so? Since both form species of a common genus, is what has been separated validly distinguished, with the result that, after the fact, it is, in fact, heave offering? Or do we impose a rigid distinction between species and species, so that, even after the fact, the distinction holds? That is what is at stake at M. 1:4C, D, with the House of Hillel in the position that species are always kept distinct. M. 1:5 goes over the same

5. MIXTURES

conception. M. 1:6 is joined to the foregoing because it deals with the distinction between what is done before and after the fact, and now we recognize the possibility that people with impaired intentionality or power to express intentionality can, after the fact, act effectively. We come to the interplay of action and intentionality, with intentionality ruled out of bounds. M. Ter. 1:8 explains how the act of separation takes place. What is required is negative: there must not be a predetermined and measured quantity of produce. The produce that falls into the classification of holy must be so classified by fortune, that is, by accident and not by intention. So the act of classification must be intentional, but carrying out the act must be left in the hands of God. That forms an important limitation upon the role of intentionality, a distinction between the arena in which my intentionality operates, and the boundaries beyond which my intentionality does not extend. The basic principles of the separation of heave offering having been set forth — intentionality as a distinction, speciation as a consideration — we come at M. Ter. 2:1–2 to the systematic composition of a grid in which the two sets of principles are joined in a common, complex expression. The established rules are [1] heave offering may not be separated from one genus of produce on behalf of produce of a different genus; [2] if the householder owns different species within the same genus of produce, heave offering should be separated from the species which is of the higher quality (Avery-Peck, p. 81). M. 2:1–3 begin the work by specifying that heave offering may not be separated from produce of one genus on behalf of another now with reference to cultic cleanness. The unclean must be treated in distinction from the clean. If one has done so, the act is valid. But what about deliberately doing so, since the unclean is useless and of less value? M. Ter. 2:2 then invokes the consideration of intentionality. If one intentionally separated unclean for clean, his act is null; if unintentionally, his act is valid. Here, therefore, intentionality joins as a principal criterion for classification. The role of intentionality in the classification of part of the crop as heave offering is spelled out at M. Ter. 3:5. The farmer must express his will distinctly and clearly, meaning he must say where, in his intentionality, that portion of the crop that is distinguished as heave offering is located within the larger batch. So the oral declaration is required, not merely a decision reached within one's heart, and that oral designation must be detailed and concrete. Only after the offering has been so designated is part of the batch separated and given to the priest. M. Ter. 4:1–6 complete the presentation of rules on the classification of produce. M. Ter. 4:1 allows for the possibility that an owner may wish to give more than the minimum portion of his crop for heave offering. The established principles are worked out within this context. The issue of intentionality is introduced, now with reference to the volume of the crop that a farmer wishes to set aside for this purpose.

Once we have completed the rules of classification, we turn to the consideration of the disposition of mixtures, that is, the confusion of what has been classified. The simple logic that governs is that first we classify an undifferentiated thing, then we deal with the reversal of the act of classification, hence, mixtures or confusion. The basic principle (Avery-Peck, p. 131) is that when heave offering is mixed with unconsecrated produce such that it constitutes a minute proportion of the mixture (approximately one per cent or less), it loses its integrity within the other produce and therefore becomes permitted for consumption by a non-priest. Joshua and Eliezer dispute whether or not heave offering which can be distinguished from the unconsecrated produce with which it is mixed simply should be recovered and given to a priest. Aqiba's principle governs: "When it is known which [type of produce in the status of heave offering] fell [into the unconsecrated produce, the two different types] do not neutralize one another. But when it is not known which [type of produce in the status of heave offering] fell [into the unconsecrated produce, the two different types of produce] neutralize one another." M. 4:10–13 go over the same ground. The rule is that if we do not know into which of several batches of unconsecrated produce heave offering has fallen, all of the produce is deemed to join together as a single batch to neutralize the heave offering. Chapter Five continues the same matter. At M. 5:1–4 we deal with cases in which either the heave offering or the unconsecrated produce with which heave offering is mixed is unclean. At M. 5:5–9 we address the question of whether or not produce taken to replace heave offering which is neutralized is true heave offering. This is a secondary question of classification. The entire composition, therefore, address the joint issues of mixtures and cases of doubt, which, here, are one and the same.

The taxonomic power of intentionality comes into play when it comes to violating the sanctity of heave-offering. If a non-priest has eaten heave-offering, how do we classify the act? If he has done so intentionally, he is subjected to one set of sanctions, and if unintentionally, a different set of sanctions, as specified at M. Ter. 6:1D: the principal and added fifth are restored to the priesthood. The added fifth is a fine through which the non-priest makes atonement for misappropriating the sanctified produce (Avery-Peck, p. 193). The task is to indicate who is liable to pay the principal and added fifth, and what produce may be used for that purpose. While the

5. MIXTURES

whole of Chapter Six works on these questions of detail, what generates the questions to begin with is the power of classification deriving from intentionality.

M. Ter. 9:1–4 address a subtle issue of classification. It concerns the yield of heave-offering, that is to say, the status of a crop grown from the seed that is in the classification of heave-offering, or of tithes, or of other produce subject to special taxic indicators ("restrictions"). Is such a crop in the status of the seed from which it was grown? If so, then in the case of a crop grown from seed in the status of heave offering, only priests may consume that produce. Along these same lines, at M. Ter. 9:5–7, we have produce that is liable to the separation of tithes but not yet tithed. If seed in that status is planted, is the crop subject to tithes from the beginning of its growth, is, like crops grown from tithed seed, is the liability incurred only at the time of harvest and processing. At M. 9:1–4 we distinguish seed in the status of heave offering from seed in any other status.. Why? Because while heave offering is consecrated, other types of produce are not. So Avery-Peck (p. 251): "The individual who plants heave offering thus misuses what is holy and intrinsically cannot be eaten by him. This consideration does not apply to other categories of produce, which, while restricted as to consumption by specified persons or in special circumstances, are not holy." The distinction between what is intrinsically holy and what is only holy as to function, e.g., value, is familiar from quite distinct areas of law, e.g., between what is sanctified for use on the altar and what is sanctified for the benefit of the sanctuary in general. That at stake is the difference between an intrinsic and a functional taxic indicator is then perfectly clear. The second group of materials, M. 9:5–7, goes over a different and secondary point. It is whether or not the crop shares in the status of the seed from which it grew is determined on the basis of the nature of that seed or the type of restriction to which it is subject. Avery-Peck explains, "If the seed constitutes part of the crop that grows from it (e.g., onions), the crop has the same status as the seed ... If ... the seed is not integral to the crop but is destroyed in the growth process, then even in the case of seed in the status of heave offering, that crop does not have the status which originally was held by the seed. The crop is deemed a separate entity and distinct from the seed."

Chapter Ten deals with cooking food in the status of heave offering along with unconsecrated produce. When does the unconsecrated produce take on the status of the heave-offering with which it is prepared? The taxic principle is simple. If the prohibited produce has imparted its character to the entire mixture, then the whole takes on the status of the forbidden produce, e.g., by reason of the flavor imparted by the heave-offering. If produce in the status of heave offering is cooked or prepared with unconsecrated food and flavors it, then the entire mixture is in the status of heave offering. This principle that what dominates also defines is familiar from a variety of areas of law, and yields no problems. The entirety of Chapter Ten illustrates this same principle. The cases describe diverse methods of preparing food, e.g., dough raised with leaven in the status of heave offering (M. Ter. 10:2), permitted food absorbing forbidden vapors (M. 10:3–4), water flavored with heave offering (M. 10:5, 6), when permitted food is pickled, boiled, or cooked, with forbidden (M. 10:7–12). The principle stated at the outset is repeatedly applied. Here we have not doubt but simple classification.

Produce in the status of heave offering may not be permitted to go to waste. It must be used for the purpose for which it has been designated, that is to say, for the benefit of the priest. So the taxic principle that governs the utilization of produce in the status of heave offering is the initial purpose for which it is intended, that is to say, the benefit of the priest. The intentionality of the farmer in designating this portion of the crop for the priest governs the disposition of the crop, yet another important way in which intentionality forms a primary taxic indicator in the formation of the rules of this tractate. Chapter Eleven spells the matter out. M. 11:1–3 presents the governing theory: produce in the status of heave offering must be prepared in the manner customary for unconsecrated produce of the same type. What this means is that the intentionality of the farmer-donor is limited by the prevailing practice or rule, though I do not think that that is a principal consideration here. All portions of the produce that normally are eaten must be available for eating (Avery-Peck, p. 295). If produced is processed in an abnormal way, so that what is usually eaten is pressed for juice, the skin would go to waste; that must not happen. M. 11:4–7 proceeds to produce that normally is not eaten but may be consumed. Such an interstitial category demands attention. How do we resolve the matter? If the priest deems that produce worthy as food, then it is in the consecrated status of heave offering. What the priest does not deem food is treated as inedible and therefore not in the status of heave offering. Here intentionality has paramount power of classification. M. 11:8–10 deal with produce of an ambiguous classification. It is unclean and may not be eaten by the priest; or he may not want it as food. But it may be used for some other purpose, e.g., fodder or lamp oil. Since it cannot be used as food, it does not have to be eaten; but it may not be permitted to go to waste.

5. MIXTURES

VIII. CONCLUSION

The catalogue leaves no doubt whatsoever that the Mishnah over all sets forth a systematic and sustained essay in the exposition of problems of classification, with special attention to the complementary issues of mixtures and distinctions. In nearly every tractate, and over the surface of the greater part of many tractates, one can learn the principles of the speciation of a genus, the relationship of the species of a genus to one another, the comparison and contrast of species, the hierarchization of genera, the division of one thing into many things, the aggregation or conglomeration of many things into one thing, and related issues, all of them subject to generalization, of hierarchical classification. The enormous catalogue that follows proves beyond doubt that the Mishnah's framers overall proposed a sustained treatise on mixtures, classification, and the issues of taxonomy, and laid out with great care not only the results of the application of fixed rules but, more to the point, lessons so planned and set forth as to teach the general rules of classification: speciation and hierarchization of the species. Indeed, in some tractates, the generalizations that can apply everywhere are set forth in correct order, much as Euclid lays out his theorems in a necessary order, from the simple to the complex, and from the fundamental to the secondary.

6.
ANALYSIS:
Intentionality

I. DEFINING INTENTIONALITY, ATTITUDE

Intentionality is the attitude that motivates a given action, the intention of the person who performs the action: what he hopes to accomplish — either effect or prevent. That act defined by intentionality, or expression of an attitude, governs the action's classification, e.g., as to effect or lack of effect, as to acceptability or lack of acceptability, e.g., in recitation of prayer. While a single word, *kavvanah*, corresponds, the category, intentionality, is shown by context to pertain even where that particular word (or any of its synonyms) does not appear.

Intentionality classifies actions, so that with one intention an action is cursed, but with the opposite, it is blessed, so T. Bik. 2:15: He who sells a Torah scroll never sees a sign of blessing. Scribes who copy Torah scrolls, Tefillin-parchments, and mezuzah-parchments — they and their dealers who buy these items from scribes, and their dealers' dealers who buy them from other merchants, and all those who deal in sacred objects for the sake of making a profit will never see a sign of blessing. But if they were dealing with these objects for the sake of Heaven, lo, they shall be blessed. Dealing in holy objects for the sake of a profit is not acceptable, for the sake of Heaven is.

One's intention affects the assessment of one's deed, whether it is for good or ill. Miriam criticized Moses and was punished, but her intention was honorable; had it been dishonorable, the punishment would have been greater, so Sif. Num. XCIX:II.2: Now it is an argument *a fortiori:* if Miriam, who intended to speak against her brother not to his detriment but to his credit, and not to lessen procreation but to increase it, and who spoke only in private, yet she was punished, if someone intends to speak ill of his fellow and not in praise, to diminish and not to increase procreation, and speaks not in private but among others — how much the more so will such a one be punished! Now it is an argument *a fortiori:* if Uzziah the king, who had no intention of arrogating greatness to himself for his own honor but for the honor of his creator, was punished as he was, one who arrogates greatness to himself for his own honor and not for the honor of his creator — how much the more so will such a one be punished!

Concrete actions take on consequence only by reference to the intention with which they are carried out. For example, what matters in the offerings is intentionality; the size of the offering makes no difference, only the intent of the person who presents it, so b. Men. 13:11 I.2/110a: It is said of the burnt offering of a beast, 'An offering by fire, a smell of sweet savor' (Lev. 1:9) and of the bird offering, 'An offering by fire, a smell of sweet savor' (Lev. 1:17) and even of the meal offering, 'An offering by fire, a smell of sweet savor' (Lev. 2:9) — to teach that all the same are the one who offers much and the one who offers little, on condition that a man will direct his intention to Heaven. Now might you say, 'Then it is because God needs the food,' Scripture states, 'If I were hungry, I would not tell you, for the world is mine and the fullness thereof' (Ps. 50:12); 'For every beast of the forest is mine and the cattle upon a thousand hills; I know all the fowl of the mountains and wild beasts of the field are mine; do I eat the meat of bulls or drink the blood of goats' (Ps. 50:10, 11, 13). I did not order you to make sacrifices so you might say, 'I will do what he wants so he will do what I want.' You do not make sacrifices for my sake but for your sake: 'you shall sacrifice at your own volition' (Lev. 19:5)."

Intentionality forms a critical theological category, since it is the actor's intention to which God responds in his evaluation of an action, its consequence, and his — God's — response. The correct attitude in serving God is on account of reverence or fear, not as an entirely votive action, out of love, e.g., M. Sot. 5:5: On that day did R. Joshua b. Hurqanos expound as follows: "Job served the Holy One, blessed be He, only out of love, since it is said, Though he slay me, yet will I wait for him (Job 13:15). But still the matter is in doubt as to whether it means, 'I will wait for him,' or 'I will not wait for him.' Scripture states, Until I die I will not put away mine integrity from me' (Job. 27:5). This teaches that he did what he did out of love." Said R. Joshua, "Who will remove the dirt from your eyes, Rabban Yohanan b. Zakkai? For you used to expound for your entire life that Job served the Omnipresent only out of awe, since it is said, The man was perfect and upright and one who feared God and avoided evil (Job. 1:8). And now has not Joshua, the disciple of your disciple, taught that he did what he did out of love."

One is permitted to fear God alone, and that is the sole correct source of intentionality, as the following story indicates (Y. B.M. 2:4 I.2): Samuel bar Suseretai went to Rome. The queen had lost her jewelry. He found it. A proclamation went forth through the city: "Whoever returns her jewelry in thirty days will receive thus and so. If he returns it after thirty days, his head will be cut off." He did not return the jewelry within thirty days. After thirty days, he returned it to her. She said to him, "Weren't you in town?" He said to her, "Yes I was here." She said to him, "And didn't you hear the proclamation?" He said to her, "Yes I heard it." She said to him, "And what did it say?" He said to her. that it said, 'Whoever returns her jewelry in thirty days will receive thus-and-so. If he returns it after thirty days. his head will be cut off.'" She said to him, "And why didn't you return it within thirty days?" "So that people should not say, 'It was because I was afraid of you that I did so.' But it was because I fear the All-Merciful." She said to him. "Blessed be the God of the Jews."

The correct intentionality involves submission to God's will, and that is what governs under all conditions, so M. Rosh Hashanah 3:8: Now it happened that when Moses held up his hand, Israel prevailed, and when he let his hand fall, Amalek prevailed (Ex. 17:11). Now do Moses's hands make war or stop it? But the purpose is to say this to you: So long as the Israelites would set their eyes upward and submit their hearts to their Father in heaven, they would grow stronger. And if not, they fell. God plays a role by responding to Man's intentionality, thus: As regards a good intention — the Omnipresent, blessed be He, refines it so that it produces a corresponding deed. As for an evil intention — the Omnipresent does not refine it, so that it does not produce a corresponding deed (T. Peah 1:4).

Intentionality is critical in doing one's religious duties; one must not utilize the Torah and the commandments for an inappropriate purpose, so B. Ned. 8:3–4 II.8–9/62a: "That you may love the Lord your God and that you may obey his voice and that you may cleave to him" (Deut. 30:20): This means that someone shouldn't say, "I shall study Scripture, so as to be called a sage, I shall repeat Mishnah teachings, so as to be called 'my lord.' I shall reason critically, so that I may be an elder and take a seat at the session. Rather: Learn out of love, and honor will come on its own: "Bind them on your fingers, write them on the table of your heart" (Prov. 7:3); "Her ways are ways of pleasantness" (Prov. 3:17); "She is a tree of life to those that hold onto her, and happy is everyone who keeps her" (Prov. 3:18). R. Eliezer b. R. Sadoq says, "Do things for the sake of the One who has made them and speak of them for their own sake, and don't turn them into a crown for self-glorification or make them into a spade with which to dig. It derives from an argument a fortiori in the case of Belshazzar, namely, if Belshazzar — who used the holy utensils that were removed from their status of sanctification, in line with the statement, 'for the robbers shall enter into it and profane it' (Ezek. 7:22), since they had broken in, the

6. ANALYSIS: Intentionality

utensils were profaned — was removed from the world — 'in that night was Belshazzar slain' (Dan. 5:30) — one who makes selfish use of the crown of the Torah, which lives and endures forever, all the more so will be uprooted from this world!"

The correct intentionality is to carry out the requirements of the Torah for their own sake, not for the sake of a reward, so Sif. Dt. CCCVI:XXII.1: "May my discourse come down as the rain, my speech distill as the dew, like showers on young growths, like droplets on the grass. For the name of the Lord I proclaim": R. Benaiah would say, "If you carry out the teachings of the Torah for their own sake, the teachings of the Torah will live for you. For it is said, 'For they are life to those that find them' (Prov. 4:22). But if you do not carry out teachings of the Torah for their own sake, they will kill you. For it is said, "My doctrine shall drop as the rain.' And the word for 'drop' yields the sense of 'killing,' in line with its usage in the following verse: 'And he shall break the heifer's neck there in the valley' (Dt. 21:4). 'For she has cast down many wounded, yes, a mighty host are all those she has slain' (Prov. 7:26)."

The right attitude furthermore involves sincerity, a total commitment to the action for its own sake, so B. Hor. 3:3 I.11/10b: Said R. Nahman bar Isaac, "A transgression committed for its own sake, in a sincere spirit, is greater in value than a religious duty carried out not for its own sake, but in a spirit of insincerity. But did not R. Judah say Rab said, "A person should always be occupied in study of the Torah and in practice of the commandments, even if this is not for its own sake but in a spirit of insincerity, for out of doing these things not for their own sake, a proper spirit of doing them for their own sake will emerge"? *Say:* it is equivalent to doing them not for their own sake.

Faith is the key. Acting in good faith, in complete sincerity, makes a person worthy of encountering the Holy Spirit, so Mekh. XXV:I.26: R. Nehemiah says, "How do you know that whoever takes upon himself the obligation to carry out a single religious duty in faith is worth that the Holy Spirit should rest upon him? For so we find in the case of our ancestors that as a reward for the act of faith that they made, they achieved merit, so that the Holy Spirit rested on them, as it is said, 'and they believed in the Lord and in his servant Moses. Then Moses and the people of Israel sang this song to the Lord, saying, 'I will sing to the Lord, for he has triumphed gloriously; the horse and his rider he has thrown into the sea.'" "So you find that Abraham our father inherited this world and the world to come only as a reward for the faith that he believed, as it is said, "And he believed in the Lord" (Gen. 15:6). So you find that the Israelites were redeemed from Egypt only as a reward for the faith that they believed, as it is said, "And the people believed" (Ex. 4:31). "The Lord preserves the faithful" (Ps. 31:25). He calls to mind the faith of the fathers.

What governs the relationship between intentionality and action? The intention to carry out one's obligation must accompany the act that effects that obligation; otherwise, the act bears no effect, so M. Ber. 2:1A-C: One who was reading the verses of the *Shema* in the Torah and the time for the recitation of the *Shema* arrived: If he directed his heart towards fulfilling the obligation to recite the *Shema*, he fulfilled his obligation to recite. And if he did not direct his heart, he did not fulfill his obligation. Whether or not the recitation of the Prayer of supplication requires intentionality is subject to discussion, e.g., M. Ber. 4:4 A. R. Eliezer says, "One who makes his prayers a fixed task — his prayers are not valid supplications of God." Intentionality may take precedence over actual activity, as at M. Ber. 4:5 A–C: If he was riding on an ass, he should dismount to recite the Prayer. But if he cannot dismount, he should turn his face toward the east. And if he cannot turn his face, he should direct his heart toward the Chamber of the Holy of Holies. When one prays, he is to direct his heart to God, e.g., M. Ber. 5:1 A–E: One may stand to pray only in a solemn frame of mind. The early pious ones used to tarry one hour before they would pray, so that they could direct their hearts to the Omnipresent. While one is praying even if the king greets him, he may not respond. And even if a serpent is entwined around his heel, he may not interrupt his prayer. Intentionality governs the effect of all rites, so M. Rosh Hashanah 3:7D–J: He who was going along behind a synagogue, or whose house was near a synagogue, and who heard the sound of the shofar or the sound of the reading of the Scroll of Esther, if he paid attention thereby intending to carry out his obligation, he has fulfilled his obligation. But if not, he has not fulfilled his obligation. That is the rule even if this one heard and that one heard, for this one paid attention, and that one did not pay attention to what he heard.

The intentional violation of the law always invalidates the consequent action. What is done in violation of the law but not by intention, by contrast, may well be accepted, since it was not an act of rebellion against the Torah, e.g., M. Ter. 2:3: One who immerses unclean utensils on the Sabbath — if he does so unintentionally, he may use them; but if he does so intentionally, he may not use them. One who tithes his produce, or who cooks on the Sabbath — if he does so unintentionally, he may eat the food he has prepared; but if he does so intentionally, he may not eat the food. One who plants a tree on the Sabbath — if he does so unintentionally, he may leave it to grow; but if he does so intentionally, he must uproot it. But in the Seventh Year of the Sabbatical cycle, whether he has planted the tree unintentionally or intentionally, he must uproot it. Along these same lines, intentionality forms the principal criterion for effecting atonement through repentance. If one manifests the inappropriate intentionality, then the rite is null, thus M. Yoma 8:9 A. He who says, "I shall sin and repent, sin and repent" — they give him no chance to do repentance. "I will sin and the Day of Atonement will atone," — the Day of Atonement does not atone. So too the law distinguishes inadvertence from deliberation in action, with appropriately diverse penalties, T. Shab. 2:17–18: He who slaughters an animal on the Sabbath — if he did so inadvertently — it may be eaten at the end of the Sabbath. If he did so deliberately, it may not be eaten. Produce which one gathered on the Sabbath — if he did so inadvertently, it may be eaten at the end of the Sabbath. If he did so deliberately, it may not be eaten.

It follows that intentionality overrides action. Thus, for example, a mere accident of speech is not binding; one must say exactly what he intended to say for the act of speech to be binding, whether in regard to oaths or offerings. Thus M. Ter. 3:8: (1) One who in designating agricultural gifts intends to say, "heave offering," but says, "tithe," "tithe," but says "heave offering," (2) or who, in designating a sacrifice, intends to say, "burnt offering," but says, "peace offering," "peace offering," but says, "burnt offering"; (3) or who, in making a vow, intends to say, "that I will not enter this house," but says, "that house," "that I will not derive benefit from this one," but says, "from that one," has not said anything, until his mouth and heart agree. Along these same lines, to incur guilt, one must intend the action that one has carried out. If he acted in a manner different from his intended action, he is not culpable as he would have been had he accomplished his purpose, so M. San. 9:4: If he intended to kill a beast and killed a man, an untimely birth and killed an offspring that was viable, he is exempt. If he intended to hit him on his loins with a blow that was not sufficient to kill him when it struck his loins, but it went and hit his heart, and there was sufficient force in that blow to kill him when it struck his heart, and he died, he is exempt. If he intended to hit him on his heart, and there was in that blow sufficient force to kill when it struck his heart, and it went and hit him on his loins, and there was not sufficient force in that blow to kill him when it struck his loins, but he died, he is exempt.

One's intentionality further governs the effect of one's deeds when it comes to dealing with consecrated produce. For example, M. Ma'aser Sheni 1:5 rules, One who buys outside Jerusalem with money in the status of second tithe, which is to be eaten only in Jerusalem pieces of fruit , if he did so (1) unintentionally not realizing the coins were consecrated, let their payment be returned to its former place to the purchaser who bought them by mistake; if he did so (2) on purpose—let the pieces of fruit be brought up and eaten in the holy place Jerusalem. And if the Temple does not exist, let the pieces of fruit rot.

When the farmer has decided that he wishes to benefit from the crop, e.g., to take it to market for sale, then God's rights of ownership are activated, and the crop must be tithed. But the crop may be subjected to random nibbling and not become liable to tithing. The actions of the farmer convey his attitude and intention vis à vis the crop, e.g., once he has covered a basket, once he has filled a vessel. So M. Maaserot 1:5: At what point after the harvest must tithes be removed from produce? (1) Cucumbers and gourds-after he removes the fuzz from them. But if he does not remove the fuzz, tithes need not be removed until he stacks them up. (2) Chatemelons—after he scalds them in order to remove the fuzz. But if he does not scald them, tithes need not be removed until he makes a store of melons. (3) Green vegetables which are normally tied in bunches-after he ties them But if he does not tie them, tithes need not be removed until the vessel into which he places the picked greens is filled. But if he does not fill the vessel, tithes need not be removed until he collects all he needs. (4) The contents of a basket need not be tithed until he covers the basket. But if he does not cover it, tithes need not be removed until he fills the vessel. But if he does not fill the vessel, tithes need not be removed until he collects all he needs in that basket. Under what circumstances do these criteria apply? If he is bringing the produce to market. But if he is bringing it home, it is not liable to the removal of tithes, and) he eats some of it as a random snack until he reaches home.

The entire system of animal sacrifices in atonement of sin rests on the distinction between an intentional and an unintentional action. A sin is atoned for by a sin-offering only when the act is inadvertent. A deliberate action is not covered, so M. Shab. 11:6J-K: "This is the general principle: All those who may be liable to sin offerings in fact are not liable unless at the beginning and the end, their sin is done inadvertently. But if the beginning of their sin is inadvertent and the end is deliberate, or the beginning deliberate and the end inadvertent, they are exempt—unless at the beginning and at the end their sin is inadvertent. The matter of intentionality governs the penalty to be paid by means of an animal sacrifice or some other form of sanction, e.g., extirpation (premature death), death at the hands of Heaven, death at the hands of an earthly court, so M. Keritot 1:2: For those transgressions are people liable, for deliberately doing them, to the punishment of extirpation, and for accidentally doing them, to the bringing of a sin offering, and for not being certain of whether or not one has done them, to a suspensive guilt offering Lev. 5:17—"except for the one who

6. ANALYSIS: Intentionality

imparts uncleanness to the sanctuary and its Holy Things, because he is subject to bringing a sliding scale offering (Lev. 5:6–7, 11)" the words of R. Meir. And sages say, "Also: except for the one who blasphemes, as it is said, You shall have one law for him that does anything unwittingly (Num. 15:29)—excluding the blasphemer, who does no concrete deed."

Intentionality governs the acceptability of some classes of animal offerings but not others. Specifically, if an animal is designated for use as a Passover offering or as a sin offering, but then the officiating priest offers the animal up under some other designation, that is, in a classification other than that specified by the donor's intent, the offering is null, so M. Zeb. 1:1 = M. Men. 1:1 for meal offerings: All animal offerings which were slaughtered not for their own name are valid so that the blood is tossed, the entrails burned, etc., but they do not go to the owner's credit in fulfillment of an obligation, except for the Passover and the sin offering-the Passover at its appointed time the afternoon of the fourteenth of Nisan." So too M. Zeb. 2:3: This is the general rule: Whoever slaughters, or receives the blood, or conveys the blood, or sprinkles the blood intending to eat something which is usually eaten flesh, to burn something which is usually burned entrails, outside of its proper place the court for Most Holy Things, Jerusalem for Lesser Holy Things—it is invalid and the flesh may not be eaten. And extirpation does not apply to it. Whoever slaughters, or receives the blood, or conveys the blood, or sprinkles (the blood), intending to eat something which is usually eaten, to burn something which is usually burned outside of its proper time—it is refuse. And they are liable on its account to extirpation even if they eat the flesh within the time limit.

The intentionality of the animal offering covers six matters, and for each of these matters, the animal must be offered up under the donor's correct intentionality: M. Zeb. 4:6: For the sake of six things is the animal offering sacrificed: (1) for the sake of the animal offering, (2) for the sake of the one who sacrifices it, (3) for the sake of the Lord, (4) for the sake of the altar fires, (5) for the sake of the odor, (6) for the sake of the pleasing smell. And as to the sin offering and the guilt offering, for the sake of the sin expiated thereby. Said R. Yosé, "Even: One who was not mindful in his heart for the sake of one all of these but slaughtered without specifying these things—it is valid, for it is a condition imposed by the court, that intention follows only the mind of the one who carries out the act not the owner; and the officiant does not specify the six things at all."

The following compositions address the general problem of intentionality in matters of uncleanness, so b. Hag. 2:7 II.3–2/18b: Said R. Jonathan b. Eleazar, "If someone's head-band fell from him and he said to his fellow,

'Give it to me,' and he gave it to him, the headband is unclean" for we cannot assume that he took it upon himself to guard it from uncleanness while he handled it, since the owner did not ask whether he was clean or not, nor can we say that the owner guarded it against defilement while it was not in his possession. Said R. Jonathan b. Amram, "If one's garments for the Sabbath were mixed up with his garments for everyday and he put them on, they are made unclean." if someone protects something assuming it is one thing and finds it to be another, it is unclean. Intentionality extends to other matters besides concrete issues of the law and its practice. Intentionality shades over into attitude, the abstract becoming concrete through feelings or emotions. The right attitude is one of accommodation of one's own will to the will of others, self-abnegation, restraint, prudence. The most prized virtue is humility, on account of which Judah merited that the monarchy be assigned to his tribe, so too Saul (T. Ber. 4:18). A person should conform to the prevailing practice of the community and not stand out, so Hillel the Elder says at T. Ber. 2:21, "Do not appear naked where others go clothed, and do not appear clothed where others go naked, and do not appear standing where others sit, and do not appear sitting where others stand, and do not appear laughing where others weep, and do not appear weeping where others laugh, because Scripture states, 'a time to weep, a time to laugh, a time to embrace, a time to refrain from embracing' (Qoh. 3:4, 5)." Along these same lines, M. Abot 3:10 advises that God is pleased by those who try to please others: "Anyone from whom people take pleasure — the Omnipresent takes pleasure. Aqiba at T. Berakhot 3:3 goes over the same ground: "One in whom mankind delights, God delights. One in whom mankind does not delight, God does not delight. One who is content with his own portion, it is a good sign for him. One who is not content with his own portion, it is a bad sign for him." And altruism is the right attitude, e.g., M. Abot 5:16: In any loving relationship that depends upon something, when that thing is gone, the love is gone. But any that does not depend upon something will never come to an end. What is a loving relationship which depends upon something? That is the love of Amnon and Tamar 11 Sam. 13:15. And one which does not depend upon something? That is the love of David and Jonathan. So too the right intention is what validates contention, M. Abot 5:17: Any dispute which is for the sake of Heaven will in the end yield results, and any which is not for the sake of Heaven will in the end not yield results. What is a dispute for the sake of Heaven? This is the sort of dispute between Hillel and Shammai. And what is one which is not for the sake of Heaven? It is the dispute of Korach and all his party. One from whom people do not take pleasure, the Omnipresent does not take pleasure."

6. ANALYSIS: Intentionality

God's response to prayer depends upon the attitude of the community. He cannot be coerced through mere recitation of the right words. Miracles respond to intentionality, so Y. Ta. 3:4 I.1: One time they had to call a fast, but it did not rain. R. Joshua carried out a fast in the South, and it rained. The Sepphoreans said, "R. Joshua b. Levi brings down rain for the people in the South, but R. Haninah holds back rain for us in Sepphoris." They found it necessary to declare a second time of fasting and sent and summoned R. Joshua b. Levi. Haninah said to him, "Let my lord go forth with us to fast." The two of them went out to fast, but it did not rain. He went in and preached to them as follows: "It was not R. Joshua b. Levi who brought down rain for the people of the south, nor was it R. Haninah who held back rain from the people of Sepphoris. But as to the Southerners, their hearts are open, and when they listen to a teaching of Torah they submit to accept it, while as to the Sepphoreans, their hearts are hard, and when they hear a teaching of Torah, they do not submit or accept it." When he went in, he looked up and saw that the cloudless air was pure. He said, "Is this how it still is? Is there no change in the weather?" Forthwith, it rained. He took a vow for himself that he would never do the same thing again. He said, "How shall I say to the creditor God not to collect what is owing to him."

It is the possibility of a minor's forming a valid intention in respect to religious obligations that determines the point at which the minor may begin to carry out those obligations, so T. Hag. 1:2: If he knows how to shake an object, he is liable to observe the commandment of the lulab. If he knows how to cloak himself, he is liable for the commandment of fringes. If he knows how to speak, his father teaches him the Shema', Torah, and the Holy Language Hebrew. And if not, it would have been better had he not come into the world. If he knows how to take care of his phylacteries, his father purchases phylacteries for him. If he knows how to take care of his person, they eat food preserved in a state of cultic cleanness depending upon the cleanness of his person. If he knows how to take care of his hands, they eat food preserved in a state of cultic cleanness depending upon the cleanness of his hands. If he has sufficient intelligence to answer a question, then a doubt involving him in private domain is resolved as unclean, and one involving him in public domain is resolved as clean. If he knows how to effect proper slaughter of an animal, then an act of slaughter on his part is valid.

The intention to do evil, even if the action is not done, is culpable and to be repented, so b. Qid. 4: 13/II.13/81b: R. Hiyya bar Ashi was accustomed, whenever he prostrated himself to his face, to say, "May the All-Merciful save us from the Evil Impulse." Once his wife heard this. She said, "Now how many years he has kept away from me, so how come he says this?"

One day he was studying in his garden, and she dressed up in disguise and walked back and forth before him. He said to him, "How are you?" She said to him, "I'm Haruta the famous whore, and I've come back today." He lusted after her. She said to him, "Bring me that pomegranate from the top bough." He climbed up and got it for her. When he went back inside his house, his wife was heating the oven, so he climbed up and sat down in it. She said to him, "So what's going on?" He told her what had happened. She said to him, "So it was really me." But he wouldn't believe her until she gave him the pomegranate. He said to her, "Well, anyhow, my intention was to do what is prohibited." For the rest of the life of that righteous man he fasted in penitence until he died on that account. So too in the following: When R. Aqiba would come to this verse, he wept, saying, "If someone intended to eat ham and really had in hand veal, yet the Torah has said that he requires atonement and forgiveness, one who intends to eat ham and really had in hand ham — all the more so!" Along these same lines: "Though he knew it not, yet he is guilty and shall bear his iniquity" (Lev. 5:17) — when R. Aqiba would come to this verse of Scripture, he would weep: "If someone intended to eat permitted fat and really had in hand forbidden fat, yet the Torah has said, 'Though he knew it not, yet he is guilty and shall bear his iniquity,' one who really did intend to eat forbidden fat and had in hand forbidden fat — all the more so is he guilty!" Issi b. Judah says, "'Though he knew it not, yet he is guilty and shall bear his iniquity' (Lev. 5:17) — for such a thing as this that we are sinful even not by intent let all those who are mournful mourn."

It would be difficult to assemble a more uniform set of diverse formulations of a single principle. Intentionality forms the systemic dynamics of the entire structure of sanctification and morality that the Halakhah constructs.

II. INTENTIONALITY AND FREEDOM OF WILL

Man matches God in possessing freedom of will. And therein sages found the source of world disorder. Man's will was the sole power in the world that matched the power of God. And it is that variable in creation that accounts for the present imperfection of creation. To understand why, we recall that by his act of will God created the orderly world of justice, one that exhibits abundant, indicative marks of perfection. Then whence chaos embodied by disorder and dissonance? And, when the rules that embody rationality — that guarantee measure for measure above all — cease to describe the everyday experience of mankind and the here and now of

6. ANALYSIS: Intentionality

Israel, where shall we find the reason why? In the logic of a world order based on exact justice, in the Torah God accords to man a statement of his own will, a commandment, and one who issues a command both wants the command to be obeyed but also accords to the other the power to disobey. That is the very premise of commandments.

For the sages, therefore, it was man's rebellion, beyond God's control but within God's dominion that explains change. And change, imperfection, the ephemerality of affairs — these signal the actualities of disorder in a world meant for perfection, stasis, balance throughout. God proposes, man disposes. Chaos begins not in God but in man, in that trait of man that endows man with the same power that the Creator has, to conceive and to do. Since God has made an orderly world, only his counterpart on earth, man, can account for the disruption of world order. For the sole player in the cosmic drama with the power to upset God's plans is man. He alone is like God, "in our image, after our likeness." In their penetrating reflection on the power of intentionality, sages explain chaos, and that prepares the way for their investigation of sin and its remedy.

That is why, explaining the imperfection of change, the advent of time in the historical sense, the inequality of exchange, the theology of the Halakhah finds in the opposite of the indicators of perfection the sources of disruption. And change comes about principally because man by an act of will corrupts perfection. Accordingly, the Halakhah takes as its critical problem the generative tension between the word of God and the will of man, in full recognition that God judges what man does by reason of the exercise of free will. Set forth in many ways, the simplest statement is made when R. Aqiba says, "Everything is foreseen, and free choice is given; in goodness the world is judged; and all is in accord with the abundance of deeds" (Tractate Abot 3:15A).

Free will, moreover, reaches concrete expression in the deeds a man does by reason of the plans or intentions that he shapes on his own. The high value accorded by God to man's voluntary act of accepting God's dominion, the enthusiastic response made by God to man's supererogatory deeds of uncoerced love and uncompelled generosity, the heavy emphasis upon the virtues of self-abnegation and self-restraint — these emblematic traits of the coherent theology attest to the uncertainty of man's response that, from the beginning, God has built into creation. For the one power that lies beyond the rules of reason, that defies predicting, is man's power to make up his own mind.

Now how to show how these convictions form the center of the theological structure and system set forth in the Halakhah? Commensurate with the claim just now set forth, that intentionality defines the center of the system and its dynamic, the demonstration must adduce evidence of a systemic and systematic character. For that purpose, sayings, however demonstrably typical, and episodic stories or exegeses of verses of Scripture, however probative in character, do not match the task. Turning, rather, to norms of behavior, we seek evidence in the authority of required, enforced law. This is of two kinds.

First, the Halakhah designs enduring structures, institutions for the governance of Israel as a Godly realm. If I can show that in its very doctrine of how holy Israel is governed, intentionality forms the critical point of differentiation even of institutional politics — the power legitimately to inflict violence — then my claim concerning the centrality of intentionality in explaining world order and its corruption will find commensurate demonstration.

Second, the Halakhah makes its theological statement not only in apodictic sayings, or in exegesis of Scripture, or in tales of sages and exemplary stories. It speaks also, and especially, through specific norms of conduct. My task is to show how intentionality governs actualities of behavior, not of mere belief. We shall see how the consideration of the will of man preoccupies sages when they define the norms of everyday conduct.

To accomplish the task of showing the normative and paramount power of intentionality or the act of will, I have selected sages' theoretical account[1] of the working of the enduring institutions of holy Israel, the theological politics of their system. When they describe the government of holy Israel, they carry out a labor of differentiation of power, indicating what agency or person has the power to precipitate the working of politics as legitimate violence at all. And, as we shall see through the provisions that they make for various institutional foci of power to carry out diverse

---

[1] I see no point in speculating on the relationship between that theory and political actualities of this-worldly Israel, before, during, or after the composition of the documents of the Halakhah. The theory of a tripartite government, in the hands of high priest and Temple, king and administration, and sage and court, does not pertain to how Israel actually was governed at any point, either in the picture of the Written Torah of ancient Israelite times, or in the historical accounts of the Second Temple period, or in the epoch after the destruction of political autonomy in 70 C.E. Not only so, but to imagine that sages anticipated in Mishnah-tractate Sanhedrin-Makkot and other passages how Israel's government would constitute itself in the return to the Land of Israel at the time of the Messiah is to ignore the entirety of sages' thought on what would and would not take place in the world to come. As we shall see in Chapter Fourteen, with the resurrection complete, the world to come fully realized, God in charge, there would be no need for the legitimate violence of high priest, king, or sage. Our account of the theology of the Halakhah does not require an answer to the question, to what circumstance do sages address their politics? which is just as well, since, in any case, I cannot answer that question.

6. ANALYSIS: Intentionality

tasks, it is at the point of intentionality, with the story of Eden in hand, that sages accomplish their goal. Were we to ignore Eden, we could make no sense of their concrete provisions for holy Israel's government. When, therefore, we understand the differentiating force of intentionality at the most practical level of sages' theory of the social order, the power of the human will that imparts to politics its activity and dynamism, we shall grasp what everywhere animates the structures of the politics and propels the system. That is why I have chosen as a principal part of my account of intentionality the sages' theological politics.

Politics concerns legitimate violence, the functioning of sanctions. Specifically, we analyze the mythic foundations of sanctions that sages assign to various authorities, on earth and in Heaven. And when we move from sanctions to the myth expressed and implicit in the application and legitimation of those sanctions, we see a complex but cogent politics sustained by a simple political theology. This survey of sanctions and their implications had best commence with a clear statement of what we shall now uncover. The encompassing political framework of rules, institutions and sanctions is explained and validated by appeal to God's shared rule. That dominion, exercised by God and his surrogates on earth, is focused partly in the royal palace, the king, partly in the Temple, the priesthood, and partly in the court and its sages. For us, the issue here is, which part falls where and why? Helpfully, the political myth explains who exercises legitimate violence and under what conditions, and furthermore specifies the source for differentiation. The myth consequently serves a particular purpose — which is to answer that particular question. Indeed, the sages' political myth comes to expression in its details of differentiation, which permit us to identify, and of course to answer, the generative question of politics.

How, exactly, do I propose to identify the political myth of the Dual Torah? And precisely what data are supposed to attest to that myth?

Institutions of political persuasion and coercion dominate not only through physical but also through mental force, through psychological coercion or appeal to good will. So my inquiry's premise is not far to seek. I take as a given that a political myth animates the structure of a politics. But the authorship of the Mishnah, upon the politics of which we concentrate for the present analysis, has chosen other media for thought and expression than narrative and teleological ones. It is a philosophical, not a historical (fictive) account; it is conveyed through masses of detailed rules about small things. While the Mishnah through its cases amply informs us on the institutions of politics, the mythic framework within which persuasion and inner compliance are supposed to bring about submission to legitimate power scarcely emerges, remaining only implicit throughout.

But it is readily discerned when we ask the right questions. If we were to bring to the authorship of the Mishnah such questions as "who tells whom what to do?" (or "who can do what to whom, and for how long?") they would point to the politics' imaginary king and its equally fictive high priest, and its court comprised by sages, all with associated authorities and functionaries. Here, they would tell us, are the institutions of politics—represented in personal rather than abstract form, to be sure. But if we were to say to them, "And tell us the story (in our language: the myth) that explains on what basis you persuade people to conform," they would find considerable difficulty in bringing to the fore the explicit mythic statements made by their writing.

How then are we to identify, on the basis of what the Mishnah does tell us, the generative myths to which the system is supposed to appeal? A myth explains the exercise of legitimate power. Now, we know, power comes to brutal expression when the state kills or maims someone or deprives a person of property through the imposition of legal sanctions for crime or sin.[2] In the absence of a myth of power, we therefore begin with power itself. We shall work our way back from the facts of power to the intimations, within the record of legitimately violent sanctions, of the intellectual and even mythic sources of legitimation for the exercise and use of that legitimate violence. For it is at the point of imposing sanctions, of killing, injuring, denying property, excluding from society, that power operates in its naked form. Then how these legitimate exercises of violence are validated will set before us such concrete evidence of the myth. And, so far as there is such evidence, that will identify the political myth of the Dual Torah that commences with the Mishnah. The relevance to the centrality of intentionality in the theology of the Dual Torah will become transparent by the end, even though it is obscure at this point.

Since the analysis of sources will prove somewhat abstruse, let me signal in advance the main line of argument. Analyzing myth by explaining sanctions draws our attention to the modes of legitimate violence that the system identifies. There we find four types of sanctions, each deriving from a distinct institution of political power, each bearing its own mythic explanation.

---

[2] I do not distinguish crime from sin, since I do not think the system does. At the same time our own world does make such a distinction, and it would be confusing not to preserve it. That accounts for the usage throughout.)

6. ANALYSIS: Intentionality

[1] The first comprises what God and the Heavenly court can do to people.

[2] The second comprises what the earthly court can do to people. That type of sanction embodies the legitimate application of the worldly and physical kinds of violence of which political theory ordinarily speaks.

[3] The third comprises what the cult can do to the people. The cult through its requirements can deprive people of their property as legitimately as can a court.

[4] The fourth comprises conformity with consensus—self-imposed sanctions. Here the issue is, whose consensus, and defined by whom?

Across these four types of sanction, four types of coercion are in play. They depend on violence of various kinds—psychological and social as much as physical. Clearly, then, the sanctions that are exercised by other than judicial-political agencies prove violent and legitimately coercive, even though the violence and coercion are not the same as those carried out by courts.

On this basis we can differentiate among types of sanctions—and hence trace evidences of how the differentiation is explained. Since our data focus upon who does what to whom, the myth of politics must explain why various types of sanctions are put into effect by diverse political agencies or institutions. As we shall see, the exercise of power, invariably and undifferentiatedly in the name and by the authority of God in Heaven to be sure, is kept distinct. And the distinctions in this case signal important differences which, then, require explanation. Concrete application of legitimate violence by

[1] Heaven covers different matters from parts of the political and social world governed by the policy and coercion of

[2] the this-worldly political classes. And both sorts of violence have to be kept distinct from the sanction effected by

[3] the community through the weight of attitude and public opinion. Here, again, we find a distinct set of penalties applied to a particular range of actions.

When we have seen the several separate kinds of sanction and where they apply, we shall have a full account of the workings of politics as the application of power, and from that concrete picture we may, I think, identify the range of power and the mythic framework that has to have accommodated and legitimated diverse kinds of power.

Our task therefore is to figure out on the basis of sanctions' distinct realms, Heaven, earth, and the mediating range of the Temple and sacrifice, which party imposes sanctions for (in modern parlance) what crimes or sins. Where Heaven intervenes, do other authorities participate, and if so, what tells me which party takes charge and imposes its sanction? Is the system differentiated so that where earth is in charge, there is no pretense of appeal to Heaven? Or do we find cooperation in coextensive jurisdiction, such that one party penalizes an act under one circumstance, the other the same act under a different circumstance? A survey of the sanctions enables us to differentiate the components of the power-structure before us. So we wonder whether each of these three estates that enjoy power and inflict sanctions of one kind or another — Heaven, earth, Temple in-between — governs its own affairs, without the intervention of the others, or whether, working together, each takes charge in collaboration with the other, so that power is parceled out and institutions simultaneously differentiate themselves from one another and also intersect. The survey of sanctions will allow us to answer these questions and so identify the myth of politics and the exercise of power that the Halakhah promulgated through the institutional arrangements set forth by the law of the Mishnah.

Clearly, simply knowing that everything is in accord with the Written Torah and that God wants Israel to keep the laws of the Torah does not reveal the systemically active component of the political myth. On the one hand, the propositions are too general; on the other hand, they do not address the critical question. The sequence of self-evident premises that runs [1] God revealed the Torah, [2] the political institutions and rules carry out the Torah, and therefore [3] people should conform, hardly sustains a concrete theory of *just* where and how God's authority serves the systemic construction at hand. The appeal to Scripture, therefore, reveals no incisive information about the Halakhah's validating myth as set forth in the laws of the Mishnah.

III. THE MANIPULATION AND APPLICATION OF POWER

In the Halakhah the manipulation and application of power, allowing the impositions of drastic sanctions in support of the law for instance, invariably flow through institutions, on earth and in Heaven, of a quite concrete and material character. "The kingdom of Heaven" may be within, but violate the law deliberately and wantonly and God will kill you sooner than you should otherwise have had to die. And, as a matter of fact, the Mishnah's framers rarely appeal in the context of politics and the legitimate exercise of violence to "the kingdom of Heaven." When we considered the same

6. ANALYSIS: Intentionality

matter earlier, we noted that Israel's acceptance of the dominion of the kingdom of Heaven involved acts of worship and obedience, but at no point invoked coercion in a this-worldly framework.

Indeed, from the Pentateuchal writings, we can hardly construct the *particular* politics, including the mythic component thereof, that operates. First of all, the Written Torah does not prepare us to make sense of the institutions that the politics of the sages for its part designs — government by king and high priest, rather than, as in the Pentateuch, prophet. Second, and concomitantly, the Pentateuchal myth that legitimates coercion — rule by God's prophet, governance through explicitly revealed laws that God has dictated for the particular occasion! — plays no active and systemic role whatsoever in the formulation and presentation of the Mishnah's theological politics. Rather, of the types of political authority contained within the scriptural repertoire, the Mishnah's philosophers reject prophetic and charismatic authority and deem critical authority exercised by the sage's disciple who has been carefully nurtured in rules, not in gifts of the spirit. The authority of sages in their theological politics does not derive from charisma, (revelation by God to the sage who makes a ruling in a given case, or even from general access to God for the sage). The myth we shall presently explore in no way falls into the classification of a charismatic myth of politics.

The data to which we now turn will tell us who does what to whom and why, and, in the reason why, we shall uncover the political myth we seek. At the very heart of matters we shall uncover the determinative power of intentionality. But the process by which we reach that conclusion is what counts, since that requires us to sift the evidence meant by sages to dictate the very governance of holy Israel, the institutions, procedures, and sanctions of government on earth and in Heaven. And out of the result we shall see a clear, powerful, and normative statement of the meaning of intentionality, how man's and God's acts of will bear equal weight. Predictably, when we work our way through sanctions to recover the mythic premises thereof, we begin with God's place in the institutionalization and execution of legitimate violence. Of course, the repertoire of sanctions does encompass God's direct intervention, but that is hardly a preferred alternative or a common one. Still, God does commonly intervene when oaths are violated, for oaths are held to involve the person who invokes God's name and God. Further, whereas when faced with an insufficiency of valid evidence under strict rules of testimony, the earthly court cannot penalize serious crime, the Heavenly court can and does impose a penalty. Clearly, then, God serves to justify the politics and account for its origin. Although God is never asked to join in making specific decisions and effecting policy in the everyday politics of the state, deliberate violation of certain rules provokes God's or the Heavenly court's direct intervention. Thus obedience to the law clearly represents submission to God in Heaven. Further, forms of Heavenly coercion such as we shall presently survey suggest a complex mythic situation, with more subtle nuance than the claim that, overall, God rules, would indicate. A politics of rules and regulations cannot admit God's *ad hoc* participation, and this system did not do so. God joined in the system in a regular and routine way, and the rules took for granted God's part in the sages' theological politics.

Now come the data of real power, the sanctions. We may divide sanctions just as the authorship of the Mishnah did, by simply reviewing the range of penalties for law-infraction as they occur. These penalties, as we mentioned above, fall into four classifications:

[1] what Heaven does,
[2] what political institutions do,
[3] what religious institutions do, and
[4] what is left to the coercion of public opinion, that is, consensus, with special attention to the definition of that "public" that has effective opinion to begin with. The final realm of power, conferring or withholding approval, proves constricted and, in this context, not very consequential.

Let us begin with the familiar, with sanctions exercised by the earthly court as they are fully described in Mishnah-tractates Sanhedrin and Makkot. Here is covered the imposition of sanctions as it is represented by the earthly court, the Temple, the heavenly court, the sages. This review allows us to identify the actors in the system of politics—those with power to impose sanctions, and the sanctions they can inflict. Only from this perspective will the initial statement of the sages, the Mishnah, in its own odd idiom, be able to make its points in the way its authorship has chosen. When we take up the myth to which that statement implicitly appeals, we shall have a clear notion of the character of the evidence, in rich detail, on which our judgment of the mythic substrate of the system has been composed.

How to proceed? By close attention to the facts of power and by sorting out the implications of those facts. A protracted journey through details of the law of sanctions leads us to classify the sanctions and the sins or crimes to which they apply. What precisely do I think requires classification? Our project to see who does what to whom and, on the basis of the consequent perception, to propose an explanation for that composition. For from these sanctions of state, that is, the legitimate exercise of coercion, including violence, we may work our way back to the reasons adduced for the legitimacy of the exercise of coercion, which is to say, the political myth. The

6. ANALYSIS: Intentionality

reason is that such a classification will permit us to see how in detail the foci of power are supposed to intersect or to relate: autonomous powers, connected and related ones, or utterly continuous ones, joining Heaven to earth, for instance, in the person of this institutional representative or that one. What we shall see is a system that treats Heaven, earth, and the mediating institution, the Temple, as interrelated, thus, connected, but that insists, in vast detail, upon the distinct responsibilities and jurisdiction accorded to each. Once we have perceived that fundamental fact, we may compose for ourselves the myth, or, at least the point and propositions of the myth, that accounted for the political structures contemplated by the Halakhah and persuaded people to obey or conform even when there was no immediate threat of penalty.

A survey of [1] types of sanctions, [2] the classifications of crimes or sins to which they apply, and [3] who imposes them, now yields these results.

The operative distinction between inflicting a flogging and requiring a sacrifice (Temple sanctions against person or property), and the sanction of extirpation (Heavenly death-penalty), is made explicit as follows: "For those [transgressions] are people liable, for deliberately doing them, to the punishment of extirpation, and for accidentally doing them, to the bringing of a sin-offering, and for not being certain of whether or not one has done them, to a suspensive guilt-offering."

This summary yields a simple and clear fact, and on the basis of that simple fact we may now reconstruct the entire political myth of the Halakhah. This myth accounts for the differentiation among penalties and institutions that impose them, and from the facts we reach backward to the myth that explains them. The basis for all conclusions, let me emphasize, is this fact: *some of the same crimes or sins for which the Heavenly court imposes the penalty of extirpation are those that, under appropriate circumstances (e.g., sufficient evidence admissible in court) the earthly court imposes the death-penalty.*

That is, the Heavenly court and the earthly court impose precisely the same sanctions for the same crimes or sins. The earthly court therefore forms down here the exact replica and counterpart, within a single system of power, of the Heavenly court up there. This no longer looms as an empty generalization; it is a concrete and systemically active and indicative detail, and the system speaks through its details.

But this is not the entire story. There is a second fact, equally indicative for our recovery of the substrate of myth. We note that there are crimes for which the earthly court imposes penalties, but for which the Heavenly court does not, as well vice versa. The earthly and Heavenly courts share jurisdiction over sexual crimes and over what I classify as serious religious crimes against God. The Heavenly court penalizes with its form of the death-penalty religious sins against God, in which instances a person deliberately violates the taboos of sanctification.

And that fact calls our attention to a third partner in the distribution and application of power, the Temple with its system of sanctions that cover precisely the same acts subject to the jurisdiction of the Heavenly and earthly courts. The counterpart on earth is now not the earthly court but the Temple. This is the institution that, in theory, automatically receives the appropriate offering from the person who inadvertently violates these same taboos of sanctification. The juxtaposition involves courts and Temple, and the upshot is that both are equally matters of theory. In the theory at hand, then, the earthly court, for its part, penalizes social crimes against the community that the Heavenly court, on the one side, and the Temple rites, on the other, do not take into account at all. These are murder, apostasy, kidnapping, public defiance of the court, and false prophecy. The earthly court further imposes sanctions on matters of particular concern to the Heavenly court, with special reference to taboos of sanctification (e.g., negative commandments). These three institutions, therefore, exercise concrete and material power, utilizing legitimate violence to kill someone, exacting penalties against property, and inflicting pain. The sages' modes of power, by contrast, stand quite apart, apply mainly to their own circle, and work through the intangible though no less effective means of inflicting shame or paying honor.

The facts we have in hand draw us back to the analysis of our differentiation of applied and practical power. In the nature of the facts before us, that differentiation tells us precisely for what the systemic myth will have to give its account. Power flows through three distinct but intersecting dominions, each with its own concern, all sharing some interests in common.

[1] The Heavenly court attends to deliberate defiance of Heaven.

[2] The Temple pays attention to inadvertent defiance of Heaven.

[3] The earthly court attends to matters subject to its jurisdiction by reason of sufficient evidence, proper witnesses, and the like, and these same matters will come under Heavenly jurisdiction when the earthly court finds itself unable to act.

Accordingly, we have a tripartite system of sanctions—Heaven cooperating with the Temple in some matters, with the court in others, and, as noted, each bearing its own distinct media of enforcing the law as well. What then can we say concerning the systemic myth of politics? The forms of power and the modes of mediating legitimate violence draw our attention to a single political myth. The unity of that myth is underlined by the simple fact that the earthly court enters into the process right along side the Heavenly court and the Temple; as to blasphemy, idolatry, and magic, its jurisdiction prevails. So a single myth must serve all three correlated institutions. It is the myth of God's authority infusing the institutions of Heaven and earth alike, an authority diffused among three principle foci or circles of power, Heaven's court, the earthly court, and the Temple in-between.

Each focus of power has its own jurisdiction and responsibility, Heaven above, earth beneath, the Temple in the position of mediation—transmitting as it does from earth to Heaven the penalties handed over as required. And all media of power in the matter of sanctions intersect at some points as well: a tripartite politics, a single myth drawing each component into relationship with a single source and origin of power, God's law set forth in the Torah. But the myth has not performed its task until it answers not only the question of why, but also the question of how. Specifically, the details of myth must address questions of the details of power. Who then tells whom to do what? And how are the relationships of dominion and dominance to compliance and obedience made permanent through myth?

We did not require this sustained survey to ascertain that God through the Torah has set forth laws and concerns. Nor on the surface did this considerable exercise claim a place in any account of the role of intentionality in the cosmic order. So God's place in transactions of power requires explanation, and the primacy of intentionality has now to be set forth. Specifically, it is where power is differentiated and parceled out that we see the workings of the political myth, and there we should find the facts that we seek. So we ask, how do we know who tells whom to do, or suffer, what sanction or penalty? It is the power of myth to differentiate that defines the generative question. The key lies in the criterion by which each mode of power, earthly, mediating, and Heavenly, identifies the cases over which it exercises jurisdiction. The criterion lies in the attitude of the human being who has done what he or she should not: did he act deliberately or unintentionally?

IV. THE POINT OF DIFFERENTIATION WITHIN THE POLITICAL STRUCTURES, SUPERNATURAL AND NATURAL ALIKE, LIES IN THE ATTITUDE AND INTENTION OF A HUMAN BEING

I state the upshot with heavy emphasis, as we identify the point of relevance to our inquiry:

the point of differentiation within the political structures, supernatural and natural alike, lies in the attitude and intention of a human being.

We differentiate among the application of power by reference to the attitude of the person who comes into relationship with that power. A person who comes into conflict with the system, rejecting the authority claimed by the powers that be, does so deliberately or inadvertently. The myth accounts in the end for the following hierarchization of action and penalty, infraction and sanction:

[1] If the deed is deliberate, then one set of institutions exercises jurisdiction and utilizes supernatural power.

[2] If the deed is inadvertent, another institution exercises jurisdiction and utilizes the power made available by that same supernatural being.

A sinner or criminal who has deliberately violated the law has by his action challenged the world order of justice that God has wrought. Consequently, God or God's surrogate imposes sanctions—extirpation (by the court on high), or death or other appropriate penalty (by the court on earth). A sinner or criminal who has inadvertently violated the law is penalized by the imposition of Temple sanctions, losing valued goods. People obey because God wants them to and has told them what to do, and when they do not obey, a differentiated political structure appeals to that single hierarchizing myth. The components of the myth are two: first, God's will, expressed in the law of the Torah, second, the human being's will, carried out in obedience to the law of the Torah or in defiance of that law.

Since the political myth has to explain the differentiation of sins or crimes, with their associated penalties or punishments, and so sanctions of power, I have to find that story in the Torah that accomplishes that labor of differentiation. And given the foci and premises of the present study of the governing theology of the Halakhah, that story must pertain to the nature of things and concern beginnings. And in Scripture there is a very precise answer to the question of how to differentiate among sins or crimes and why to do so. Not only so, but, in the framework of the present chapter of that theology, the point of differentiation must rest with one's attitude or intentionality And, indeed, I do have two stories of how the power of God — the power to command — conflicts with the power of humanity — the power to obey or to rebel — in such wise as to invoke the penalties and sanctions in precisely the differentiated modes we have before us. Where do I find such stories of the conflict of wills, God's and humanity's, captured by the words, "will," or "intentionality"?

The first such story of power differentiated by the will of the human being in communion or conflict with the word of the commanding God comes to us from the Garden of Eden/ We cannot too often reread the following astonishing words:

6. ANALYSIS: Intentionality

> The Lord God took the man and placed him in the garden of Eden...and the Lord God commanded the man, saying, "Of every tree of the garden you are free to eat; but as for the tree of knowledge of good and bad, you must not eat of it; for as soon as you eat of it, you shall die."
> ...When the woman saw that the tree was good for eating and a delight to the eyes, and that the tree was desirable as a source of wisdom, she took of its fruit and ate; she also gave some to her husband, and he ate...
> The Lord God called out to the man and said to him, "Where are you?"
> He replied, "I heard the sound of You in the garden, and I was afraid, because I was naked, so I hid."
> Then He asked, "Who told you that you were naked? Did you eat of the tree from which I had forbidden you to eat?"
> ...And the Lord God said to the woman, "What is this you have done!"
> The woman replied, "The serpent deceived me, and I ate."
> Then the Lord said to the serpent, "Because you did this, more cursed shall you be than all cattle..."
> So the Lord God banished him from the garden of Eden...
> *Genesis 2:15ff.*

Now a reprise of the exchange between God, Adam, and Eve, tells us that at stake was responsibility: who has violated the law, but who bears responsibility for deliberately violating the law. Each blames the next, and God sorts things out, responding to each in accord with the facts of the case: whose intentionality matches the actual deed?

> "The woman You put at my side — she gave me of the tree, and I ate."
> "The serpent duped me, and I ate."
> Then the Lord God said to the serpent, *"because you did this..."*

The ultimate responsibility lies with the one who acted deliberately, not under constraint or on account of deception or misinformation, as did Adam because of Eve, and Eve because of the serpent

True enough, all are punished, the serpent, but also woman, "I will make most severe your pangs in childbearing," and Adam, "Because you did as your wife advised and ate of the tree about which I commanded you, 'you shall not eat of it,' cursed be the ground because of you." Thus all then are punished — but the punishment is differentiated. Those who were duped are distinguished from the one who acted wholly on his own, the serpent himself is cursed; the woman is subjected to pain in childbearing, which ought to have been pain-free; because of man, the earth is cursed — a diminishing scale of penalties, each in accord with the level of intentionality or free, uncoerced will, involved in the infraction. Then the sanction applies most severely to the one who by intention and an act of will has violated God's intention and will.

To establish what I conceive to be the generative myth, I turn to a second story of disobedience and its consequences, the tale of Moses's hitting the rock:

> The community was without water, and they joined against Moses and Aaron... Moses and Aaron came away from the congregation to the entrance of the Tent of Meeting and fell on their faces. The Presence of the Lord appeared to them, and the Lord spoke to Moses, saying, "You and your brother Aaron take the rod and assemble the community, and before their very eyes order the rock to yield its water. Thus you shall produce water for them from the rock and provide drink for the congregation and their beasts."
>
> Moses took the rod from before the Lord as He had commanded him. Moses and Aaron assembled the congregation in front of the rock; and he said to them, "Listen, you rebels, shall we get water for you out of this rock?" And Moses raised his hand and struck the rock twice with his rod. Out came copious water, and the community and their beasts drank.
>
> But the Lord said to Moses and Aaron, "Because you did not trust me enough to affirm My sanctity in the sight of the Israelite people, therefore you shall not lead this congregation into the land that I have given them."
>
> Those are the waters of Meribah, meaning that the Israelites quarreled with the Lord — through which He affirmed His sanctity.
>
> Numbers 20:1–13

Here we have not only intentional disobedience, but also the penalty of extirpation. Both this myth and the myth of the fall make the same point. They direct attention to the generative conception that at stake in power is the will of God over against the will of the human being, and in particular, the Israelite human being.

What we see is quite striking. The political myth of the Halakhah emerges in the Mishnah in all of its tedious detail as a reprise — in now-consequential and necessary detail — of the story of God's commandment, humanity's disobedience, God's sanction for the sin or crime, and humanity's atonement and reconciliation. The Mishnah omits all explicit reference to myths that explain power and sanctions, but invokes in its rich corpus of details the absolute given of the story of the distinction between what is deliberate and what is mitigated by an attitude that is not culpable, a distinction set forth in the tragedy of Adam and Eve, in the failure of Moses and Aaron, in the distinction between murder and manslaughter that the Written Torah works out, and in countless other passages in the Pentateuch, Prophetic Books, and Writings. Then the Mishnah's halakhah sets forth a politics of life after Eden and outside of Eden. The upshot of the matter is that the political myth of the Halakhah sets forth the constraints of freedom, the human will brought to full and unfettered expression, imposed by the constraints of revelation, God's will made known.

V. THE SOURCES OF POWER: THE WILL OF GOD AND THE WILL OF MAN

Since it is the freedom of humanity to make decisions and frame intentions that forms the point of differentiation among the political media of power, we are required, in my view, to return to the paradigmatic exercise of that same freedom, that is, to Eden, to the moment when Adam and Eve exercise their own will and defy God. Since the operative criterion in the differentiation of sanction — that is, the exercise of legitimate violence by Heaven or by earth or by the Temple — is the human attitude and intention in carrying out a culpable action, we must recognize the politics before us rehearses the myth of Adam and Eve in Eden—it finds its dynamic in the correspondence between God's will and humanity's freedom to act however it chooses, thus freely incurring the risk of penalty or sanction for the wrong exercise of freedom.

At stake is what Adam and Eve, Moses and Aaron, and numerous others intend, propose, and plan, for that is the point at which the politics intervenes, making its points of differentiation between and among its sanctions and the authorities that impose those penalties. For that power to explain difference, which is to say, the capacity to represent and account for hierarchy, we are required, in my opinion, to turn to the story of the fall of Adam and Eve from Eden and to counterpart stories. The reason is that the political myth derives from that same myth of origins its points of differentiation and explains by reference to the principal components of that myth — God's and humanity's will and power— the dynamics of the political system at hand. God commands, but humanity does what it then chooses, and in the interplay, each power in its own right, the sanctions and penalties of the system apply.

Power comes from two conflicting forces, the commanding will of God and the free will of the human being. Power expressed in immediate sanctions is also mediated through these same forces, Heaven above, human beings below, with the Temple mediating between the two. Power works its way in the interplay between what God has set forth in the law of the Torah and what human beings do, whether intentionally, whether inadvertently, whether obediently, whether defiantly. That is why the politics of the Halakhah is a politics of Eden.³ True we listen in vain in the creation-myth of Genesis for echoes resounding in the shape of the institutions such as those the theology of politics actually invents. But the points of differentiation of one political institution from another will serve constantly to remind us of what, in the end, serves to distinguish this from that, to set forth not a generalized claim that God rules through whoever is around with a sword (or the right, that is, Roman sponsorship). At every point we are therefore reminded of the most formidable source of power, short of God, in all. That always is the will of the human being. And that is why only man has the power to disrupt that world order so painstakingly created and maintained by God. Only man is sufficiently like God to possess the utterly free will to corrupt perfection.

The theology of Rabbinic Judaism, like its law, therefore identifies free will as the principal point of correspondence between God and man, the point at which God's image makes its deepest mark upon man's visage. Just as God freely chooses, so does man. In man God has made and therefore has met his match. Man has the power to violate the rules of order, the rationality of justice then dictates the result. When man rebels against God, rejecting God's dominion instead of loving God, that sin disrupts world order. Punishment "with the proper fruit of his deeds" follows. But man's free will in response may inaugurate the process by which world order is restored, creation renewed. And that process leads to the last things of all, eternal life embodied in the resurrection of the dead and the world to come. So the theology of Halakhah accounts for life, death, and life restored.

---

[3] Here we may claim that the Halakhah understands the Written Torah in its full implications even better than do those who set forth the Authorized History that is conveyed by the sequence from Genesis through Kings. For that Authorized History does not identify creation and the fall as the governing paradigm of Israel's life, but the sages do. The Authorized History looks backward from the destruction in 586 and forward to the restoration. Sages' Halakhah, by contrast, encompasses not only 586 but 70, not only a singular event but a series and therefore defines the paradigm that the series realizes. And therein lies all the difference. Reading forward from Scripture, sages followed what, in the nature of things, was simply a much longer narrative; but it was not one that they conceived either as linear or as cyclical. The one model lead nowhere, the other defied all rationality. That is the foundation for paradigmatic thinking on their part. That is the argument of *The Presence of the Past, the Pastness of the Present. History, Time, and Paradigm in Rabbinic Judaism.* Bethesda, 1996: CDL Press.

INTEGRAL JUDAISM

7.
Integrating the System

I. AT THE CENTER OF THE SYSTEM

How do the three theological principles outlined in Chapters One through Three and the three philosophical ones set forth in Chapters Four through Six coalesce into a single coherent Judaic system of the social order? If we ask, what has the theology that God hears all and remembers all to do with the philosophy of intentionality, the answer is obvious. Mixtures form a consideration important in the Halakhah of Hullin. But it is not the integration of components that portrays an integrated system but the cogency of the system viewed whole. That leads us to the question dealt with in this chapter and the next.

The answer is, the concept of Zekhut — defined in a moment — accomplished the integration of the theology and philosophy of Judaism into an encompassing system. That protean conception formed into a cogent political economy for the social order of Israel the economics and the politics that made powerlessness into power, disinheritance into wealth.[1] Intentionality figures too. Acts of will consisting of submission, on one's own, to the will of Heaven endowed Israel with a lien and entitlement upon Heaven. What we cannot by will impose, we can by will evoke. What we cannot accomplish through coercion, we can achieve through submission. God will do for us what we cannot do for ourselves, when we do for God what God cannot make us do. In a wholly concrete and tangible sense, love God with all the heart, the soul, the might, we have.

---

[1] In my *Judaism: The Evidence of the Mishnah*, pp. 230–286, I have asked and answered in terms of the power of intentionality as the medium of classification the question of what holds the system together, and in the counterpart study of the philosophical system of Judaism attested by the Mishnah, *Judaism as Philosophy. The Method and Message of the Mishnah*. Columbia, 1991: University of South Carolina Press, I have identified the integrating and generative problematic, that of hierarchical classification. These two answers seem to me cogent with one another, even though the one appeals to psychological, the other to philosophical considerations.

Zekhut stands for the empowerment of a supernatural character that derives from the virtue of one's ancestry or from one's own virtuous deeds of a very particular order. No single word in English bears the same meaning, nor can I identify a synonym for *zekhut* in the canonical writings in the original either. The difficulty of translating a word of systemic primacy with a single word in some other language (or in the language of the system's documents themselves) tells us we deal with what is unique to that system, beyond comparison and therefore contrast and comprehension. What is most particular to, distinctive of, the systemic structure and its functioning requires definition through circumlocution, such as I gave earlier: "the heritage of virtue and its consequent entitlements."[2] The word *zekhut* for the successor-system forms the systemic counterpart to the mythologoumenon of the resurrection of Jesus Christ, unique son of God, for important Christianities.

It must follow that *zekhut*, not Torah, in a single word defines the generative myth, the critical symbol of the Judaism in the documents of which that symbol figures. A single case amplifies the claim. Ordinary folk, not disciples of sages, have access to *zekhut* entirely outside of study of the Torah. In stories not told about rabbis, a single remarkable deed, exemplary for its deep humanity, sufficed to win for an ordinary person the *zekhut*—"the heritage of virtue and its consequent entitlements"—that elicits the same marks of supernatural favor enjoyed by some rabbis on account of their lifelong, perpetual Torah-study.

Accordingly, the systemic centrality of *zekhut* in the structure, the critical importance of the heritage of virtue together with its supernatural entitlements—these emerge in a striking claim. It is framed in extreme form—another mark of the unique place of *zekhut* within the system. Even though a man was degraded and existed at the margins of the community of Judaism, one single action sufficed to win for him that heavenly glory to which rabbis in lives of Torah-study aspired. The mark of the system's integration around *zekhut* lies in its insistence that all Israelites, not only

---

[2] The commonly-used single word, "merit," does not apply, but "merit" bears the sense of reward for carrying out an obligation, e.g., by doing such and such, he merited so and so. *Zekhut*, by contrast, commonly refers to acts of supererogatory free will, and therefore while such acts are meritorious in the sense of being virtuous (by definition), they are not acts that one owes but that one gives. And the rewards that accumulate in response to such actions are always miraculous or supernatural or signs of divine grace, e.g., an unusually long life, the power to prevent a delapidated building from collapsing. I return to this matter below, when I take up the amplification of the meaning of *zekhut* in response to concrete usages of the word in the earliest document in which it plays a significant role, tractate Abot and also appears in a context sufficiently broad to allow for philological exegesis to take place.

sages, could gain *zekhut* for themselves (and their descendants). That is what I meant when I said, a single remarkable deed, exemplary for its deep humanity, sufficed to win for an ordinary person the *zekhut* that elicits supernatural favor enjoyed by some rabbis on account of their Torah-study. The centrality of *zekhut* in the systemic structure, the critical importance of the heritage of virtue together with its supernatural entitlements therefore emerge in a striking claim. Even though a man was degraded, one action sufficed to win for him that heavenly glory to which rabbis in general aspired. The rabbinical storyteller whose writing we shall consider assuredly identifies with this lesson, since it is the point of his story and its climax.

In all three instances that follow, defining what the individual must do to gain *zekhut,* the point is that the deeds of the heroes of the story make them worthy of having their prayers answered, which is a mark of the working of *zekhut*. It is deeds beyond the strict requirements of the Torah, and even the limits of the law altogether, that transform the hero into a holy man, whose holiness served just like that of a sage marked as such by knowledge of the Torah The following stories should not be understood as expressions of the mere sentimentality of the clerks concerning the lower orders, for they deny in favor of a single action of surpassing power sages' lifelong devotion to what the sages held to be the highest value, knowledge of the Torah:

Yerushalmi Taanit 1:4.I

F. A certain man came before one of the relatives of R. Yannai. He said to him, "Rabbi, attain *zekhut* through me [by giving me charity]."
G. He said to him, "And didn't your father leave you money?"
H. He said to him, "No."
I. He said to him, "Go and collect what your father left in deposit with others."
J. He said to him, "I have heard concerning property my father deposited with others that it was gained by violence [so I don't want it]."
K. He said to him, "You are worthy of praying and having your prayers answered."

The point of K, of course, is self-evidently a reference to the possession of entitlement to supernatural favor, and it is gained, we see, through deeds that the law of the Torah cannot require but must favor: what one does on one's own volition, beyond the measure of the law. Here I see the opposite of sin. A sin is what one has done by one's own volition beyond all limits of the law. So an act that generates *zekhut* for the individual is the counterpart and opposite: what one does by one's own volition that also is beyond all requirements of the law.

INTEGRAL JUDAISM

Yerushalmi Taanit 1:4.I

L. A certain ass driver appeared before the rabbis [the context requires: in a dream] and prayed, and rain came. The rabbis sent and brought him and said to him, "What is your trade?"

M. He said to them, "I am an ass driver."

N. They said to him, "And how do you conduct your business?"

O. He said to them, "One time I rented my ass to a certain woman, and she was weeping on the way, and I said to her, 'What's with you?' and she said to me, 'The husband of that woman [me] is in prison [for debt], and I wanted to see what I can do to free him.' So I sold my ass and I gave her the proceeds, and I said to her, 'Here is your money, free your husband, but do not sin [by becoming a prostitute to raise the necessary funds].'"

P. They said to him, "You are worthy of praying and having your prayers answered."

The ass-driver clearly has a powerful lien on Heaven, so that his prayers are answered, even while those of others are not. What he did to get that entitlement? He did what no law could demand: impoverished himself to save the woman from a "fate worse than death."

Yerushalmi Taanit 1:4.I

Q. In a dream of R. Abbahu, Mr. Pentakaka ["Five sins"] appeared, who prayed that rain would come, and it rained. R. Abbahu sent and summoned him. He said to him, "What is your trade?"

R. He said to him, "Five sins does that man [I] do every day, [for I am a pimp:] hiring whores, cleaning up the theater, bringing home their garments for washing, dancing, and performing before them."

S. He said to him, "And what sort of decent thing have you ever done?"

T. He said to him, "One day that man [I] was cleaning the theater, and a woman came and stood behind a pillar and cried. I said to her, 'What's with you?' And she said to me, 'That woman's [my] husband is in prison, and I wanted to see what I can do to free him,' so I sold my bed and cover, and I gave the proceeds to her. I said to her, 'Here is your money, free your husband, but do not sin.'"

U. He said to him, "You are worthy of praying and having your prayers answered."

Q moves us still further, since the named man has done everything sinful that one can do, and, more to the point, he does it every day. So the singularity of the act of *zekhut*, which suffices if done only one time, encompasses its power to outweigh a life of sin — again, an act of *zekhut* as the mirror-image and opposite of sin. Here again, the single act of saving a woman from a "fate worse than death" has sufficed.

7. Integrating the System

Yerushalmi Taanit 1:4.I

V. A pious man from Kefar Imi appeared [in a dream] to the rabbis. He prayed for rain and it rained. The rabbis went up to him. His householders told them that he was sitting on a hill. They went out to him, saying to him, "Greetings," but he did not answer them.

W. He was sitting and eating, and he did not say to them, "You break bread too."

X. When he went back home, he made a bundle of faggots and put his cloak on top of the bundle [instead of on his shoulder].

Y. When he came home, he said to his household [wife], "These rabbis are here [because] they want me to pray for rain. If I pray and it rains, it is a disgrace for them, and if not, it is a profanation of the Name of Heaven. But come, you and I will go up [to the roof] and pray. If it rains, we shall tell them, 'We are not worthy to pray and have our prayers answered.'"

Z. They went up and prayed and it rained.

AA. They came down to them [and asked], "Why have the rabbis troubled themselves to come here today?"

BB. They said to him, "We wanted you to pray so that it would rain."

CC. He said to them, "Now do you really need my prayers? Heaven already has done its miracle."

DD. They said to him, "Why, when you were on the hill, did we say hello to you, and you did not reply?"

EE. He said to them, "I was then doing my job. Should I then interrupt my concentration [on my work]?"

FF. They said to him, "And why, when you sat down to eat, did you not say to us 'You break bread too'?"

GG. He said to them, "Because I had only my small ration of bread. Why would I have invited you to eat by way of mere flattery [when I knew I could not give you anything at all]?"

HH. They said to him, "And why when you came to go down, did you put your cloak on top of the bundle?"

II. He said to them, "Because the cloak was not mine. It was borrowed for use at prayer. I did not want to tear it."

JJ. They said to him, "And why, when you were on the hill, did your wife wear dirty clothes, but when you came down from the mountain, did she put on clean clothes?"

KK. He said to them, "When I was on the hill, she put on dirty clothes, so that no one would gaze at her. But when I came home from the hill, she put on clean clothes, so that I would not gaze on any other woman."

LL. They said to him, "It is well that you pray and have your prayers answered."

The pious man of V, finally, enjoys the recognition of the sages by reason of his lien upon Heaven, able as he is to pray and bring rain. What has so endowed him with *zekhut*? Acts of punctiliousness of a moral order: concentrating on his work, avoiding an act of dissimulation, integrity in the disposition of a borrowed object, his wife's concern not to attract other men and her equal concern to make herself attractive to her husband. None of these stories refers explicitly to *zekhut*; all of them tell us about what it means to enjoy not an entitlement by inheritance but a lien accomplished by one's own supererogatory acts of restraint.

Zekhut integrates what has been differentiated. It holds together learning, virtue, and supernatural standing, by explaining how Torah-study transforms the learning man. Hierarchical classification, with its demonstration of the upward-reaching unity of all being, gives way to a different, and more compelling proposition: the unity of all being within the heritage of *zekhut*, to be attained equally and without differentiation in all the principal parts of the social order. The definition of *zekhut* therefore carries us to the heart of the integrating and integrated religious system of Judaism.

II. DEFINING ZEKHUT

The word *zekhut* bears a variety of meanings, as Jastrow summarizes the data,[3] and the pertinence of each possible meaning is to be determined in context: [1] acquittal, plea in favor of the defendant; [2] doing good, blessing; [3] protecting influence of good conduct, merit; [4] advantage, privilege, benefit. The first meaning pertains solely in juridical (or metaphorically-juridical) contexts; the second represents a very general and imprecise use of the word, since a variety of other words bear the same meaning. Only the third and the fourth meanings pertain, since they are particular to this word, on the one side, and also religious, on the other. That is to say, only through using the word *zekhut* do authors of compositions and authorships of composites express the sense given at No. 3. Moreover, it will rapidly become clear, in context that No. 4 is not to be distinguished from No. 3, since "protecting influence of good conduct" when the word *zekhut* appears always yields "advantage, privilege, benefit." It follows that, for the purposes of systemic analysis, passages in which the word *zekhut* bears the sense, in Jastrow's words, of "the protecting influence of good conduct" that yields "advantage, privilege, or benefit" will tell us how the word *zekhut* functions.

My simple definition emphasizes "heritage," because the advantages or privileges conferred by *zekhut* may be inherited and also passed on; it stresses "entitlements" because advantages or privileges always,

---

[3] Marcus Jastrow, *A Dictionary of the Targumim, The Talmud Babli and Yerushalmi, and the Midrashic Literature* (repr. N. Y., 1950: Pardes Publishing House, Inc.), p. 398.

7. Integrating the System

invariably result from receiving *zekhut* from ancestors or acquiring it on one's own; and I use the word "virtue" to refer to those supererogatory acts that demand a reward because they form matters of choice, the gift of the individual and his or her act of free will, an act that is at the same time [1] uncompelled, e.g., by the obligations imposed by the Torah, but [2] also valued by the Torah. The systemic importance of the conception of *zekhut*, we shall see in Chapter Nine, derives from its capacity to unite the generations in a heritage of entitlements; *zekhut* is fundamentally a historical category and concept, in that, like all historical systems of thought, it explains the present in terms of the past, and the future in terms of the present.[4]

Because *zekhut* is something one may receive as an inheritance, out of the distant past, *zekhut* imposes upon the definition of the social entity, "Israel," a genealogical meaning. It furthermore imparts a distinctive character to the definitions of way of life. So the task of the political component of a theory of the social order, which is to define the social entity by appeal to empowerment, and of the economic component, which is to identify scarce resources by specification of the rationality of right management, is accomplished in a single word, which stands for a conception, a symbol, and a myth. All three components of this religious theory of the social order turn out to present specific applications, in context, for the general conception of *zekhut*. For the first source of *zekhut* derives from the definition of Israel as family; the entitlements of supernatural power deriving from virtue then care inherited from Abraham, Isaac, and Jacob. The second source is personal: the power one can gain for one's own heirs, moreover, by virtuous deeds. *Zekhut* deriving from either source is to be defined in context: what can you do if you have *zekhut.*, that you cannot do if you do not have *zekhut.* and to whom can you do it. The answer to that question tells you the empowerment of *zekhut.*

Now in the nature of things, a theory of power or violence that is legitimately exercised falls into the category of a politics, and a conception of the scarce resource, defined as supernatural power that is to be rationally managed, falls into the category of an economics. That is why in the concept of *zekhut*, we find the union of economics and politics into a political economy: a theory of the whole society in its material and social relationships as expressed in institutions that permanently are given

---

[4] That of course is not the whole story, and one of the subtleties of zekhut emerges when we realize that it is a basically anti-historical reading of history, the point at which zekhut integrates theology into its larger system.

the right to impose order through real or threatened violence and in the assignment of goods and benefits, as systemically defined to be sure, through a shared rationality.

III. SPECIFIC MEANINGS OF ZEKHUT IN PARTICULAR CONTEXTS

Since I have identified as systemically active not the conception but the word and its usages, we shall focus not upon general situations, e.g., in which one receives some sort of benefit by reason of in inheritance from some other person, but upon specific usages of the word at hand. That focus is required not only by the logic of this study, but also by the difficulty of knowing what belongs and what does not belong when *zekhut* bears the confusing translation of "merit," and when "merit" promiscuously refers to pretty much anything that one gets *not* by one's own merit or just desserts at all, but despite what one has done. Scripture for example knows that God loves Israel because he loved the patriarchs (Dt. 4:37); the memory or deeds of the righteous patriarchs and matriarchs appear in a broad range of contexts, e.g., "Remember your servants, Abraham, Isaac, and Jacob" (Ex. 32:13), for Moses, and "Remember the good deeds of David, your servant" (II Chr. 6:42), for David. At stake throughout is giving people what they do not merit, to be sure. But in these contexts, "remembering" what X did as an argument in behalf of favor for Y does not invoke the word *zekhut*, and the context does not require use of that word either.[5] Accordingly, our problem of definition requires limitation to precise usages of a given word. Were we to propose to work our way back from situations that seem to exhibit conceptual affinities to the concept represented by the word under consideration, cases, for instance, in which someone appeals to what is owing the fathers in behalf of the children, we shall not accomplish the goal at hand, which is one of definition of a word that in this system, meaning, in these documents in particular, bears a very particular meaning, and, more to the point, carries out a highly critical role.

At M. San. 4:1, 5:4, 5:5, and 6:1 we find *zekhut* in the sense of "acquittal," as against conviction; at M Ket 13:6 the sense is, "right," as in "right of ownership;" at M Git 8:8 the sense is not "right of ownership"

---

[5] In line with Chapter One, God's "remembering" is the principal point in the scriptural situations adduced as evidence for the ancient origins of the concept of *zekhut*. Then the other part of the same concept, that there are deeds I may do that gain *zekhut* for myself, is excluded, and hence *zekhut* as it is revealed in the systemic sources is not represented in the scriptural ones.

in a narrow sense, but "advantage," in a broader one of prerogative: "It is not within the power of the first husband to render void the right of the second." These usages of course bear no point in common with the sense of the word later on. But the evidence of the Mishnah seems to me to demonstrate that the sense of *zekhut* paramount in the successor-documents is not original to them. The following usage at M. Qid. 4:14 seems to me to invite something very like the sense that I have proposed here. So states M. Qid. 4:14E–I:

> R. Meir says, "A man should always teach his son a clean and easy trade. And let him pray to him to whom belong riches and possessions. For there is no trade which does not involve poverty or wealth. For poverty does not come from one's trade, nor does wealth come from one's trade. But all is in accord with a man's *zekhut*."
>
> *M. Qiddushin 4:14E–I*

Quite how to translate our key-word in this passage is not self-evident. The context permits a variety of possibilities. The same usage seems to me to be located at M. Sot. 3:4, 3:5, and here there is clear indication of the presence of a conception of an entitlement deriving from some source other than one's own deed of the moment:

> 3:4. E. There is the possibility that *zekhut* suspends the curse for one year, and there is the possibility that *zekhut* suspends the curse for two years, and there is the possibility that *zekhut* suspends the curse for three years.
> F. On this basis Ben Azzai says, "A man is required to teach Torah to his daughter.
> G. "For if she should drink the water, she should know that [if nothing happens to her], *zekhut* is what suspends [the curse from taking effect]."
> 3:5 A. R. Simeon says, "*Zekhut* does not suspend the effects of the bitter water.
> B. "And if you say, '*Zekhut* does suspend the effects of the bitter water,' you will weaken the effect of the water for all the women who have to drink it.
> C. "And you give a bad name to all the women who drink it who turned out to be pure.
> D. "For people will say, 'They are unclean, but *zekhut* suspended the effects of the water for them."
> E. Rabbi says, "*Zekhut* does suspend the effects of the bitter water. But she will not bear children or continue to be pretty. And she will waste away, and in the end she will have the same [unpleasant] death."
>
> *Mishnah-tractate Sotah 3:4–5*

Now if we insert for *zekhut* at each point, "the heritage of virtue and its consequent entitlements," (thus: "For people will say, 'They are unclean, but *zekhut* suspended the effects of the water for them, then, "For people will say, 'They are unclean, but the heritage of virtue and its consequent entitlements suspended the effects of the water for them).'" We have good sense. That is to say, the woman may not suffer the penalty to which she is presumably condemnable, not because her act or condition (e.g., her innocence) has secured her acquittal or nullified the effects of the ordeal, but because she enjoys some advantage extrinsic to her own act or condition. She may be guilty, but she may also possess a benefice deriving by inheritance, hence, heritage of virtue, and so be entitled to a protection not because of her own, but because of someone else's action or condition.

That meaning may be sustained by the passage at hand, even though it is not required by it; still, it seems to me plausible that the word *zekhut* in the Mishnah bears not only a juridical but a religious sense. But, if, as I think, it does, that usage is not systemically critical, or even very important. If we search the pages of the Mishnah for places in which, absent the word *zekhut*, the conception in hand is present, we find none — not one. For example, there simply is no reference to gaining *zekhut* through doing one's duty, e.g., in reciting the *Shema* or studying the Torah, and references to studying the Torah, e.g., at M. Peah 1:1, do not encompass the conception that, in doing so, one gains an advantage or entitlement for either one's own descendants or for all Israel. On that basis we are on firm ground in holding the twin-positions [1] that the word bore, among its meanings, the one important later on, and also [2] that the word played no systemic role, in the philosophical system adumbrated by the Mishnah, commensurate with the importance accorded to the word and its sense in the religious system that took shape and came to expression in the successor-writings.[6]

The evidence of tractate Abot is consistent with that of the Mishnah. The juridical sense of *zekhut* occurs at 1:6, "Judge everybody as though

---

[6] A rapid review of the Tosefta's usages of the word *zekhut* suffices, since there are no surprises. Juridical usages are at these passages: T. Git. 1:5 (*zekhut* in the sense of an advantage or a benefit); Sanhedrin 1:8, 3:3, 9:1, 2, 3, 4, 10:11; T. Qid. 1:13. An indeterminate sense of *zekhut* in the sense of "advantage" or "entitlement," without a clear definition of what one must do or why one gains a benefit therefrom, is at T. Pe. 1:2, T. Yoma 5:12 = T. Ta. 4:9 (*zekhut* in contrast to disadvantage or liability, conceivably a juridical usage). The sense, "by reason of the claim..." or "the entitlement of..." seems to me justified in context at T. M. S. 5:27, 29, T. Sot. 11:10, and T. B. B. 7:9. Overall, I do not find here anything as decisive as what we see in tractate-Abot, though the case may be made that some of the Tosefta's passages use the word in the same sense as is revealed in that tractate. In the balance, nonetheless, I judge that a full-scale review of Tosefta's usages would not greatly change the results just now given for the Mishnah.

7. Integrating the System

to be acquitted," more comprehensibly translated, "And give everybody the benefit of the doubt," forming a reasonably coherent with the usages important in Mishnah-tractate Sanhedrin. In Abot, however, we have clear evidence for the sense of the word that seems to me demanded later on. At M. Abot 2:2 we find the following:

- C. "And all who work with the community—let them work with them for the sake of Heaven.
- D. "For the [1] *zekhut* of their fathers strengthens them, and their [fathers'] [2] righteousness stands forever.
- E. "And as for you, I credit you with a great reward, as if you had done [all of the work required by the community on your own merit alone]."

Tractate Abot 2:2

Here there is no meaning possible other than that I have given above: "the heritage of virtue and its consequent entitlements." The reference to an advantage that one gains by reason of inheritance out of one's fathers' righteousness is demanded by the parallel between *zekhut* of clause [1] and *righteousness* of clause [2]. Whatever the conceivable ambiguity of the Mishnah, none is sustained by the context at hand, which is explicit in language and pellucid in message. That the sense is exactly the same as the one I have proposed is shown at the following passages, which seem to me to exhibit none of the possible ambiguity that characterized the usage of *zekhut* in the Mishnah:

- A. He who causes *zekhut* to the community never causes sin.
- B. And he who causes the community to sin—they never give him a sufficient chance to attain penitence.

Here the contrast is between causing *zekhut* and causing sin, so *zekhut* is the opposite of sin. The continuation is equally clear that a person attained *zekhut* and endowed the community with *zekhut*, or sinned and made the community sin:

- C. Moses attained *zekhut* and bestowed *zekhut* on the community.
- D. So the *zekhut* of the community is assigned to his [credit],
- E. as it is said, "He executed the justice of the Lord and his judgments with Israel" (Dt. 33:21).
- F. Jeroboam sinned and caused the community to sin.
- G. So the sin of the community is assigned to his [debit],
- H. as it is said, "For the sins of Jeroboam which he committed and wherewith he made Israel to sin" (I Kings 15:30).

Tractate Abot 5:18

The appropriateness of interpreting the passage in the way I have proposed will now be shown to be self-evident. All that is required is to substitute for *zekhut* the proposed translation:

- C. Moses attained the heritage of virtue and bestowed its consequent entitlements on the community.
- D. So the heritage of virtue end its entitlements enjoyed by the community are assigned to his [credit].

The sense then is simple. Moses through actions of his own (of an unspecified sort) acquired *zekhut,* which is the credit for such actions that accrued to him and bestowed upon him certain supernatural entitlements; and he for his part passed on as an inheritance that credit, a lien on Heaven for the performance of these same supernatural entitlements: *zekhut,* pure and simple.

If we may now define *zekhut* as the initial system explicated in tractate Abot has used the word, we must pay close attention to the antonymic structure before us. The juridical opposites are guilty as against innocent, the religious ones, as we have now seen, sin as against the opposite of sin. That seems to me to require our interpreting *zekhut* as [1] an action, as distinct from a (mere) attitude; that [2] is precisely the opposite of a sinful one; it is, moreover, an action that [3] may be done by an individual or by the community at large, and one that [4] a leader may provoke the community to do (or not do). The contrast of sin to *zekhut* requires further attention. Since, in general, two classes that are compared to begin with, if different, must constitute opposites, the ultimate definition of *zekhut* requires us to ask how *zekhut* is precisely the opposite of sin. For one thing, as we recall, Scripture is explicit that the burden of sins cannot be passively inherited, willy-nilly, but, to form a heritage of guilt, must be actively accepted and renewed; the children cannot be made to suffer for the sins of the parents, unless they repeat them. Then *zekhut,* being a mirror-image, can be passively inherited, not by one's own merit[7] but

---

[7] Indeed, the conception of merit is so alien to the concept of *zekhut,* which one enjoys whether or not one personally has done something to merit it, that I am puzzled on how "merit" ever seemed to anyone to serve as a translation of the word *zekhut.* If I can inherit the entitlements accrued by my ancestors, then these entitlements not only cannot be classed as merit(ed by me), they must be classed as a heritage bestowed by others and not merited by me at all. And, along these same lines, the *zekhut* that I gain for myself may entitle me to certain benefits, but it may also accrue to the advantage of the community in which I live (as is made explicit by Abot for Moses' *zekhut*) and also of my descendants. The transitive character of zekhut, the power we have of receiving it from others and handing it

7. Integrating the System

by one's good fortune alone. But what constitute these *actions* that form mirror-images of sins? Answers to that critical question must emerge from the systemic documents before us, since they do not occur in those of the initial system.

That simple fact, too, attests to the systemic centrality of *zekhut*: it defines a principal point of exegesis.[8] For the question left open by the Mishnah's merely episodic, and somewhat opaque, reference to the matter and the incomplete evidence provided by its principal apologetic's representation as well, alas, is the critical issue. Precisely what actions generate *zekhut*, and which ones do not? To find answers to those questions, we have to turn to the successor-documents, since not a single passage in the Mishnah or in tractate-Abot provides me with information on the matter of what I must do to secure for myself or my descendents a lien upon Heaven, that is, an entitlement to supernatural favor and even action of a miraculous order.

We turn first to the conception of the *zekhut* that has been accumulated by the patriarchs and been passed on to Israel, their children. The reason is that the single distinctive trait of *zekhut*, as we have seen it to this point, is its transitive quality: one need not earn or merit the supernatural power and resource represented by the things you can do if you have *zekhut* but cannot do if you do not have it. One can inherit that entitlement from others, dead or living. Moses not only attains *zekhut* but he also imparts *zekhut* to the community of which he is leader, and the same is so for any Israelite. That conception is broadened in the successor-documents into the deeply historical notion of *zekhut abot*, empowerment of a supernatural character to which Israel is entitled by reason of what the patriarchs and matriarchs in particular did long ago. That conception forms the foundation for the paramount sense of *zekhut* in the successor-system: the Israelite possesses a lien upon Heaven by reason of God's love for the patriarchs and matriarchs, his appreciation for certain things they did, and his response to those actions not only in favoring them but also in entitling their descendants to do or benefit from otherwise unattainable miracles. *Zekhut*, as we noted earlier, explains the present — particularly what is odd and unpredictable in the presence — by appeal to the past, hence forms a distinctively historical conception.

---

on to others, serves as the distinctive trait of this particular entitlement, and, it must follow from that definitive characteristic, zekhut is the opposite of merit, as I said, and its character is obscured by the confusion created through that long-standing and conventional, but wrong translation of the word.

[8] Here again, the exegesis of exegesis defines the history of religion.

Within the historically-grounded metaphor of Israel as a family expressed by the conception of *zekhut abot,* Israel was a family, the children of Abraham, Isaac, and Jacob, or children of Israel, in as concrete and genealogical sense. Israel hence fell into the genus, family, as the particular species of family generated by Abraham and Sarah. The distinguishing trait of that species was that it possessed the inheritance, or heritage, of the patriarchs and matriarchs, and that inheritance, consisting of *zekhut,* served the descendants and heirs as protection and support. It follows that the systemic position of the conception of *zekhut* to begin with lies in its power to define the social entity, and hence, *zekhut* (in the terms of the initial category-formation, the philosophical one) forms a fundamentally political conception[9] and only secondarily an economic and philosophical one.

But *zekhut* serves, in particular, that counterpart category that speaks of not legitimate but illegitimate violence, not power but weakness. In context, time and again, we observe that *zekhut* is the power of the weak. People who through their own merit and capacity can accomplish nothing, can accomplish miracles through what others do for them in leaving a heritage of *zekhut.* And, not to miss the stunning message of the triplet of stories cited above, *zekhut* also is what the weak and excluded and despised can do that outweighs in power what the great masters of the Torah have accomplished. In the context of a system that represents Torah as supernatural, that claim of priority for *zekhut* represents a considerable transvaluation of power, as much as of value. And, by the way, *zekhut* also forms the inheritance of the disinherited: what you receive as a heritage when you have nothing in the present and have gotten nothing in the past, that scarce resource that is free and unearned but much valued. So let us dwell upon the definitive character of the transferability of *zekhut* in its formulation, *zekhut* abot, the *zekhut* handed on by the ancestors, the transitive character of the concept and its standing as a heritage of entitlements.

---

[9] And that political definition of the systemic role and function of *zekhut* is strengthened by the polemical power of the concept vis à vis the Christian critique of Israel after the flesh. The doctrine of the *zekhut* of the ancestors served as a component of the powerful polemic concerning Israel. Specifically, that concrete, historical Israel, meaning for Christian theologians "Israel after the flesh," in the literature before us manifestly and explicitly claimed fleshly origin in Abraham and Sarah. The extended family indeed constituted precisely what the Christian theologians said: an Israel after the flesh, a family linked by genealogy. The heritage then became an inheritance, and what was inherited from the ancestors was a heavenly store, a treasure of *zekhut,* which protected the descendants when their own *zekhut* proved insufficient. The conflict is a political one, involving the legitimacy of the power of the now-Christian empire, denied by this "Israel," affirmed by the other one.

7. Integrating the System

It is in the successor-documents such as Genesis Rabbah that the concept of *zekhut* is joined with *abot*, that is, the *zekhut* that has been left as Israel's family inheritance by the patriarchs or ancestors, yielding the very specific notion, defining the systemic politics, its theory of the social entity, of Israel not as a (mere) community (e.g., as in tractate Abot's reference to Moses' bestowing *zekhut* upon the community) but as a family, with a history that takes the form of a genealogy, precisely as Genesis has represented that history.[10] Now *zekhut* was joined to the metaphor of the genealogy of patriarchs and matriarchs and served to form the missing link, explaining how the inheritance and heritage were transmitted from them to their heirs. Consequently, the family, called "Israel," could draw upon the family estate, consisting of the inherited *zekhut* of matriarchs and patriarchs in such a way as to benefit today from the heritage of yesterday. This notion involved very concrete problems. If "Israel, the family" sinned, it could call upon the "*zekhut*" accumulated by Abraham and Isaac at the binding of Isaac (Genesis 22) to win forgiveness for that sin. True, "fathers will not die on account of the sin of the sons," but the children may benefit from the *zekhut* of the forebears. That concrete expression of the larger metaphor imparted to the metaphor a practical consequence, moral and theological, that was not at all neglected.

IV. ZEKHUT IN GENESIS RABBAH

A survey of Genesis Rabbah proves indicative of the character and use of the doctrine of *zekhut*, because that systematic reading of the book of Genesis dealt with the founders of the family and made explicit the definition of Israel as family. What we shall see is that *zekhut* draws in its wake the notion of the inheritance of an on-going (historical) family, that of Abraham and Sarah, and *zekhut* worked itself out in the moments of crisis of that family in its larger affairs. So the Israelites later on enjoy enormous *zekhut* through the deeds of the patriarchs and matriarchs. That conception comes to expression in what follows:

---

[10] And it is by no means an accident, therefore, that Genesis was one of the two pentateuchal books selected by the system-builders for their Midrash-exegesis. The systemic centrality of *zekhut* accounts for their selection. In my *Judaism and Scripture*, pp. 94–125, I have accounted for the selection of the book of Leviticus, an explanation that accords in a striking way with the one pertaining to Genesis. That means that any system-analysis must explain why one scriptural book, and not some other, has been chosen for the Midrash-compilation(s) that that system sets forth alongside its Mishnah-amplification.

2. A. "...for with only my staff I crossed this Jordan, and now I have become two companies:"
   B. R. Judah bar Simon in the name of R. Yohanan: "In the Torah, in the Prophets, and in the Writings we find proof that the Israelites were able to cross the Jordan only on account of the *zekhut* achieved by Jacob:
   C. "In the Torah: '...for with only my staff I crossed this Jordan, and now I have become two companies.'
   D. "In the prophets: 'Then you shall let your children know, saying, "Israel came over this Jordan on dry land"' (Josh. 4:22), meaning our father, Israel.
   E. "In the Writings: 'What ails you, O you sea, that you flee? You Jordan, that you burn backward? At the presence of the God of Jacob' (Ps. 114:5ff.)."

   Genesis Rabbah LXXVI:V

Here is a perfect illustration of my definition of *zekhut* as an entitlement I enjoy by reason of what someone else — an ancestor — has done; and that entitlement involves supernatural power. Jacob did not only leave *zekhut* as an estate to his heirs. The process is reciprocal and on-going. *Zekhut* deriving from the ancestors had helped Jacob himself:

   A. "When the man saw that he did not prevail against Jacob, [he touched the hollow of his thigh, and Jacob's thigh was put out of joint as he wrestled with him]" (Gen. 32:25):
   B. Said R. Hinena bar Isaac, "[God said to the angel,] 'He is coming against you with five "amulets" hung on his neck, that is, his own *zekhut*, the *zekhut* of his father and of his mother and of his grandfather and of his grandmother.
   C. "'Check yourself out, can you stand up against even his own *zekhut* [let alone the *zekhut* of his parents and grandparents].'
   D. "The matter may be compared to a king who had a savage dog and a tame lion. The king would take his son and sick him against the lion, and if the dog came to have a fight with the son, he would say to the dog, 'The lion cannot have a fight with him, are you going to make out in a fight with him?'
   E. "So if the nations come to have a fight with Israel, the Holy One, blessed be he, says to them, 'Your angelic prince could not stand up to Israel, and as to you, how much the more so!'"

   Genesis Rabbah LXXVII:III.3

The collectivity of *zekhut*, not only its transferability, is illustrated here as well: what an individual does confers *zekhut* on the social entity. It is, moreover, a matter of the legitimate exercise of supernatural power. And the reciprocity of the process extended in all directions. Accordingly, what we have in hand is first and foremost a matter of the exercise of legitimate violence, hence a political power. *Zekhut* might project not only backward, deriving from an ancestor and serving a descendant, but forward as well.

7. Integrating the System

Thus Joseph accrued so much *zekhut* that the generations that came before him were credited with his *zekhut*:

A. "These are the generations of the family of Jacob. Joseph [being seventeen years old, was shepherding the flock with his brothers]" (Gen. 37:2):
B. These generations came along only on account of the *zekhut* of Joseph.
C. Did Jacob go to Laban for any reason other than for Rachel?
D. These generations thus waited until Joseph was born, in line with this verse: "And when Rachel had borne Joseph, Jacob said to Laban, 'Send me away'" (Gen. 30:215).
E. Who brought them down to Egypt? It was Joseph.
F. Who supported them in Egypt? It was Joseph.
G. The sea split open only on account of the *zekhut* of Joseph: "The waters saw you, O God" (Ps. 77:17). "You have with your arm redeemed your people, the sons of Jacob and Joseph" (Ps. 77:16).
H. R. Yudan said, "Also the Jordan was divided only on account of the *zekhut* of Joseph."

Genesis Rabbah LXXXIV:V.2

The passage at hand asks why only Joseph is mentioned as the family of Jacob. The inner polemic is that the *zekhut* of Jacob and Joseph would more than suffice to overcome Esau. Not only so, but Joseph survived because of the *zekhut* of his ancestors:

A. "She caught him by his garment... but he left his garment in her hand and fled and got out of the house. [And when she saw that he had left his garment in her hand and had fled out of the house, she called to the men of her household and said to them, 'See he has brought among us a Hebrew to insult us; he came in to me to lie with me, and I cried out with a loud voice, and when he heard that I lifted up my voice and cried, he left his garment with me and fled and got out of the house']" (Gen. 39:13–15):
B. He escaped through the *zekhut* of the fathers, in line with this verse: "And he brought him forth outside" (Gen. 15:5).
C. Simeon of Qitron said, "It was on account of bringing up the bones of Joseph that the sea was split: 'The sea saw it and fled' (Ps. 114:3), on the *zekhut* of this: '...and fled and got out.'"

Genesis Rabbah LXXXVII:VIII.1

Zekhut, we see, is both personal and national. B refers to Joseph's enjoying the *zekhut* he had inherited, C referring to Israel's enjoying the zekhut that they gained through their supererogatory loyalty to that same *zekhut*-rich personality. How do we know that the *zekhut* left as a heritage by ancestors is in play? Here is an explicit answer:

A. "If the God of my father, the God of Abraham and the Fear of Isaac, had not been on my side, surely now you would have sent me away empty-handed. God saw my affliction and the labor of my hand and rebuked you last night" (Gen. 31:41–42):
B. Zebedee b. Levi and R. Joshua b. Levi:
C. Zebedee said, "Every passage in which reference is made to 'if' tells of an appeal to the *zekhut* accrued by the patriarchs."[11]
D. Said to him R. Joshua, "But it is written, 'Except we had lingered' (Gen. 43:10) [a passage not related to the *zekhut* of the patriarchs]."
E. He said to him, "They themselves would not have come up except for the *zekhut* of the patriarchs, for it if it were not for the *zekhut* of the patriarchs, they never would have been able to go up from there in peace."

Genesis Rabbah LXXIV:XII.1

The issue of the *zekhut* of the patriarchs comes up in the reference to the God of the fathers. The conception of the *zekhut* of the patriarchs is explicit, not general. It specifies what later benefit to the heir, Israel the family, derived from which particular action of a patriarch or matriarch.

A. "And Abram gave him a tenth of everything" (Gen. 14:20):
B. R. Judah in the name of R. Nehorai: "On the strength of that blessing the three great pegs on which the world depends, Abraham, Isaac, and Jacob, derived sustenance.
C. "Abraham: 'And the Lord blessed Abraham in *all* things' (Gen. 24:1) on account of the *zekhut* that 'he gave him a tenth of *all* things' (Gen. 14:20).
D. "Isaac: 'And I have eaten of *all*' (Gen. 27:33), on account of the *zekhut* that 'he gave him a tenth of *all* things' (Gen. 14:20).
E. "Jacob: 'Because God has dealt graciously with me and because I have all' (Gen. 33:11) on account of the *zekhut* that 'he gave him a tenth of *all* things' (Gen. 14:20).

Genesis Rabbah XLIII:VIII.2

A. Whence did Israel gain the *zekhut* of receiving the blessing of the priests?
B. R. Judah said, "It was from Abraham: 'So shall your seed be' (Gen. 15:5), while it is written in connection with the priestly blessing: 'So shall you bless the children of Israel' (Num. 6:23)."
C. R. Nehemiah said, "It was from Isaac: 'And I and the lad will go so far' (Gen. 22:5), therefore said the Holy One, blessed be he, 'So shall you bless the children of Israel' (Num. 6:23)."
D. And rabbis say, "It was from Jacob: 'So shall you say to the house of Jacob' (Ex. 19:3) (in line with the statement, 'So shall you bless the children of Israel' (Num. 6:23)."

Genesis Rabbah XLIII:VIII.3

---

[11] Freedman, *Genesis Rabbah* (London, 1948), p. 684, n. 2: It introduces a plea for or affirmation of protection received for the sake of the patriarchs.

No. 2 links the blessing at hand with the history of Israel. Now the reference is to the word "all," which joins the tithe of Abram to the blessing of his descendants. Since the blessing of the priest is at hand, No. 3 treats the origins of the blessing. The picture is clear. "Israel" constitutes a family as a genealogical and juridical fact. It inherits the estate of the ancestors. It hands on that estate. It lives by the example of the matriarchs and patriarchs, and its history exemplifies events in their lives. And *zekhut* forms that entitlement that one generation may transmit to the next, in a way in which the heritage of sin is not to be transmitted except by reason of the deeds of the successor-generation. The good that one does lives onward, the evil is interred with the bones.

To conclude this brief survey of *zekhut* as the medium of historical existence, that is, the *zekhut* deriving from the patriarchs or *zekhut abot*, let me present a statement of the legitimate power — sufficient to achieve salvation, which, in this context, always bears a political dimension — imparted by the *zekhut* of the ancestors. That *zekhut* will enable them to accomplish the political goals of Israel: its attaining self-rule and avoiding government by gentiles. This statement appeals to the binding of Isaac as the source of the *zekhut*, deriving from the patriarchs and matriarchs, which will in the end lead to the salvation of Israel. What is important here is that the *zekhut* that is inherited joins together with the *zekhut* of one's own deeds; one inherits the *zekhut* of the past, and, moreover, if one does what the progenitors did, one not only receives an entitlement out of the past, one secures an entitlement on one's own account. So the difference between *zekhut* and sin lies in the sole issue of transmissibility:

A. Said R. Isaac, "And all was on account of the *zekhut* attained by the act of prostration.
B. "Abraham returned in peace from Mount Moriah only on account of the *zekhut* owing to the act of prostration: '…and we will worship [through an act of prostration] and come [then, on that account] again to you' (Gen. 22:5).
C. "The Israelites were redeemed only on account of the *zekhut* owing to the act of prostration: And the people believed…then they bowed their heads and prostrated themselves' (Ex. 4:31).
D. "The Torah was given only on account of the *zekhut* owing to the act of prostration: 'And worship [prostrate themselves] you afar off' (Ex. 24:1).
E. "Hannah was remembered only on account of the *zekhut* owing to the act of prostration: 'And they worshipped before the Lord' (1 Sam. 1:19).
F. "The exiles will be brought back only on account of the *zekhut* owing to the act of prostration: 'And it shall come to pass in that day that a great horn shall be blown and they shall come that were lost…and that were dispersed…and they shall worship the Lord in the holy mountain at Jerusalem' (Is. 27:13).

G. "The Temple was built only on account of the *zekhut* owing to the act of prostration: 'Exalt you the Lord our God and worship at his holy hill' (Ps. 99:9).

H. "The dead will live only on account of the *zekhut* owing to the act of prostration: 'Come let us worship and bend the knee, let us kneel before the Lord our maker' (Ps. 95:6)."

Genesis Rabbah LVI:II.5

The entire history of Israel flows from its acts of worship ("prostration") beginning with that performed by Abraham at the binding of Isaac. Every sort of advantage Israel has ever gained came about through that act of worship done by Abraham and imitated thereafter. Israel constitutes a family and inherits the *zekhut* laid up as a treasure for the descendants by the ancestors. It draws upon that *zekhut* but, by doing the deeds they did, it also enhances its heritage of *zekhut* and leaves to the descendants greater entitlement than they would enjoy by reason of their own actions. But their own actions — here, prostration in worship — generate *zekhut* as well.

Accordingly, as I claimed at the outset, *zekhut* may be personal or inherited. The *zekhut* deriving from the prior generations is collective and affects all Israel. But one's own deeds can generate *zekhut* for oneself, with the simple result that *zekhut* is as much personal as it is collective. Specifically, Jacob reflects on the power that Esau's own *zekhut* had gained for Esau. He had gained that *zekhut* by living in the land of Israel and also by paying honor and respect to Isaac. Jacob then feared that, because of the *zekhut* gained by Esau, he, Jacob, would not be able to overcome him. So *zekhut* worked on its own; it was a credit gained by proper action, which went to the credit of the person who had done that action. What made the action worthy of evoking Heaven's response with an act of supernatural favor is that it was an action not to be required but if done to be rewarded, an act of will that cannot be coerced but must be honored. In Esau's case, it was the simple fact that he had remained in the holy land:

2. A. "Then Jacob was greatly afraid and distressed" (Gen. 32:7): [This is Jacob's soliloquy:] "Because of all those years that Esau was living in the Land of Israel, perhaps he may come against me with the power of the *zekhut* he has now attained by dwelling in the Land of Israel.

B. "Because of all those years of paying honor to his father, perhaps he may come against me with the power of the *zekhut* he attained by honoring his father.

C. "So he said: 'Let the days of mourning for my father be at hand, then I will slay my brother Jacob' (Gen. 27:41).

D. "Now the old man is dead."

Genesis Rabbah LXXVI:II

The important point, then, is that *zekhut* is not only inherited as part of a collective estate left by the patriarchs. It is also accomplished by an individual in his or her own behalf. By extension, we recognize, the successor-system opens a place for recognition of the individual, both man and woman as a matter of fact, within the system of *zekhut*. As we shall now see, what a man or a woman does may win for that person an entitlement upon Heaven for supernatural favor of some sort. So there is space, in the system, for a private person, and the individual is linked to the social order through the shared possibilities of generating or inheriting an entitlement upon Heaven.[12]

V. DEEDS THAT GENERATE ZEKHUT

For if we now ask, what are the sorts of deeds that generate *zekhut*, we realize that those deeds produce a common result of gaining for their doer, as much as for the heirs of the actor, an entitlement for Heavenly favor and support when needed. And that fact concerning gaining and benefiting from *zekhut* brings us to the systemic message to the living generation, its account of what now is to be done. And that message proves acutely contemporary, for its stress is on the power of a single action to create sufficient *zekhut* to outweigh a life of sin. Then the contrast between sin and *zekhut* gains greater depth still. One sin of sufficient weight condemns, one act of *zekhut* of sufficient weight saves; the entire issue of entitlements out of the past gives way, then, when we realize what is actually at stake.

We recall that Torah-study is one — but only one — means for an individual to gain access to that heritage, to get *zekhut*. There are other equally suitable means, and, not only so, but the merit gained by Torah-study is no different from the merit gained by acts of a supererogatory character. If one gets *zekhut* for studying the Torah, then we must suppose there is no holy deed that does not generate its share of *zekhut*. But when it comes to specifying the things one does to get *zekhut*, the documents before us speak of what the Torah does not require but does recommend: not what we are commanded to do in detail, but what the right attitude, formed within the Torah, leads us to do on our own volition:

---

[12] The philosophical system, by contrast, had regarded as important principally the issue of classifying persons, e.g., by castes or by other indicators; the Mishnah's paramount system of hierarchical classification had treated the individual in the way it treated all other matters, and so, we now see, does the system of *zekhut*: now to be broadened into the definition, accomplishing a lien upon Heaven.

C. There was a house that was about to collapse over there [in Babylonia], and Rab set one of his disciples in the house, until they had cleared out everything from the house. When the disciple left the house, the house collapsed.
D. And there are those who say that it was R. Adda bar Ahwah.
E. Sages sent and said to him, "What sort of good deeds are to your credit [that you have that much merit]?"
F. He said to them, "In my whole life no man ever got to the synagogue in the morning before I did. I never left anybody there when I went out. I never walked four cubits without speaking words of Torah. Nor did I ever mention teachings of Torah in an inappropriate setting. I never laid out a bed and slept for a regular period of time. I never took great strides among the associates. I never called my fellow by a nickname. I never rejoiced in the embarrassment of my fellow. I never cursed my fellow when I was lying by myself in bed. In the marketplace I never walked over to someone who owed me money.
G. "In my entire life I never lost my temper in my household."
H. This was meant to carry out that which is stated as follows: "I will give heed to the way that is blameless. Oh when wilt thou come to me? I will walk with integrity of heart within my house" (Ps. 101:2).

Y. Taanit 3:11.IV

What I find striking in this story is that mastery of the Torah is only one means of attaining the merit that enabled the sage to keep the house from collapsing. For what the sage did to gain such remarkable merit is not to master such-and-so many tractates of the Mishnah. Nor does the storyteller refer to carrying out the commandments of the Torah as specified. It was rather acts that expressed courtesy, consideration, restraint. These acts, which no specification can encompass in detail, produced the right attitude, one of gentility, that led to gaining merit. Acts rewarded with an entitlement to supernatural power are those self-abnegation or the avoidance of power over others — not taking great strides among the associates, not using a nickname, not rejoicing in the embarrassment of one's fellow, not singling out one's debtor — and the submission to the will and the requirement of self-esteem of others.

Here, in a moral setting, we find the politics replicated: the form of power that the system promises derives from the rejection of power that the world recognizes — legitimate violence replaced by legitimation of the absence of the power to commit violence or of the failure to commit violence. Not exercising power over others, that is, the counterpart politics, moreover, produced that scarcest of all resources, supernatural favor, by which the holy man could hold up a tottering building. Here then we find politics and economics united in the counterpart-category formed of *zekhut*: the absence of power yielding supernatural power, the valuation of the intangible, Torah, yielding supernatural power. It was, then, that entitlement to supernatural favor that formed the systemic center.

What about what we have to do to secure an inheritance of *zekhut* for our heirs? Here is a concrete example of how acts of worth or *zekhut* accrue to the benefit of the heirs of those that do them. What makes it especially indicative is that here gentiles have the power to acquire zekhut for their descendants, which is coherent with the system's larger interest in not only Israel (as against the faceless, undifferentiated outsider) but the gentiles as well. Here we see that the successor-system may hold within the orbit of its generative conception even the history of the gentiles:

A. "When they came to the threshing floor of Atad, which is beyond the Jordan, they lamented there with a very great and sorrowful lamentation, and he made a mourning for his father seven days" (Gen. 50:10):

B. Said R. Samuel bar Nahman, "We have reviewed the entire Scripture and found no other place called Atad. And can there be a threshing floor for thorns [the Hebrew word for thorn being *atad*]?

C. "But this refers to the Canaanites. It teaches that they were worthy of being threshed like thorns. And on account of what *zekhut* were they saved? It was on account of the acts of kindness that they performed for our father, Jacob [on the occasion of the mourning for his death]."

D. And what were the acts of kindness that they performed for our father, Jacob?

E. R. Eleazar said, "[When the bier was brought up there,] they unloosened the girdle of their loins."

F. R. Simeon b. Laqish said, "They untied the shoulder-knots."

G. R. Judah b. R. Shalom said, "They pointed with their fingers and said, 'This is a grievous mourning to the Egyptians' (Gen. 50:11).

H. Rabbis said, "They stood upright."

I. Now is it not an argument *a fortiori*: now if these, who did not do a thing with their hands or feet, but only because they pointed their fingers, were saved from punishment, Israel, which performs an act of kindness [for the dead] whether they are adults or children, whether with their hands or with their feet, how much the more so [will they enjoy the *zekhut* of being saved from punishment]!

J. Said R. Abbahu, "Those seventy days that lapsed between the first letter and the second match the seventy days that the Egyptians paid respect to Jacob. [Seventy days elapsed from Haman's letter of destruction until Mordecai's letter announcing the repeal of the decree (cf. Est. 3:12, 8:9). The latter letter, which permitted the Jews to take vengeance on their would-be destroyers, should have come earlier, but it was delayed seventy days as a reward for the honor shown by the Egyptians to Jacob."[13]

Genesis Rabbah C:VI.1

---

[13] Freedman, *Genesis Rabbah* (London, 1948: Soncino), p. 992, n. 6.

The Egyptians gained *zekhut* by honoring Jacob in his death, so Abbahu. This same point then registers for the Canaanites. The connection is somewhat farfetched, that is, through the reference to the threshing floor, but the point is a strong one. And the explanation of history extends not only to Israel's, but also the Canaanites', history.

If the Egyptians and the Canaanites, how much the more so Israelites! What is it that Israelites as a nation do to gain a lien upon Heaven for themselves or entitlements of supernatural favor for their descendants? Here is one representative answer to that question:

A. "If the God of my father, the God of Abraham and the Fear of Isaac, had not been on my side, surely now you would have sent me away empty-handed. God saw my affliction and the labor of my hand and rebuked you last night" (Gen. 31:41–42):
B. Zebedee b. Levi and R. Joshua b. Levi:
C. Zebedee said, "Every passage in which reference is made to 'if' tells of an appeal to the *zekhut* accrued by the patriarchs."[14]
D. Said to him R. Joshua, "But it is written, 'Except we had lingered' (Gen. 43:10) [a passage not related to the *zekhut* of the patriarchs]."
E. He said to him, "They themselves would not have come up except for the *zekhut* of the patriarchs, for it if it were not for the *zekhut* of the patriarchs, they never would have been able to go up from there in peace."
F. Said R. Tanhuma, "There are those who produce the matter in a different version." [It is given as follows:]
G. R. Joshua and Zebedee b. Levi:
H. R. Joshua said, "Every passage in which reference is made to 'if' tells of an appeal to the *zekhut* accrued by the patriarchs except for the present case."
I. He said to him, "This case too falls under the category of an appeal to the *zekhut* of the patriarchs."

So much for *zekhut* that is inherited from the patriarchs, a now familiar notion. But what about the deeds of Israel in the here and now?

J. R. Yohanan said, "It was on account of the *zekhut* achieved through sanctification of the divine name."
K. R. Levi said, "It was on account of the *zekhut* achieved through faith and the *zekhut* achieved through Torah.

Faith despite the here and now, study of the Torah—these are what Israel does in the here and now with the result that they gain an entitlement for themselves or their heirs.

---

[14] Freedman, *Genesis Rabbah*, p. 684, n. 2: It introduces a plea for or affirmation of protection received for the sake of the patriarchs.

L. "The *zekhut* achieved through faith: 'If I had not believed...' (Ps. 27:13).
M. "The *zekhut* achieved through Torah: 'Unless your Torah had been my delight' (Ps. 119:92)."
2. A. "God saw my affliction and the labor of my hand and rebuked you last night" (Gen. 31:41–42):
B. Said R. Jeremiah b. Eleazar, "More beloved is hard labor than the *zekhut* achieved by the patriarchs, for the *zekhut* achieved by the patriarchs served to afford protection for property only, while the *zekhut* achieved by hard labor served to afford protection for lives.
C. "The *zekhut* achieved by the patriarchs served to afford protection for property only: 'If the God of my father, the God of Abraham and the Fear of Isaac, had not been on my side, surely now you would have sent me away empty-handed.'
D. "The *zekhut* achieved by hard labor served to afford protection for lives: 'God saw my affliction and the labor of my hand and rebuked you last night.'"

Genesis Rabbah LXXIV:XII.1

Here is as good an account as any of the theology of *zekhut*. The issue of the *zekhut* of the patriarchs comes up in the reference to the God of the fathers. The conception of the *zekhut* of the patriarchs is explicit, not general. It specifies what later benefit to the heir, Israel the family, derived from which particular action of a patriarch or matriarch. But acts of faith and Torah-study form only one medium; hard labor, that is, devotion to one's calling, defines that source of *zekhut* that is going to be accessible to those many Israelites unlikely to distinguish themselves either by Torah-study and acts of faith, encompassing the sanctification of God's name, or by acts of amazing gentility and restraint.

VI. RELATIONSHIPS

The system here speaks to everybody, Jew and gentile. It posits that eternity in time that we encountered in Chapter Two, for it speaks of the unity of past and present and future. So too *zekhut* therefore defines the structure of the cosmic social order and explains how it is supposed to function. It is the encompassing quality of *zekhut*, its pertinence to past and future, high and low, rich and poor, gifted and ordinary, that marks as the systemic statement the message of *zekhut*, now fully revealed as the conception of reciprocal response between Heaven and Israel on earth, to acts of devotion beyond the requirements of the Torah but defined all the same by the Torah. As Scripture had said, God responds to the faith of the ancient generations by supernatural acts to which, on their own account, the moderns are not entitled, hence a heritage of entitlement.

But those acts, now fully defined for us, can and ought to be done, also, by the living generation. And, as a matter of fact, no one today, meaning, at the time of the system-builders, is exempt from the systemic message and its demands: even steadfastness in accomplishing the humble work of the everyday and the here and now.

The systemic statement made by the usages of *zekhut* speaks of relationship, function, the interplay of humanity and God. One's store of *zekhut* derives from a relationship, that is, from one's forebears. That is one dimension of the relationships in which one stands. *Zekhut* also forms a measure of one's own relationship with Heaven, as the power of one person, but not another, to pray and so bring rain attests. What sort of relationship does *zekhut*, as the opposite of sin, then posit? It is not one of coercion, for Heaven cannot force us to do those types of deeds that yield *zekhut*, and that, story after story suggests, is the definition of a deed that generates *zekhut:* doing what we ought to do but do not have to do. But then, we cannot coerce Heaven to do what we want done either, for example, by carrying out the commandments. These are obligatory, but do not obligate Heaven.

Whence then the Israelite's lien on Heaven? It is through deeds of a supererogatory character—to which Heaven responds by deeds of a supererogatory character: supernatural favor to this one, who through deeds of ingratiation of the other or self-abnegation or restraint exhibits the attitude that in Heaven precipitates a counterpart attitude, hence generating *zekhut*, rather than to that one, who does not. The simple fact that rabbis cannot pray and bring rain, but a simple ass-driver can, tells the whole story. The relationship measured by *zekhut*—Heaven's response by an act of uncoerced favor to a person's uncoerced gift, e.g., act of gentility, restraint, or self-abnegation—contains an element of unpredictability for which appeal to the *zekhut* inherited from ancestors accounts. So while I cannot coerce heaven, I can through *zekhut* gain acts of favor from Heaven, and that is by doing what Heaven cannot require of me. Heaven then responds to my attitude in carrying out my duties—and more than my duties. That act of pure disinterest—giving the woman my means of livelihood—is the one that gains for me Heaven's deepest interest.

So *zekhut* forms the political economy of the religious system of the social order put forward by the Talmud of the Land of Israel, Genesis Rabbah, Leviticus Rabbah, and related writings. Here we find the power that brought about the transvaluation of value, the reversal of the meaning of power and its legitimacy. *Zekhut* expresses and accounts for the economic valuation of the scarce resource of what we should call moral authority. *Zekhut* stands for the political valorization of weakness, that which endows the weak with a power that is not only their own but their ancestors'. It enables the weak to accomplish goals through not their own power, but their very incapacity to accomplish acts of violence — a transvaluation as radical as that effected in economics. And *zekhut* holds together both the economics and the politics of this Judaism: it makes the same statement twice.

Zekhut as the power of the powerless, the riches of the disinherited, the valuation and valorization of the will of those who have no right to will. In the context of Christian Palestine, Jews found themselves on the defensive. Their ancestry called into question, their supernatural standing thrown into doubt, their future denied, they called themselves "Israel," and the land, "the Land of Israel." But what power did they possess, legitimately, if need be through violence, to assert their claim to form "Israel"? And, with the holy land passing into the hands of others, what scarce resource did they own and manage to take the place of that measure of value that now no longer was subjected to their rationality? Asserting a politics in which all violence was illegitimate, an economics in which nothing tangible, even real property in the Holy Land, had value, the system through its counterpart-categories made a single, simple, and sufficient statement. But those whom Judaism knows as "our sages of blessed memory" were not the only system-builders, and theirs was not the only question about the social order framed in historical and theological, rather than analytical and philosophical terms. Their contemporary, the Bishop of Hippo whom Christianity knows as Saint Augustine, set forth an account of the social order framed in the same terms and addressed to the same urgent and critical question. It is in the context of comparison that, in the end, we interpret the system that has now been described and analyzed: the Judaism transformed from a philosophy to a religion and defined by the theological and philosophical principles outlined in chapters one through six.

8.
Living in the kingdom of God

I. THE RATIONALITY OF THE ISRAELITE SOCIAL ORDER

"Make his wishes yours, so that he will make your wishes his...Anyone from whom people take pleasure, God takes pleasure" (Abot 2:4). These two statements hold together the two principal elements of the conception of the relationship to God that in a single word *zekhut* conveys. Give up, please others, do not impose your will but give way to the will of the other, and Heaven will respond by giving a lien that likewise is not coerced but evoked. By the rationality of interior discipline we have the power to form rational relationships beyond ourselves, with Heaven; and that is how the system expands the boundaries of the social order to encompass not only the natural but also the supernatural world.[1]

For it is the rationality of that relationship to God that governs the social order, defining the three components thereof: ethics, ethnos, ethos. For within that relationship we discern the model of not merely ethics but economics, not merely private morality in society but the public policy, the politics that delineates the limns of the ethnic community, and not alone the right attitude of the virtuous individual but the social philosophy of an entire nation — so the system proposes. And that is the this-worldly social order that joins with Heaven, the society that is a unique and holy family, so transformed by *zekhut*-inherited and *zekhut*-accomplished as to transcend the world-order. That ordering of humanity in society, empowered and enriched in an enchanted political economy, links private person to the public polity through the union of a common attitude: the one of renunciation that tells me how to behave at home and in the streets, and that instructs Israel how to conduct its affairs among the nations and throughout history.

---

[1] I use the word "rationality" in the sense in which it is used in the thought of Max Weber: the systemic sense of what is appropriate and proper. The comparison of the rationalities of the initial and the successor systems is undertaken in the closing paragraphs of this chapter. This is not, of course, an account of the concept of rationality in the thought of Weber. I believe my characterization, for the limited purpose of these remarks, is entirely accurate.

8. Living in the kingdom of God

Treating every deed, every gesture as capable of bringing about enchantment, the later documents of the Rabbinic canon — the two Talmuds and the Midrash-compilations of the fifth and sixth centuries — imparted to the givens of everyday life remarkable power. The conviction that, by dint of special effort, I the Israelite may so conduct myself as to acquire an entitlement of supernatural power turns my commonplace circumstance into an arena encompassing Heaven and earth. God responds to my — and holy Israel's — virtue, filling the gap that we leave when we forebear, withdraw, and give up what is ours: our space. When I do, then God responds; my sacrifice — my surrender of my claim — evokes memories of Abraham's readiness to sacrifice Isaac.[2] My devotion to the other calls up from Heaven what by demanding I cannot coerce. That accounts for the definition of legitimate power in politics as only weakness, economics as the rational increase of resources that are, but need not be, scarce, valued things that are capable of infinite increase.

The Mishnah's God can scarcely compete with the God of the Yerushalmi and the Midrash-compilations.[3] For the God of the philosophers, the apex of the hierarchy of all being as the framers of the Mishnah have positioned God, has made the rules and is shown by them to form the foundation of world order. All things reach up to one thing, one thing contains within itself many things: these twin-propositions of monotheism, which the philosophical system demonstrates in theory and proposes to realize in the facts of the social order, define a God who in an orderly way governs all the palpable relationships of nature as of supernature — but who finds a place, who comes to puissant expression, in not a single one of them. The God of the philosophers assures, sustains, supports, nourishes, guarantees, governs. But the way that God responds to what we do is all according to the rule. That is, after all, what natural philosophy proposes to uncover and discern, and what more elevated task can God perform than the nomothetic one accomplished in the daily creation of the world.

---

[2] Note the fine perception of S. Levy, *Original Virtue and Other Studies*, pp. 2–3: "Some act of obedience, constituting the Ascent of man, is the origin of virtue and the cause of reward for virtue... What is the conspicuous act of obedience which, in Judaism, forms the striking contrast to Adam's act of disobedience, in Christianity? The submission of Isaac in being bound on the altar... is regarded in Jewish theology as the historic cause of the imputation of virtue to his descendants." It is not an accident, then, as we shall see, that Augustine selected as his paradigmatic historical exemplum the conflict of Cain and Abel, the city of God being inhabited by Abel and his descendants; he required a virtue pertinent to all of humanity, not to Israel alone, for his argument, so it seems to me as an outsider to the subject.

[3] My initial comments on that matter are in *The Incarnation of God: The Character of Divinity in Formative Judaism* (Philadelphia, 1988: Fortress Press).

But God in the later documents of the Rabbinic canon gains what the philosophical God lacks, which is personality, active presence, pathos and empathy. The God of the religious system breaks the rules, accords an entitlement to this one, who has done some one remarkable deed, but not to that one, who has done nothing wrong and everything right. So a life in accord with the rules — even a life spent in the study of the Torah — in Heaven's view is outweighed by a single moment, a gesture that violates the norm, extending the outer limits of the rule, for instance, of virtue. And who but a God who, like us, feels, not only thinks, responds to impulse and sentiment, not only judges and declares truth, can be portrayed in such a way as this?

> So I sold my ass and I gave her the proceeds, and I said to her, 'Here is your money, free your husband, but do not sin [by becoming a prostitute to raise the necessary funds].'"
> They said to him, "You are worthy of praying and having your prayers answered."

No rule exhaustively describes a world such as this. If the God of the philosophers' Judaism portrayed in Chapters Four through Six makes the rules, the God of the theological Judaism of Chapters One through Three breaks them. The systemic difference, of course, is readily extended outward from the personality of God: the philosophers' God thinks, the God of the theologians responds, and we are in God's image, after God's likeness, not only because we through right thinking penetrate the principles of creation, but through right attitude replicate the heart of the Creator. Humanity on earth incarnates God on high, the Israelite family in particular, and, in consequence, earth and Heaven join — within.

Perhaps the philosophers' system contained within itself — as I shall argue in a moment — the flaw that, like a grain of sand in an oyster, so irritated the innards as to form a pearl. And perhaps even the philosophers, with their exquisitely ordered and balanced social world, can have made a place for God to act; but, knowing how they thought, we must imagine that like philosophers later on, they will have insisted that miracles too follow rules and demonstrate the presence of rules. But now, in the theological Judaism, the world now is no longer what it seems. At stake in what is remarkable is what falls beyond all power of rules either to describe or to prescribe.

What is asked of Israel and of the Israelite individual now is Godly restraint, supernatural generosity of soul that is "in our image, after our likeness:" that is what sets aside all rules. And, since as a matter of simple fact, that appeal to transcend the norm defined not personal virtue but the sainthood of all Israel, living all together in the here and in the now, we must conclude that, within Israel's society, within what the Greco-Roman world will have called its *polis*, its political and social order, the bounds of earth have now extended to Heaven. In terms of another great system composed in the same time and in response to a world-historical catastrophe of the same sort, Israel on earth dwells in the city of God. And, it must follow, God dwells with Israel, in Israel: "today, if you will it."

That insistence upon the systemic centrality of the conception of *zekhut*, with all its promise for the reshaping of value, draws our attention once more to the power of a single, essentially-theological, conception to impart shape and structure to the social order. The Judaism set forth in the successor-documents portrayed a social order in which, while taking full account of circumstance and historical context, individuals and nation alike controlled their own destiny. The circumstance of genealogy dictated whether or not the moral entity, whether the individual or the nation, would enjoy access to entitlements of supernatural favor without regard to the merit of either one. But, whether favored by a rich heritage of supernatural empowerment as was the nation, or deprived, by reason of one's immediate ancestors, of any lien upon Heaven, in the end both the nation and the individual had in hand the power to shape the future. How was this to be done? It was not alone by keeping the Torah, studying the Torah, dressing, eating, making a living, marrying, procreating, raising a family, burying and being buried, all in accord with those rules.

That life in conformity with the rule, obligatory but merely conventional, did not evoke the special interest of Heaven. Why should it? The rules describe the ordinary. But (in language used only in a later document) "God wants the heart," and that is not an ordinary thing. Nor was the power to bring rain or hold up a tottering house gained through a life of merely ordinary sanctity. Special favor responded to extraordinary actions, in the analogy of special disfavor, misfortune deemed to punish sin. And just as culpable sin, as distinct from mere error, requires an act of will, specifically, arrogance, so an act of extraordinary character requires an act of will. But, as mirror image of sin, the act would reveal in a concrete way an attitude of restraint, forbearance, gentility, and self-abnegation. A sinful act, provoking Heaven, was on that one did deliberately to defy Heaven. Then an act that would evoke Heaven's favor, so imposing upon Heaven a lien that Heaven freely gave, was one that, equally deliberately and concretely, displayed humility.

But the systemic focus upon the power of a single act of remarkable generosity, the surrender to the other of what is most precious to the self, whether that constituted an opinion or a possession or a feeling, in no way will have surprised the framers of the philosophical Judaism. They had laid heavy emphasis upon the power of human intentionality to settle questions of the status of interstitial persons, objects, or actions, within the larger system of hierarchical classification. So in the philosophical Judaism attitude and intentionality classified what was of doubtful status, that is to say, forming the active and motivating component of the structure and transforming the structure, a tableau of fixed and motionless figures, into a system of action and reaction. Then, in the process of transformation, we should hardly find surprising the appeal to the critical power of attitude and intentionality. For what we find in the later documents of the Rabbinic canon is a fundamental point of connection. What was specific before, intentionality, is now broadened and made general through extension to all aspects of one's attitude.

Now the powerful forces coalescing in intentionality gained very precise definition. They underwent the transformation from merely concrete cases of the taxonomic power of intentionality that worked one way here, another way there, into very broad-ranging but quite specific and prescribed attitudes. The later documents of the Rabbinic canon took their leave from the initial ones without a real farewell. Then what is the point of departure? It is marked by the intense interest, in the religious Judaism, upon not the fixed given of normative intentionality,[4] but rather changing people, both individually and nationally, from what they were to something else. And, if the change is in a single direction, it is, nonetheless, also always personal and individual.

The change is signaled — briefly to sum up the conclusions of Chapter Seven and this chapter as well — by the conception that study of the Torah not only illuminated and educated but transformed, and, moreover, so changed the disciple that he gained in supernatural standing and authority. Torah-study produced *zekhut*, and all things depended upon the *zekhut* that a person, or the nation as a whole, possessed. Mastery of what we classify as "the system's worldview" changed a person by generating *zekhut*, that is, by so affecting the person as to inculcate attitudes that would produce remarkable actions (often: acts of omission, restraint, and forbearance) to generate *zekhut*. The change was the end, the Torah-study, the medium.

---

[4] That is, an assessment of what people will ordinarily think or propose or wish to have happen. The rule is set by that norm, not by exceptions, and on that basis, in the initial system, we are able to determine what (an ordinary person's) intentionality will dictate in a given interstitial case.

But the system's worldview was not the sole, or even the principal, component that showed how the received system was transformed by the new one. The conception of *zekhut* came to the fore to integrate of the system's theory of the way of life of the social order, its economics, together with its account of the social entity of the social order, its politics. The remarkable actions — perhaps those of omission more than those of commission — that produced *zekhut* yielded an increase in the scarcest of all resources, supernatural favor. At the same time those actions of self-denial endowed a person rich in entitlements to Heavenly intervention with that power to evoke that vastly outweighed the this-worldly power to coerce in the accomplishment of one's purpose.

This rapid account of the systemic structure and system, its inversion of the received categories and its formation of anti-categories of its own, draws our attention to the specificity of the definition of right attitude and puissant intentionality by contrast to the generality of those same matters when represented in the philosophical system of the Mishnah. We have, therefore, to ask ourselves whether the quite concrete and definition of those attitudes and correct will and proper intentionality that lead to acts that generate *zekhut* will have surprised framers of documents prior to those that attest the transformed Judaism before us, the Talmuds and the late Midrash-compilations. The answer is negative, and that fact alerts us to yet another fundamental continuity between the earlier and the later components of the Rabbinic canon.

II. APPROVED EMOTIONS

As a matter of fact, the doctrine defining the appropriate attitude persisted pretty much unchanged from the beginning components of the Rabbinic canon.[5] The repertoire of approved and disapproved attitude and intentionality remained constant through the half-millennium of the unfolding of the canon of Judaism from the Mishnah onward: humility, forbearance, accommodation, a spirit of conciliation. For one thing, Scripture itself is explicit that God shares and responds to the attitudes and intentionality of human beings. God cares what humanity feels — wanting love from Israelites, for example — and so the conception that actions that express right attitudes of humility will evoke in Heaven a desired

---

[5] I have demonstrated that fact in my *Vanquished Nation, Broken Spirit. The Virtues of the Heart in Formative Judaism*. (New York, 1987: Cambridge University Press).

response will not have struck as novel the authors of the Pentateuch or the various prophetic writings, for example. The biblical record of God's feelings and God's will concerning the feelings of humanity leaves no room for doubt. What is fresh in the system before us is not the integration of the individual with the nation but the provision, for the individual, of a task and a role analogous to that of the nation.

With its interest in classifying large-scale and collective classes of things, the Mishnah's system treats matters of attitude and emotion in that same taxic context. For instance, while the Mishnah casually refers to emotions, e.g., tears of joy, tears of sorrow, where feelings matter, it always is in a public and communal context. Where there is an occasion of rejoicing, one form of joy is not to be confused with some other, or one context of sorrow with another. Accordingly, marriages are not to be held on festivals (M. M. Q. 1:7). Likewise mourning is not to take place then (M. M. Q. 1:5, 3:7–9). Where emotions play a role, it is because of the affairs of the community at large, e.g., rejoicing on a festival, mourning on a fast day (M. Suk. 5:1–4). Emotions are to be kept in hand, as in the case of the relatives of the executed felon (M. San. 6:6). If I had to specify the single underlying principle affecting all forms of emotion, for the Mishnah it is the profoundly philosophical attitude that attitudes and feelings must be kept under control, never fully expressed without reasoning about the appropriate context. Emotions must always lay down judgments.

We see in most of those cases in which emotions play a systemic and indicative, not merely an episodic and random, role, that the basic principle is the same. We can, and must so frame our feelings as to accord with the appropriate rule. In only one case does emotion play a decisive role in settling an issue, and that has to do with whether or not a farmer was happy that water came upon his produce or grain. That case underlines the conclusion just now drawn. If people feel a given sentiment, it is a matter of judgment, therefore invokes the law's penalties. So in this system emotions are not treated as spontaneous, but as significant aspects of a person's judgment.

Whence then the doctrine that very specific attitudes bear the weight of the systemic structure as a whole? It is in tractate Abot, which supplies those phrases cited at the outset to define the theology that sustains the conception of *zekhut*. Tractate Abot, free-standing in form and content but conventionally attached to the Mishnah and serving as the Mishnah's advocate, turns out to form the bridge from the Mishnah to the Yerushalmi and its associated compilations of scriptural exegeses. That tractate presents the single most comprehensive account of religious affections.

8. Living in the kingdom of God

The reason is that, in that document above all, how we feel defines a critical aspect of virtue. The issue proves central, not peripheral. The very specific and concrete doctrine emerges fully exposed. A simple catalogue of permissible feelings comprises humility, generosity, self-abnegation, love, a spirit of conciliation of the other, and eagerness to please. A list of impermissible emotions is made up of envy, ambition, jealousy, arrogance, sticking to one's opinion, self-centeredness, a grudging spirit, vengefulness, and the like. Nothing in the wonderful stories about remarkable generosity does more than render concrete the abstract doctrine of the heart's virtue that tractate Abot sets forth.

People should aim at eliciting from others acceptance and good will and should avoid confrontation, rejection, and humiliation of the other. This they do through conciliation and giving up their own claims and rights. So both catalogues form a harmonious and uniform whole, aiming at the cultivation of the humble and malleable person, one who accepts everything and resents nothing. True, these virtues, in this tractate as in the system as a whole, derive from knowledge of what really counts, which is what God wants. But God favors those who please others. The virtues appreciated by human beings prove identical to the ones to which God responds as well. And what single virtue of the heart encompasses the rest? Restraint, the source of self-abnegation, humility, serves as the antidote for ambition, vengefulness, and, above all, for arrogance. It is restraint of our own interest that enables us to deal generously with others, humility about ourselves that generates a liberal spirit towards others. And the correspondence of Heavenly and mortal attitudes is to be taken for granted — as is made explicit.

So the emotions prescribed in tractate Abot turn out to provide variations of a single feeling, which is the sentiment of the disciplined heart, whatever affective form it may take. And where does the heart learn its lessons, if not in relationship to God? So: "Make his wishes yours, so that he will make your wishes his" (Abot 2:4). Applied to relationships between human beings, this inner discipline of the emotional life will yield exactly those virtues of conciliation and self-abnegation, humility and generosity of spirit, that the framers of tractate Abot spell out in one example after another. Imputing to Heaven exactly those responses felt on earth, e.g., "Anyone from whom people take pleasure, God takes pleasure" (Abot 3:10), makes the point at the most general level.

Then what have the later documents of the Rabbinic canon contributed? Two things: [1] the conception that acts of omission or commission expressing an attitude of forbearance and self-abnegation generate *zekhut* in particular; [2] the principle that *zekhut* functions in those very specific ways that the system deems critical: as the power to attest to human transformation and regeneration, affording, in place of philosophical politics and philosophical economics, that power inhering in weakness, that wealth inhering in giving up what one has, that in the end promise the attainment of our goals. I may state the matter in a single sentence:

the path from one system to the other is in three stages:

[1] the philosophical Judaism, portrayed by the Mishnah, assigns to intentionality and attitude systemic centrality;

[2] tractate Abot, in presenting in general terms the rationale of the Mishnah's system, defines precisely the affective attitude and intentionality that are required;

[3] the religious Judaism of the Yerushalmi and associated writings joins together the systemic centrality of attitude and intentionality with the doctrine of virtue laid out in tractate Abot.

But in joining these received elements the new system emerges as distinct from the old.[6] For when we deem the attitude of affirmation and acceptance, rather than aggression, and the intentionality of self-abnegation and forbearance, to define the means for gaining *zekhut*, what we are saying is contrary and paradoxical: if you want to have, then give up, and if you want to impose your judgment, then make the judgment of the other into your own, and if you want to coerce Heaven, then evoke in Heaven attitudes of sympathy that will lead to the actions or events that you want, whether rain, whether long life, whether the salvation of Israel and its hegemony over the nations: to rule, be ruled by Heaven; to show Heaven rules, give up what you want to the other. *Zekhut* results: the lien upon Heaven, freely given by Heaven in response to one's free surrender to the will and wish of Heaven. And by means of *zekhut*, whether one's own, whether one's ancestors', the social order finds its shape and system, and the individual his or her place within its structure.

The correspondence of the individual to the nation, both capable of gaining *zekhut* in the same way, linked the deepest personal emotions

---

[6] This is not to suggest that the substance of the doctrine of virtue was richly revised in the successor-writings. That is not so. The transformation was systemic, not doctrinal. Emotions not taken up earlier in the pages of the Yerushalmi did not come under discussion. Principles introduced earlier enjoyed mere restatement and extensive exemplification. Some principles of proper feelings might even generate secondary developments of one kind or another. But nothing not present at the outset — in tractate Abot — drew sustained attention later on. The system proved essentially complete in the earliest statement of its main points. What then do the authors or compilers of the Yerushalmi contribute? Temper marks the ignorant person, restraint and serenity, the learned one. These are mere details.

to the cosmic fate and transcendent faith of that social group of which each individual formed a part. The individual Israelite's innermost feelings, the inner heart of Israel, the microcosm, correspond to the public and historic condition of the nation, of Israel, the macrocosm. In the innermost chambers of the individual's deepest feelings, the Israelite therefore lives out the public history and destiny of the people, Israel.

III. COMPETITION FOR THE STATUS OF "BEING ISRAEL"

What precipitated deep thought upon fundamental questions of social existence was a simple fact. From the time early in the fourth century that Christianity attained the status of a licit religion, the Jews of Palestine witnessed the formation of circumstances that had formerly been simply unimaginable: another Israel, in the same place and time, competed with them in their terms, quoting their Scriptures, explaining who they were in their own categories but in very different terms from the ones that they used. We need not explain the profundities of religious doctrine by reducing them to functions and necessities of public policy. But it is, a matter of simple fact, that the Jews in the fourth century had witnessed a drastic decline in their power to exercise legitimate violence (which is to say, violence you can make stick), as well as in their command of the real estate of Palestine that they knew as the Holy Land and its wealth. The system's stress upon matters of intentionality and attitude, subject to the governance of even the most humble of individuals, even the most insignificant of nations, exactly corresponded to the political and social requirements of the Jews' condition in that time. The transformed Judaism made of necessity a theological virtue, and, by the way, the normative condition of the social order.

In the fourth century, from Constantine's great victory and legitimation of Christianity in the beginning, to the Theodosian code that subordinated Jewry and limited its rights at nearly the end of the fourth century, Jews confronted a remarkable shift in the character of the Roman empire. The state first legalized Christianity, then established Christianity as most favored religion, and — by the end of that century — finally undertook to extirpate paganism, and, by the way, to subordinate Judaism. Therein lies the urgency of the critical question addressed by the system as a whole — if not the self-evidence of the truth of its response to that question. Dealing with world-historical change in the character of the Roman Empire consequent on the legalization of Christianity by Constantine and the establishment of Christianity as the state-religion by his successors, the transformed Judaism made its statement in answer to the fundamental question confronting the social order: precisely what are we now to do?

That political question concerning the assessment of the legitimate use of violence in this Judaism called into doubt the legitimacy of any kind of violence at all, Jews' having none. But no less subject to reflection was that "doing" that referred to making a living, the economics of the acquisition and management of scarce resources, and, it goes without saying, the making of a life, the philosophy of rational explanation of all things in some one way. At stake, then, were the very shape and structure of the social order, reconsidered at what was, and was certainly perceived as, the critical turning.

This utter reordering of society framed a question that had to be faced and could not be readily answered.[7] It concerned the meaning and end of history, Israel's history, now that the prophetic promises were claimed by the Christian competition to have been kept in the past, leaving nothing in the future for which to hope. When, for a brief moment, in 361–3 the emperor Julian disestablished Christianity and restored paganism, proposing also to rebuild the Jews' Temple in Jerusalem, Christianity met the challenge and regained power. The Temple was not rebuilt, and Julian's brief reign brought in its wake a ferocious counter-revolution, with the Christian state now suppressing the institutions of paganism, and Christian men in the streets of the towns and villages taking an active role on their own as well. Julian's successors persecuted pagan philosophy. In 380 the emperor Theodosius (379–395) decreed the end of paganism:

> It is our desire that all the various nations which are subject to our clemency and moderation should continue in the profession of that religion which was delivered to the Romans by the divine Apostle Peter.

Paganism found itself subjected to penalties. The state church — a principal indicator of the Christian civilization that the West was to know — now

---

[7] And certainly had not been answered by the Mishnah's system, which treated history — composed of events in particular — as mere occasions for taxonomic inquiry: classifying this event in one way, according to one overriding rule, that event in some other, according to another rule; and neither rule bore any relationship to history. The regularization and ordering of disorderly events — counterpart to what we know as social science today — denied to history all status as the source of category-formation. I have spelled all this out in my *Messiah in Context* [= *The Foundations of Judaism. Method, Teleology, Doctrine.* (Philadelphia, 1983–5: Fortress Press. Second printing: Lanham, 1988: University Press of America. Studies in Judaism series). I–III. II. *Messiah in Context. Israel's History and Destiny in Formative Judaism*].

came into being. In 381 Theodosius forbade sacrifices and closed most temples. In 391–392 a new set of penalties was imposed on paganism. And, while tolerated, Judaism, together with the Jews, suffered drastic change in their legal standing as well.

The upshot is simple. In the beginning of the fourth century Rome was pagan, in the end, Christian. In the beginning Jews in the Land of Israel administered their own affairs. In the end their institution of self-administration lost the recognition it had formerly enjoyed. In 300 the area of Palestine where Jews lived was mainly settled by Jews, hence, palpably and visibly, the Land of Israel, while in 400, the country was populated with Christian shrines.[8] In the beginning Judaism enjoyed entirely licit status, and the Jews, the protection of the state. In the end Judaism suffered abridgement of its former liberties, and the Jews of theirs. In the beginning, the Jews lived in the Land of Israel, and in some numbers. In the end they lived in Palestine.

As a matter of fact, each of the important changes in the documents first redacted at the end of the fourth century dealt with a powerful challenge presented by the triumph of Christianity in Constantine's age.[9] The first change revealed in the unfolding of the sages' canon pertains to the use of Scripture. The change at hand specifically is in making books out the collection of exegeses of Scripture. That represents an innovation because the Mishnah, and the exegetical literature that served the Mishnah, did not take shape around the order of biblical passages, even when relevant, let alone the explanation of verses of Scripture. In the third, and especially, in the later fourth centuries, other writings, entering the canon, took shape around the explanation of verses of Scripture, not a set of topics. What this meant was that a second mode of organizing ideas, besides the topical mode paramount for the Mishnah, the Tosefta, the Yerushalmi (and the Bavli later on), now made its way.

The second concerned extensive consideration of the topic of the Messiah, formerly not accorded a principal place among the parts of the social

---

[8] Constantine and his mother had built churches and shrines all over the country, especially in Jerusalem, so the Land of Israel received yet another name, for another important group, now becoming the Holy Land.

[9] I have spelled these matters out in *Judaism and Christianity in the Age of Constantine. Issues of the Initial Confrontation.* (Chicago, 1987: University of Chicago Press); *Midrash in Context* [= *The Foundations of Judaism. Method, Teleology, Doctrine.* (Philadelphia, 1983–5: Fortress Press. Second printing: Atlanta, 1988: Scholars Press for Brown Judaic Studies) I–III. I. *Midrash in Context. Exegesis in Formative Judaism]*; .and, in summary, in *Judaism in the Matrix of Christianity.* (Philadelphia, 1986: Fortress Press. British edition, Edinburgh, 1988, T. & T. Collins).

system.[10] The philosophers of the Mishnah did not make use of the Messiah myth in the construction of a teleology for their system. They found it possible to present a statement of goals for their projected life of Israel which was entirely separate from appeals to history and eschatology. The appearance in the Talmuds of a messianic eschatology fully consonant with the larger characteristic of the rabbinic system — with its stress on the viewpoints and proof-texts of Scripture, its interest in what was happening to Israel, its focus upon the national-historical dimension of the life of the group — indicates that the encompassing rabbinic system stands essentially autonomous of the prior, Mishnaic system.

Third, the Mishnah had presented an ahistorical and, in the nature of things, non-eschatological teleology, and did not make use of the messiah-theme to express its teleology. By contrast, the Talmud not only provides an eschatological and therefore a messiah-centered teleology for its system. Its authorship also formed a theory of history and found it appropriate to compose important narratives, episodic to be sure, concerning events that, in prior systemic writings, were treated as mere taxic indicators. Now what happened counted, not only that something happened, and the details of events were to be narrated and preserved. So far as the definition of an event comprises a cultural indicator, the telling of stories about events tells us that, for the Talmud of the Land of Israel and related writings, the very formation of culture has been transformed.

IV. FROM PHILOSOPHY TO RELIGION: THE KINGDOM OF HEAVEN AND THE CITY OF GOD

No wonder, then, that the Mishnah's philosophical (therefore also social-scientific) and ahistorical Judaism, a Judaism of rules, gave way to the religious and historical (therefore also eschatological) Judaism of the Talmud of the Land of Israel and associated Midrash-compilations — a Judaism of exceptions to the rules. These important shifts show that the later system set forth a Judaism topically intersecting with the Mishnah's but essentially asymmetrical with it. Given the political changes of the age, with their implications for the meaning and end of history as Israel would experience it, the foci of the connected but autonomous system now directed attention to the media for salvation in the here and now, for Israel and the individual alike, and in time to come for all Israel.

---

[10] This is worked out in *Messiah in Context*, cited above.

8. Living in the kingdom of God

A single now-familiar word captured the whole: *zekhut* yielded a broad variety of answers to one urgent question. It was a question encompassing society and history, now and the coming age, Israel and the nations, the social order in the here and now and the great society comprised by nature and supernature. To the question posed by the simple statement of the religious system set forth in the late fourth and fifth century documents is this: the entire social order forms one reality, in the supernatural world and in nature, in time and in eternity.

The sages who wrote and compiled the Talmud of the Land of Israel, Genesis Rabbah, Leviticus Rabbah, and Pesiqta deRab Kahana, did not stand alone in their profound reflections on how earth and Heaven intersect, and how the here and the now forms a moment in history. As it happens, at the same time and under similar circumstances of historical crisis, another system-builder was at work. When we appreciate the commonalities of the task facing each party and the dimensions that turn out to take the measure of the results of each, we realize how different men, speaking each to his own world, delivering each his own statement, turn out in the same time to answer the same question in what is, as a matter of fact, pretty much the same cosmic dimensions, and, it would turn out, with the same enduring results for the formation of Western civilization.

Augustine of Hippo's life, in North Africa and Italy, (354–430) roughly coincided with the period in which, to the east, the sages of the Land of Israel produced their Talmud in amplification of the Mishnah as well as their Midrash-compilations in extension of Moses' books of Genesis and Leviticus. But he comes to mind, for comparison and contrast, not merely because of temporal coincidence. Rather, the reason is that, like the sages of Judaism, he confronted the same this-worldly circumstance, one in which the old order was deemed to be coming to an end — and was acknowledged to be closing. And the changes were those of power and politics.

In 410 — a century after the advent of Christianity to political legitimacy and then hegemony — after the Goths took Rome, some refugees of Alaric's conquest fled to North Africa (as well, as a matter of fact, as to the Land of Israel/Palestine, as events even early in the story of Jerome in Jerusalem tell us[11]). At the very hour of his death, some decades later, Augustine's own city, Hippo lay besieged by the Vandals. So it was at what seemed the twilight of the ancient empire of Rome that Augustine

---
[11] I refer to J. N. D. Kelly, *Jerome: His Life, Writings, and Controversies* (N.Y., 1975: Harper & Row).

composed his account of the theology of the social order known as the *City of God*. Within his remarkable *oeuvre*, it was that work that renders of special interest here the sages' contemporary and their counterpart as a system-builder.

Like the critical issue of political calamity facing sages in the aftermath of the triumph of Christianity and the failure of Julian's brief restoration of both paganism and (as to Jerusalem) Judaism, the question Augustine addressed presented a fundamental challenge to the foundations of the Christian world order, coming as it did from Roman pagan aristocrats, taking refuge in North Africa.[12] What caused the fall of Rome, if not the breaches

---

[12] The bibliography for this chapter lists the books I have consulted. In no way claiming to know the scholarship on Augustine, even in the English language, I chose to rely mostly upon a single work, consulting others mostly for my own illumination. It is the up-to-date and, I think, universally respected account by Peter Brown, *Augustine of Hippo* (Berkeley and Los Angeles, 1967: University of California Press). The pertinent passage is on p. 302. All otherwise unidentified page references to follow are to this work. My modest generalizations about the intersection of the two systems on some points important to each rests, for Augustine, entirely on Brown. I found very helpful the outline of the work presented by John Neville Figgis, *The Political Aspects of S. Augustine's 'City of God'* (London, 1921: Longmans Green and Co.), pp. 1–31, and the characterization of Augustine's thought by Herbert A. Deane, *The Politician and Social Ideas of St. Augustine* (New York & London, 1963: Columbia University Press). In Deane's lucid account, anyone in search of specific doctrinal parallels between sages' system and that of Augustine will find ample evidence that there is none of consequence. As will become clear, what I find heuristically suggestive are structural and functional parallels, not points of doctrinal coincidence of any material importance. My sense is that the success of Brown's book overshadowed the important contribution of Gerald Bonner, *St. Augustine of Hippo. Life and Controversies* (London, 1963: SCM Press, Ltd.), a less dazzling, but more systematic and (it seems to me) useful presentation. A brief and clear account of the two cities is in Eugene Teselle, *Augustine the Theologian* (N.Y., 1970: Herder and Herder), pp. 268–278, who outlines the variety of approaches taken to the description and interpretation of the work: polemical, apologetic; philosophy or theology of history; analysis of political ideology; source of principles of political and moral theory; and of ecclesiastical policy; and the like. The achievement of F. Van der Meer, *Augustine the Bishop. Religion and Society at the Dawn of the Middle Ages* (New York, 1961: Harper & Row). Translated by Brian Battershaw and G. R. Lamp, is not to be missed: a fine example of the narrative-reading of religion by a historian of religion of one useful kind. Precisely what Augustine means by "the city of God" is worked out by John O'Meara, *The Charter of Christendom: The Significance of the City of God* (New York, 1961: The Macmillan Co.), who says (p. 43) that "the city of God exists already in heaven and, apart from certain pilgrim men who are on their way to it while they are on this earth, in heaven only." When I speak of sages' having extended the boundaries of the social system from earth to Heaven, I mean to suggest something roughly parallel, in that, when women and men on earth conform to the Torah, they find themselves in the image and after the likeness of Heaven. The sense of the concept "history," then, is "the story of two cities," so Hardy, pp. 267ff. (cf. Edward R. Hardy, Jr., "The City of God," in Roy W. Battenhouse, *A Companion to the Study of St. Augustine* (New York, 1955: Oxford University Press), pp. 257–286. I find the story of Israel among the nations as the equivalent, unifying and integrating conception of history in the doctrine(s) of history in the Yerushalmi and Leviticus Rabbah; this then means Israel forms the counterpart to the city of God, and I think that is the beginning of all systemic comparison in this context (and, I should suspect, in all others).

8. Living in the kingdom of God

in its walls made from within the city by Christianity? The first three books of *The City of God* responded, in 413, and twenty-two books in all came to a conclusion in 426: a gigantic work.[13] While *The City of God* (re)presents Christian faith "in the form of biblical history, from Genesis to Revelation,[14] just as sages present important components of their system in historical form of narrative, I see no important doctrinal points in common between the program of Israel's sages in the Land of Israel and that of the great Christian theologian and philosopher. Each party presented in an episodic way what can be represented as an orderly account of the social order,[15] each for the edification of its chosen audience; neither, I think, would have understood a line of the composition of the other, in writing or in concept. And that unbridgeable abyss makes all the more striking the simple fact that, from one side of the gap to the other, the distance was slight. For each party addressed questions entirely familiar, I think, to the other, and the gross and salient traits of the system of the one in some striking ways prove symmetrical to those of the other.[16]

---

[13] p. 303.

[14] John H. S. Burleigh, *The City of God. A Study of St. Augustine's Philosophy. Croall Lectures, 1944* (London, 1949: Nisbet & Co. Ltd.), p. 153.

[15] But the two parties have in common the simple fact that the representation of their respective systems is the accomplishment of others later on, indeed, in the case of sages, much later on indeed. Note the judgment of Deane, Augustine "was not a system-builder...Virtually everything that Augustine wrote...was an occasional piece" (Herbert A. Deane, *The Political and Social Ideas of St. Augustine* (New York & London, 1963: Columbia University Press, p. viii). Sages' documents, it is quite obvious, do not utilize the categories for the description of the social order that I have imposed: ethos, ethics, ethnos; worldview, way of life, doctrine of the social entity. But systemic description in its nature imputes and of necessity imposes system, and that is so, whether the system is deemed social or theological in its fundamental character. I have no difficulty in defending the proposition that sages' system was in its very essence a system of society, that is, of the holy people, Israel, and the union of social and theological thought in Augustine is signaled by the very metaphors he selected for his work, in his appeal to "the city."

[16] When William Green recommended the choice of Augustine and I accepted it, the recommendation and recognition of its rightness bore a certain rationality too. Drawing a comparison with Augustine is by no means capricious, based merely on the temporal coincidence of the sages in the Yerushalmi and related writings and Augustine. What I think more compelling is the fact that sages inherited a Middle Platonic doctrine concerning the unity of all being and reworked it in historical-narrative terms, therefore finding in (among other concepts) the notion of *zekhut* a medium for the unification of the generations, past and present. Augustine, for his part, is everywhere described as a reworking the heritage of Platonism, drawing chiefly from Plotinus, so for instance Burleigh, p. 157. As a guess, therefore, I would venture that the principal shift in the large-scale modes of thought from the Mishnah through to the Yerushalmi along with Genesis Rabbah, Leviticus Rabbah, and Pesiqta deRab Kahana, was the movement away from Aristotelian modes of thought, such as characterized the Mishnah, to those of Middle Platonism. But not being a historian of philosophy in antiquity, I am able only to suggest that hypothesis as a subject for further inquiry. In any event one did not have to adopt the inheritance of Plato, in the formulation of Middle Platonism, Neo-Platonism, or Plotinus,

The relationship of the opposing cities of God and the devil, embodied in the pilgrim Church and the empirical state, presents the chief systematic problem of *The City of God*.[17] Augustine covered, in five books, "those who worshipped the gods for felicity on earth;" in five, "those who worshipped them for eternal felicity;" and twelve, the theme of the origin of "two cities, one of God, the other of the world," "their unfolding course in the part," "their ultimate destinies."[18] True, sages reconsidered the prior disinterest in history, but they did not then produce a continuous account of everything that had ever happened, and Augustine did. Nor do the two literary monuments, Augustine's and sages', bear anything in common as to form, style, sources, mode of argument, selection of audience, literary convention of any kind. Then why treat the system of sages and the systematic statement of Augustine as so connected as to warrant comparison? For the obvious reason that the authorship of Israel and the Christian author not only responded to the same circumstance but also framed the question deemed posed by that common circumstance in the same terms: a recasting, in historical terms, of the whole of the social order, a rethinking, in the image of Augustine, of God's city.

What then was the value of the *polis*, which throughout these pages I have rendered as "the social order," and exactly who lived in the city of the earth? It was "any group of people tainted by the Fall," any that failed to regard "the 'earthly' values they had created as transient and relative."[19] To this Augustine responds, "Away with all this arrogant bluffing: what, after all, are men but men!"[20] The rise of Rome is reduced, in Brown's words, "to a simple common denominator…the 'lust for domination.'" The Romans were moved by "an overweening love of praise: 'they were, therefore, "grasping for praise, open-handed with their money; honest in the pursuit of wealth, they wanted to hoard glory."'"[21] But the true glory resides not in Rome but in the city of God: "the virtues the Romans had ascribed to their heroes would be realized only in the citizens of this other city; and it is only within the walls of the Heavenly Jerusalem that Cicero's noble

---

to focus upon the social order as the centerpiece of philosophical, systematic thought and system-building. Aristotle (much less influential in this period, to be sure) provided an equally accessible model for anyone who might wish to rethink the foundations of the polis or of the social being of Israel, the holy people, in the Land of Israel, the holy land.

[17] So Teselle, p. 270.
[18] *Ibid.*, pp. 303–304. Cf. also Burleigh, pp. 166ff. on Augustine's attitude toward "the concrete political structures of history."
[19] *Ibid.*, p. 309.
[20] *Ibid.*, p. 309.
[21] *Ibid.*, p. 310.

definition of the essence of the Roman Republic could be achieved."[22] The Judaic sages — we now realize — assuredly concurred on whence comes glory, whence shame: the one from humility, the other, pride.

The system of Augustine addresses the crisis of change with an account of history, and it is, therefore, in the same sense as is the system of the Judaic sages, a deeply historical one: "The whole course of human history...could be thought of as laden with meanings which might be seized, partially by the believer, in full by the seer."[23] So Brown: "In his *City of God*, Augustine was one of the first to sense and give monumental expression to a new form of intellectual excitement." God communicates through both words and events. Specifically, history proves the presence of a division between an earthly and a heavenly city.[24] Why do I find this historical interest pertinent to my picture of a Judaism's social order? Because, in Brown's words, "there is room, in Augustine's view of the past, for the consideration of whole societies..."[25] But the building block of society is relationship, and the whole of human history emerges out of the relationship of Cain and Abel, natural man after the fall, citizen of this world, against a man who built no city, "by hoping for something else...he waited upon the name of the Lord."[26] Brown says:

> Augustine treats the tension between Cain and Abel as universal, because he can explain it in terms applicable to all men. All human society...is based on a desire to share some good. Of such goods, the most deeply felt by human beings is the need for 'peace:' that is, for a resolution of tensions, for an ordered control of unbalanced appetites in themselves, and of discordant wills in society...the

---

[22] *Ibid.*, pp. 311–312.
[23] *Ibid.*, p. 317.
[24] *Ibid.*, p. 319. See Burleigh, pp. 185ff., "A philosophy of history." He cites the following: "St. Augustine's De Civitate Dei...may be regarded as the first attempt to frame a complete philosophy of history...It was...a singularly unsuccessful attempt; for it contained neither philosophy nor history, but merely theology and fiction." Whether or not so of Augustine, that statement seems to me an apt description of the form of history as invented in the pages of the Talmud of the Land of Israel. My presentation of sages' thought on history is in my *The Foundations of Judaism. Method, Teleology, Doctrine.* Philadelphia, 1983–5: Fortress Press. II. *Messiah in Context. Israel's History and Destiny in Formative Judaism.* Second printing: Lanham, 1988: University Press of America. Studies in Judaism series. This matter has not played a principal role in my exposition of the successor-system, because it seems to me ancillary and not categorically-definitive. Burleigh describes the dominant philosophy of the age, characteristic of Augustine as well, as anti-historical. But Augustine's "Platonic Biblicism in effect brings them [history and philosophy] into the closest relation. Biblical History is Platonic idealism in time." That statement seems to me to run parallel to the characterization of the rabbinic uses of history in the form of persons and events as exemplary and cyclical, rather than unique and linear.
[25] *Ibid.*, p. 320.
[26] *Ibid.*, p. 320.

members of the [city of earth[, that is, fallen men, tend to regard their achievement of such peace in society as sufficient in itself...²⁷

The city of Heaven is "the consecrated commonwealth of Israel," the city of earth, everybody else.²⁸ Brown's summary of Augustine's main point with slight alteration serves as epitome of sages' views:

What was at stake, in the City of God and in Augustine's sermons, was the capacity of men to 'long' for something different, to examine the nature of their relationship with their immediate environment; above all, to establish their identity by refusing to be engulfed in the unthinking habits of their fellows.²⁹

How alien can sages, concerned as they were with the possibilities of extraordinary conduct or attitude, have found Augustine's interest in establishing identity by reflection on what others deemed routine? The obvious answer justifies juxtaposing the two systems as to not only their ineluctable questions, but also their self-evidently valid answers.

Two further rhetorical questions seem justified: if Augustine spoke of "resident aliens" when referring to the citizens of God's city,³⁰ then how difficult can sages have found interpreting the identity of their social entity, their Israel, in the same way: here now, but only because of tomorrow: the pilgrim people, *en route* to somewhere else. And why should we find surprising, as disciples of Israel's sages, a city of God permeated, as was Augustine's, by arguments for hope:³¹

"'Lord, I have loved the beauty of Thy house.' From his gifts, which are scattered to good and bad alike in this, our most grim life, let us, with His help, try to express sufficiently what we have yet to experience."³²

Two systems emerged from the catastrophes of the fifth century, Augustine's³³ for the Christian, sages' for the Judaic West. Constructed

---

²⁷ *Ibid.*, p. 322.
²⁸ *Ibid.*, p. 322.
²⁹ *Ibid.*, p. 322.
³⁰ *Ibid.*, p. 323
³¹ *Ibid.*, p. 328.
³² *Ibid.*, p. 328.
³³ Note Burleigh, p. 218: "The Fifth Century...was a period of radical historical change." But just as Augustine expressed no sense of "the end of an era," so in the pages of the documents surveyed here I find no world-historical foreboding, only an optimistic and unshakeable conviction that Israel governed by its own deeds and attitudes its own destiny every day. That seems to me the opposite of a sense that all things are changing beyond repair. I can find no more ample representation of the historical convictions of the Rabbinic sages than Bur-

in the same age and in response to problems of the same character and quality, the systems bore nothing in common, except the fundamentally same messages about the correspondence of the individual's life to the social order, the centrality of relationship, the rule of God, and the response of God to what transcended all rules.

By both systems, each in its own way, God is joined to the social order because it is in relationships that society takes shape and comes to expression, and all relationships, whether between one person and another or between mortals and God, are wholly consubstantial.[34] That is why, for Augustine, the relationship between the individuals, Cain and Abel, can convey and represent the relationships characteristic of societies or cities, and that is why, for sages, the relationships between one person and another can affect God's relationship to the village needing rain or the householder needing to shore up his shaky dwelling-place.

True, we deal with the two utterly unrelated systems of the social order, fabricated by different people, talking about different things to different people, each meant to join the society of humanity (or a sector thereof) with the community of Heaven. But both formed quite systematic and well-crafted responses to one and the same deep perception of disorder. And that produced a profound sense that the rules had been broken, generating that condition that in our time we call alienation. And that was overcome by Augustine in his way, by sages in theirs.[35]

How, in the language of Judaism as the Rabbinic sages formulated it, may we express the answer to the question of the times? The shaking of the foundations of the social order shows how Israel is estranged from God. The old rules have been broken, therefore the remarkable and the

---

leigh's representation of Augustine's: "Rome might pass away. The protecting fostering power of her emperors might be withdrawn. But God endured. His purpose of gathering citizens into His Eternal City was not frustrated by transient circumstances. St. Augustine had no anxiety for the Empire or for civilization, even 'Christian' civilization, because he found a better security in God." It is interesting to note that Burleigh gave his lectures in 1944, responding it seems to me to the impending dissolution of the British Empire in his rereading of Augustine — and dismissing an interest in the fate of Empires as essentially beside the point for Augustine. So I think it was for the Rabbinic sages.

[34] Burleigh characterizes matters in this way: "He seems to have been satisfied to show...that the exposition and defense of the Christian faith necessitates a survey of all History, which is in its essence God's providential government of the human race" (p. 202).

[35] The basic motif of alienation, personal, cosmic, political, theological, as much as affective characterizes the two systems, because it defines the condition that provokes for each system the generative question, and because it is in the mode of reintegration that each system finds its persistent statement. True, alienation defines a purely contemporary category and forms a judgment made by us upon the circumstance or attitude of ancients. But the category does serve to specify, for our own understanding, what is at stake.

exceptional succeeds. What is unnatural to the human condition of pride is humility and uncertainty, acceptance and conciliation. And when — so the system maintains — God recognizes in Israel's heart the proper feelings, He will respond by ending that estrangement that marks the present age. So the single word encompassing the question addressed by the entire social system of the successor-Judaism must be *alienation*. The human and shared sense of crisis — whether Augustine reflecting on the fall of Rome, or sages confronting the end of the old order — finds its response in the doctrine of God's assessment, God's response.

God enters the social order imagined by sages because God in the natural order proves insufficient, a Presence inadequate to the human situation. God must dwell in the city of humanity, and Israel in the kingdom of God, counterpart to Augustine's city of God. So what in secular terms we see as a historical crisis or in psychological terms as one of alienation, in religious terms we have to identify as a caesura in the bounds of eternity. The psychological theology of the system joins the human condition to the fate of the nation and the world — and links the whole to the broken heart of God.

And yet that theological observation about the incarnate God of Judaism does not point us toward the systemic center, which within my definitions of what a system is must be social and explain the order of things here and now. For in the end, a religious theory of the social order describes earth, not Heaven.[36] It simply begs the question to claim that the system in the end attended to the condition of God's heart, rather than humanity's mundane existence. For a religious system is not a theological one, and questions about the way of life, world-view, and social entity, admittedly bearing theological implications or even making theological statements, in the end find their answers in the reconstruction of the here and now. It is for identifying that generative problematic of the Judaism of the fifth century documents that the comparison between the Judaism of the sages and the Christianity of Augustine in his *City of God* proves particularly pertinent. Augustine's personal circumstance and that of the Rabbinic sages correspond, so do Augustine's central question and the fundamental preoccupation of the Rabbinic sages. Augustine's *City of God* and the Talmud of the Land of Israel took shape in times that were radically changing, and both systemic statements accommodated questions of history. Both did so in the same way.

---

[36] To be sure, earth in the model of Heaven, or, as we might prefer, Heaven in the model of earth.

Specifically, Augustine, bringing to fruition the tradition of Christian historical thought commencing with Eusebius, provided for Christianity a theory of history that placed into the right perspective the events of the day. And the Rabbinic sages did the same, first of all affirming that events required recognition for the unique lessons contained in each, second, then providing a theory of events that acknowledged their meaning, that is, their historicity, but that also subordinated history to considerations of eternity. The generative problematic of the later documents of the Rabbinic canon concerned history: vast changes in the political circumstance of Israel, perceived mutations in the tissue of social relationship, clearly an interest in revising the plain meaning of ordinary words: value, power, learning. And the systemic answer for its part addressed questions of long-term continuity, framed in genealogical terms for the now-genealogically-defined Israel: the past lives in us, and the system explains in very precise and specific terms just how that takes place, which is through the medium of inherited entitlement or attained entitlement. The medium was indeed the same. The message carried by *zekhut* counseled performance of actions of renunciation, in the hope that Heaven would respond. Power was weakness, value was knowledge, and knowledge was power: all things formed within the Torah.

V. THE QUESTION OF HISTORY ONCE AGAIN

But if that was the message by way of answer to the historical question of change and crisis, then what how had the question of history come to be formulated? We come back to the issues of Chapter Two. It was, of course, precisely what events should be deemed to constitute history, what changes matter, and what are we to do. The answer — the Rabbinic sages' and Augustine's alike — was that only certain happenings are eventful, bear consequence, require attention. And they are eventful because they form paradigms, Cain and Abel for Augustine and for the rabbis alike ("God favors the pursued over the pursuer), Israel's patriarchs and matriarchs for the Rabbinic sages alone.[37] Then what has happened to history as made by the barbarians at Rome and Hippo, the Byzantine Christians at Tiberias and Sepphoris? It has ceased to matter, because what happened

---

[37] But while I think they are primary, as the formation of Genesis Rabbah at this time indicates, they are not alone; Israel at Sinai, David on the throne, and other historical moments serve as well. It is a mere impression, not a demonstrable fact, that the patriarchs and matriarchs provide the primary paradigm.

at Rome, what happened at Tiberias, is no happening at all, but a mere happenstance. The upshot is not that history follows rules, so we can predict what will be, not at all.

Augustine did not claim to know what would happen tomorrow morning, and the Rabbinic sages interpreted events but did not claim to shape them, except through the Torah. The upshot is that what is going on really may be set aside in favor of what is really happening, and the story that is history has already been told in (for Augustine) the Bible and (for the Rabbinic sages) the Torah. But, then, that is no longer history at all, but merely, a past made into an eternal present. So, if I may specify what I conceive to be the systemic answer, it is, there are some things that matter, many that do not, and the few that do matter echo from eternity to eternity, speaking in that voice, the voice of God, that is the thin voice of silence.

The systemic question, urgent and critical, not merely chronic, then, concerned vast historical change, comprising chains of events. The answer was that, in an exact sense, "event" has no meaning at all. Other than historical modes of organizing existence governed, and history in the ordinary sense did not form one of them. Without the social construction of history, there also is no need for the identification of events, that is, individual and unique happenings that bear consequence, since, within the system and structure of the successor-Judaism, history forms no taxon, being replaced by *zekhut*, a historical category that was — we now realize — in the deepest sense anti-historical. So, it must follow, no happening is unique, and, on its own, no event bears consequence.

Neither Augustine nor the Rabbinic sages — both of them theologians of history — produced narrative history. Both, rather, wrote reflections *on* history, a very different matter. For neither did narrative history, ordinarily a sustained paraphrastic chronicle, serve as a medium for organizing and explaining perceived experience. True, both referred to events in the past, but these were not strung together in a continuing account. They were cited because they were exemplary, not because they were unique. These events then were identified out of the unlimited agenda of the past as what mattered, and these occasions of consequence, as distinct from undifferentiated and unperceived happenings were meant to explain the things that mattered in the chaos of the everyday.

In responding as they did to what we conceive to be historical events of unparalleled weight, Augustine and the Rabbinic sages took positions that, from our perspective, prove remarkably contemporary. For we now understand that all histories are the creation of an eternal present, that is, those moments in which histories are defined and distinguished, in which

8. Living in the kingdom of God

events are identified and assigned consequence, and in which sequences of events, "this particular thing happened here *and therefore*...," are strung together, pearls on a string, to form ornaments of intellect. Fully recognizing that history is one of the grand fabrications of the human intellect, facts not discovered but invented, explanations that themselves form cultural indicators of how things are in the here and now, we may appreciate as far more than merely instrumental and necessary the systemic responses to the urgent questions addressed in common by the Rabbinic sages and by Augustine.

Shall we then represent the Judaism of the later documents of the classical canon as a historical religion. After all, iit appeals for its worldview to not myth about gods in heaven but the history of Israel upon earth — interpreted in relationship to the acts of God in heaven to be sure? And shall we characterize that Judaism as a religion that appeals to history, that is, to events, defined in the ordinary way, important happenings, for its source of testing and establishing truth? I think not. That Judaism identifies an event through its own cognitive processes. Just as the canon that recapitulates the system, so events — things that happen given consequence — recapitulate the system. Just as the system speaks in detail through the canon, so too through its repertoire of events granted recognition the system delivers its message. But just as the canon is not the system, so the recognition of events does not classify the system as historical.

This brings me directly to the final question of systemic description: what exactly does the successor-Judaism mean by events? To answer that question succinctly is simple. In the canonical literature of the successor-Judaism, events find their place, within the science of learning of *Listenwissenschaft* that characterizes this literature, along with sorts of things that, for our part, we should not characterize as events at all. Events have no autonomous standing; events are not unique, each unto itself; events have no probative value on their own. Events form cases, along with a variety of other cases, making up lists of things that, in common, point to or prove one thing. Not only so, but among the taxonomic structure at hand, events do not make up their own list at all, for what is truly eventful generates *zekhut*. It is the act of *zekhut* that unites past and present, and it is the act that gains *zekhut* that makes history for tomorrow.

Events of other kinds, even those that seem to make an enormous, and awful, difference in Israel's condition, will appear on the same list as persons, places, things. And the contrary lists — very often in the form of stories as we have seen — tell us events that in and of themselves change biography (the life and fate of an ass-driver) and make history. That means that events other than those that gain *zekhut* not only have no autonomous standing on their own, but also that events constitute no species even within a genus of a historical order. For persons, places, and things in our way of thinking do not belong on the same list as events; they are not of the same order. Within the logic of our own minds, we cannot classify the city, Paris, within the same genus as the event, the declaration of the rights of man, for instance, nor is Sinai or Jerusalem of the same order of things as the Torah or the Temple, respectively. But in the logic of the Judaism before us, Jerusalem stands for sanctity and for Temple; it is of precisely the same taxic order.

What then shall we make of a list that encompasses within the same taxic composition events and things? Answering that question shows us how the Rabbinic sages sort out what matters from what does not, and events, by themselves, do not form a taxon and on their own bear no means and therefore do not matter. For one such list made up of events, persons, and places, is as follows: [1] Israel at the sea; [2] the ministering angels; [3] the tent of meeting; [4] the eternal house [= the Temple]; [5] Sinai. That mixes an event (Israel redeemed at the sea), a category of sensate being (angels), a location (tent of meeting, Temple), and then Sinai, which can stand for a variety of things but in context stands for the Torah. In such a list an event may or may not stand for a value or a proposition, but it does not enjoy autonomous standing; the list is not defined by the eventfulness of events and their meaning, the compilation of matters of a single genus or even a single species (tent of meeting, eternal house, are the same species here). The notion of event as autonomous, even unique, is quite absent in this taxonomy. And once events lose their autonomy, that process of selection gets under way that transforms one event into history bearing meaning and sets aside as inconsequential in the exact sense all other events.

Since this point is systemically so fundamental, let me give the case of another such list, which moves from events to other matters altogether, finding the whole subject to the same metaphor, hence homogenized. First come the events that took place at these places or with these persons: Egypt, the sea, Marah, Massah and Meribah, Horeb, the wilderness, the spies in the Land, Shittim, for Achan/Joshua and the conquest of the Land. Now that mixture of places and names clearly intends to focus on particular things that happened, and hence, were the list to which I refer to conclude at this point, we could define an event for the successor-Judaism as a happening that bore consequence, taught a lesson or exemplified a truth, in the present case, an event matters because it the mixture of rebellion and obedience. But there would then be no doubt that "event" formed a genus unto itself, and that a proper list could not encompass both events, defined conventionally as we should, and also other matters altogether.

But the textual community at hand, the same literary context, proceeds to the following items: [1] the Ten Commandments; [2] the show-fringes and phylacteries; [3] the *Shema* and the Prayer; [4] the tabernacle and the cloud of the Presence of God in the world to come. Why we invoke, as our candidates for the metaphor at hand, the Ten Commandments, show-fringes and phylacteries, recitation of the *Shema* and the Prayer, the tabernacle and the cloud of the Presence of God, and the mezuzah, seems to me clear from the very catalogue. These reach their climax in the analogy between the home and the tabernacle, the embrace of God and the Presence of God. So the whole is meant to list those things that draw the Israelite near God and make the Israelite cleave to God. And to this massive catalogue, events are not only exemplary—which historians can concede without difficulty—but also subordinated.

They belong on the same list as actions, things, persons, places, because they form an order of being that is not to be differentiated between events (including things that stand for events) and other cultural artifacts altogether. A happening is no different from an object, in which case "event" serves no better, and no worse, than a hero, a gesture or action, recitation of a given formula, or a particular locale, to establish a truth. It is contingent, subordinate, instrumental.[38] And why find that fact surprising, since all history comes to us in writing, and it is the culture that dictates how writing is to take place; that is why history can only paraphrase the affirmations of a system, and that is why events recapitulate in acute and concrete ways the system that classifies one thing that happens as event, but another thing is not only not an event but is not classified at all. In the present instance, an event is not at all eventful; it is merely a fact that forms part of the evidence for what is, and what is eventful is not an occasion at all, but a condition, an attitude, a perspective and a viewpoint. Then, it is clear, events are subordinated to the formation of attitudes, perspectives, viewpoints—the formative artifacts of not history in the conventional sense but culture in the framework of Sahlin's generalization,

---

[38] I can think of no more apt illustration of Geertz's interesting judgment: "an event is a unique actualization of a general phenomenon, a contingent realization of the cultural pattern." But my principal master in the present matter is Sahlin, cited in the next note.

"history is culturally ordered, differently so in different societies, according to meaningful schemes of things."[39]

Events not only do not form a taxon, they also do not present a vast corpus of candidates for inclusion into some other taxon. Among the candidates, events that are selected by our documents are few indeed. They commonly encompass Israel at the Sea and at Sinai, the destruction of the first Temple, the destruction of the second Temple, events as defined by the actions of some holy men such as Abraham, Isaac, and Jacob (treated not for what they did but for who they were), Daniel, Mishael, Hananiah and Azariah, and the like. It follows that the restricted repertoire of candidates for taxonomic study encompasses remarkably few events, remarkably few for a literary culture that is commonly described as quintessentially historical!

Then what taxic indicator dictates which happenings will be deemed events and which not? What are listed throughout are not data of nature or history but of theology: the issue of history is one of relationship, just as with Augustine. Specifically, God's relationship with Israel, expressed in such facts as the three events, the first two in the past, the third in the future, namely, the three redemptions of Israel, the three patriarchs, and holy persons, actions, events, what-have-you—these are facts that are assembled and grouped. What we have is a kind of recombinant theology given narrative form through tales presented individually but not in a sustained narrative. This recombinant theology through history is accomplished when the framer ("the theologian") selects from a restricted repertoire a few items for combination. What we have is a kind of subtle restatement, through an infinite range of possibilities, of the combinations and recombinations of a few essentially simple facts (data).

The net effect, then, is to exclude, rather than to include: the world is left outside. The key to systemic interpretation lies in the exegesis of that exegetical process that governs selection: what is included, what is excluded. In this context I find important Jonathan Z. Smith's statement:

> An almost limitless horizon of possibilities that are at hand...is arbitrarily reduced...to a set of basic elements...Then a most intense ingenuity is exercised to overcome the reduction...to introduce interest and variety. This ingenuity is usually accompanied by a complex set of rules.[40]

---

[39] See his *Islands of History* (Chicago, 1985: The University of Chicago Press),.
[40] "Sacred Persistence: Towards a Redescription of Canon," in William Scott Green, ed., *Approaches to Ancient Judaism* 1978, 1:11–28. Quotation: p. 15.

If we know the complex set of rules in play here, we also would understand the system that makes this document not merely an expression of piety but a statement of a theological structure: orderly, well-composed and proportioned, internally coherent and cogent throughout.

The canonical, therefore anything but random, standing of events forms a brief chapter in the exegesis of a canon. That observation draws us back to Smith, who observes:

> the radical and arbitrary reduction represented by the notion of canon and the ingenuity represented by the rule-governed exegetical enterprise to apply the canon to every dimension of human life is that most characteristic, persistent, and obsessive religious activity... The task of application as well as the judgment of the relative adequacy of particular applications to a community's life situation remains the indigenous theologian's task; but the study of the process, particularly the study of comparative systematics and exegesis, ought to be a major preoccupation of the historian of religions.[41]

Smith speaks of religion as an "enterprise of exegetical totalization," and he further identifies with the word "canon" precisely what we have identified as the substrate and structure of the list. If I had to define an event in this canonical context, I should have to call it merely another theological thing: something to be manipulated, combined in one way or in another, along with other theological things.

The later documents of the Rabbinic canon sustain the generative mode of thought of the initial one, the Mishnah and the Tosefta, which was list-making. But now the lists derive from data supplied by Scripture (as with the bulk of Augustine's historical events of paradigmatic consequence), rather than by nature. Now as before, list-making is accomplished within a restricted repertoire of items that can serve on lists; the list-making then presents interesting combinations of an essentially small number of candidates for the exercise. But then, when making lists, one can do pretty much anything with the items that are combined; the taxic indicators are unlimited, but the data studied, severely limited. So the successor-system in mode of thought and medium of expression has recapitulated the initial system.

---

[41] *ibid.*, p. 18.

Index of Ancient Sources

Hebrew Bible/Old Testament
Genesis
2:15ff. 173
14:20 196
15:5 .... 195, 196
15:6 153
18:25 10
22 193
22:5 .... 196, 197
22:15 8
24:1 196
27:41 198
30:25 195
31:41–42 .... 196, 202, 203
32:7 198
32:25 194
32:32 77
33:11 196
37:2 195
39:9 11
39:13–15 195
43:10 .... 196, 202
50:10 201
50:11 201
Exodus
4:31 .... 154, 197
14:29 43
15:8 43
16:35 36
17:11 152
19:3 196
20:2 9
20:3 9
20:7 9
22:30 .... 65, 70, 83

23:19 .... 72, 77
24:1 197
29:37 115
32:13 186
34:26 72
Leviticus
1:9 151
1:17 151
2:9 151
3:17 77
5:1–6 94
5:6–7 .... 92, 157
5:11 .... 92, 157
5:17 .... 92, 156, 160
5:17–19 91
7:23 77
7:34 77
8:1–3 10
11:34 .... 103, 104, 106, 115
11:37 .... 102, 103, 106, 115
11:38 104
17:5–7 54
17:8–9 53
17:13 41
17:13–14 .... 72, 76
19:2 .... 9, 70
19:4 9
19:5 151
19:12 9
19:19 91
20:10 39
21:1 91
22:28 72
23:7 91
25:4 90

Numbers

1:1	36
3:12	52
6:2	33
6:6	91
6:23	196
7:18	37
8:16–18	52
9:1–14	35
11:24–26	38
15:29	92, 157
20:1–13	174
30:1–16	15

Deuteronomy

4:37	186
12:9	52, 53
12:13	54
12:14	54
12:20–24	65, 66, 83, 84
12:21	72, 73, 77
14:21	65, 83
18:3	72, 77
18:4	77
21:4	153
22:6–7	72, 77
22:9	90
22:10	90
28:65	32
30:20	152
32:13	43
33:21	189

Joshua

4:22	194

1 Samuel

1:19	197
26:10	11

2 Samuel

12:13	39
13:15	158

1 Kings

15:30	189

2 Chronicles

6:42	186

Esther

3:12	201
8:9	201

Job

13:15	151
27:5	151

Psalms

3:2–3	39
3:4	39
10:4	33
27:13	203
31:25	154
45:7	10
50:10	151
50:11	151
50:13	151
74:13	43
77:16	195
77:17	195
78:13	42
95:6	198
101:2	200
106:9	43
114:5ff.	194
119:92	203
136:13	42

Proverbs

3:17	152
3:18	152
4:22	153
7:26	153
13:16	33
16:4	32
29:22	33

Qohelet

1:18	33
3:4	158
3:5	158
11:10	32

Song of Songs

2:7	11
3:5	11
4:15	43

Isaiah

27:13	197
39:1	40
42:21	5
54:9	10
63:14	42
64:1	43

Ezekiel
    7:22 152
    24:7 41
    24:8 41
Daniel
    5:30 153
Hosea
    4:2 41
Micah
    7:6 57
Habakkuk
    3:14 42
    3:15 42

Rabbinic Works
  Abot
    1:6 188
    2:2 189
    2:4 ....206, 213
    3:10 ....158, 213
    3:15 .... 4, 161
    3:16 4
    3:21 4
    5:16 158
    5:17 158
    5:18 189
  Bavli
    Haggal
      18b 157
    Horayot
      10b 153
    Menahot
      110a 151
    Nedarim
      22a 32
      22b 33
      62a 152
    Qiddushin
      81b 159
  Mishnah
    Baba Qamma
      8:4 26
    Berakot
      2:1 154
      4:4 154

    4:5 154
    5:1 154
  Bikkurim
    1:1–2 128
    2:1–11 129
  Demai
    5:3–11 129
    6:1–2 130
    6:3–5 130
    6:7–10 130
    7:6 130
    7:7 130
    7:8 130
  Gittin
    8:8 186
  Hagigah
    2:5ff 63
  Hallah
    1:1 130
    1:3 131
    1:5 131
    1:6 131
    1:8 131
    2:1 131
    2:4 131
    2:8 131
    3:7 132
    3:8–9 132
    3:10 132
  Hullin
    1:1 .... 73, 85
    2:1 73
    2:7 74
    2:8 74
    5:1 76
    5:2 78
    6:1 .... 76, 78
    7:1 77
    8:1 77
    9:1 79
    10:1–2 77
    11:1 77
    12:1 77
  Kelim
    1:1–4 63
    1:6 60

237

1:6–9	62	Makhshirin	
1:7	60	1:5	104, 105
1:8	60	1:6	105
1:9	61	2:1	127
Keritot		2:2	127
1:1	93	2:3	113, 127
1:2	93, 156	3:2	112
1:7	93	3:5–7	104
3:1–3	93	4:1	107
3:2	93	4:2	107
3:4	93	4:3	108
3:4–6	93	4:4	108
3:9	91	4:5	109
Ketubot		4:6	111
13:6	186	4:7	112
Kilayim		4:8	112
1:1–4	132	4:9	104, 113
1:4–6	132	4:10	113
1:7–9	132	5:4	104
3:7	132	Makkot	
4:1–7:8	132	3:15	5
8:1	132	Menahot	
8:2	132	1:1	157
9:1–10	132	10:1–4	75
9:2	133	Miqvaot	
Maaser Sheni		3:1	125
1:1–2	133	3:2	126
1:3–7	133	3:4	126
1:5	155	4:4	126
2:5	134	6:1	126
2:6	134	6:3	126
2:10–3:4	134	6:7	127
4:1–8	134	6:8	127
Maaserot		Moed Qatan	
1:1	137	1:5	212
1:1ff	134	1:7	212
1:5	156	3:7–9	212
2:1	134	Nedarim	
2:2–4	134	9:1	31
2:5–6	134	9:9	31
3:5–10	135	Orlah	
4:1	135	1:1	135
4:6	135	1:6	135
5:1–2	135	1:7	136
5:3–5	135	1:7–8	136
5:6–7	135	1:9	136

2:1–3	136
2:4	136
2:5	136
2:6	136
2:7	136
2:8	136
2:9	136
2:10	136
2:11	136
2:12	136
2:13	136
2:14	136
2:15	136
2:16	136
2:17	136
3:1	137
3:2	137
3:3	137
3:4	137
3:5	137
3:6	137
3:7	137
3:8	137

Peah

1:1	188
1:1–2	137
1:4–6	137
2:1–8	137
2:5–8	138
5:1–2	138
5:7ff	138
7:6	139
7:7	139
8:1	139
8:2–4	139

Qiddushin

4:1	48
4:14	187

Rosh Hashanah

3:7	154
3:8	152
4:1–3	50

Sanhedrin

4:1	186
5:4	186
5:5	186
6:1	186

6:6	212
9:4	155

Shabbat

1:1	94
11:6	156

Shebiit

1:1	140
1:6–8	140
2:1	140
2:2–5	140
2:6	140
2:6–10	140
3:1–4:1	141
3:2	141
3:5–4:1	141
5:1–5	142
7:1–2	142
7:6	143
8:1–2	141
8:1–6	141
8:2	141
8:3ff	141
8:7–11	141
9:1–6	143
10:7	144

Shebuot

1:1–2	95
1:1–7	95
2:1	95
2:1–5	95
3:1–8:6	96

Sotah

3:4–5	187
5:5	151
9:15	57

Sukkot

3:12	51
5:1–4	212

Ta'anit

4:6–7	45, 47
4:7	54

Temurah

6:1	125

Terumot

1:1–2	144
1:3	144
1:4–5	144

1:6	145	8:2	123
1:8	145	8:3	125
2:1–2	145	8:6	124
2:1–3	145	9:1	115
2:3	154	9:5	115
3:5	145	11:8	124
3:8	155	14:4	54
4:1–6	145	14:4–9	52
4:10–13	146	14:6	54
5:1–4	146	14:7	54
5:5–9	146	14:9	54
6:1	146		

Tosefta

Baba Batra

7:9	188

9:1–4	147		
9:5–7	147		

Berakot

2:21	158
3:3	158
4:18	158

10:2	148		
10:3–4	148		
10:5	148		
10:6	148		

Bikkurim

2:15	150

10:7–12	148		
11:1–3	148		

Gittin

1:5	188

11:4–7	148		
11:8–10	148		

Haggai

1:2	159

Tohorot

Kelim

1:9	118	1:8	61
2:1	118	1:10	61
2:2	118	1:11	61
2:3	118	1:12	61, 64

2:3–6	121
2:4	118

Maaser Sheni

5:27	188
5:29	188

2:5	119
2:6	119

Makhshirin

1:7	128

2:7	119, 121
2:8	119

Miqvaot

3:7	127

2:9	119
3:1	119

Nazir

4:7	33

3:1–4	121

Peah

Yoma

1:2	188
1:4	152

8:9	155

Qiddushin

Zabim

1:13	188

2:1	28		
2:2	28		

Sanhedrin

Zebahim

1:8	188
3:3	188
9:1	188

1:1	157
2:3	157
4:6	157
6:5	125
8:1	123

9:2 188
9:3 188
9:4 188
10:11 188
Shabbat
   2:17–18 155
Sotah
   11:10 188
Taanit
   4:9 188
Yoma
   5:12 188
Zebahim
   10:14 124
Yerushalmi
   Baba Mesia
      2:4 151
   Taanit
      1:4 .... 181, 182, 183
      3:4 159
      3:11 200

Ruth Rabbah
   72:3.1 11
Sifré to Deuteronomy
   306:22.1 153
Sifré to Numbers
   52:1 37
   64:1 36
   95:2 38
   99:2.2 150
Song of Songs Rabbah
   24:2.1 11
   38:2 40

Midrash and Other Rabbinic Works
   Fathers According to Rabbi Nathan
      33:5.1 43
   Genesis Rabbah
      39:6 10
      43:8.2 196
      43:8.3 196
      56:2.5 198
      74:12.1 .... 196, 203
      76:2 198
      76:5 194
      77:3.3 194
      84:5.2 195
      87:8.1 195
      100:6.1 201
   Lamentations Rabbati
      113:1.1 42
   Leviticus Rabbah
      10:1–3.1 10
      24:5 9
   Mekilta
      25:1.26 153
   Pesiqta deRab Kahana
      2:1.1 39

Index of Subjects

A
Abot, 48, 212–214
Abraham, 11
action, and intention, 100–103, 151, 154, 155
adjuration, oath of, 5
Aggadah
    and oaths, 9–12
    and vows, 32–33
animal offerings, 156–157
Aristotle, 89, 96, 97–100
arrogance, 209, 213
atonement, 155, 156–157
attitude, 3, 211–215. *See also* intentionality
Augustine, 207n2, 219–228
Augustine of Hippo (Brown), 220n12
Augustine the Bishop (Van der Meer), 220n12
Augustine the Theologian (Tesselle), 220n12

B
bailment, oath of, 6, 13
bailments, false claim in connection with, 5
Bavli, and vows, 32–33
Bikkurim, 128–129
blood, 70
Bonner, Gerald, 220n12
Brown, Peter, 220n12, 224
Burleigh, John H.S., 221n14, 223n24, 224n33, 225n34

C
Cain and Abel, 207n2, 223
Canaanites, 202
causation, 18–19
The Charter of Christendom: The Significance of the City of God (O'Meara), 220n12
Christianity, 215–216, 219–220
The City of God: A Study of St. Augustine's Philosophy (Burleigh), 221n14, 223n24, 224n33, 225n34
City of God (Augustine), 220–225
claims, and oaths, 13
classification
    Aristotelianism, 97–100
    and intentionality, 100–116, 150
    in patterning events, 44–47
    and sanctity of Israel, 64–65
    and truth of monotheism, 89–97
    in vows, 15, 18, 27
consecration, acts of, 17
contamination. *See* uncleanness
courts, and oaths, 7, 13
crime, sanctions against, 164–175
cult, history of, 51–55
cultic contamination, 62–63

D
David, 39
Day of Atonement, 155
Deane, Herbert A., 220n12, 221n15
death, 16
deductive reasoning, 97–100

Dema'i, 129–130
dietary rules. *See* food-preparation
divorce, 16

E
Egyptians, 202
emotion, 211–215
eschatology, 218
euphemisms, 26–27

F
faith, 153
Figgis, John Neville, 220n12
food-preparation, 64–70
The Foundations of Judaism: Method, Teleology, Doctrine (Neusner), 223n24

G
Genesis Rabbah, 193–199
gentiles, and Temple-offerings, 74
Gittin, 16, 17, 30
God
    and human intentionality, 100–102
    name of, 8–9
    and oaths, 5–14
    omnipotence of, 3–5
Green, William, 221n16

H
Halakhah
    and intentionality, 162
    and oaths, 9–10, 13–14
    and vows, 16–17
Hallah, 130–132
hierarchization. *See* classification
history, and temporal order, 35–37, 47–49, 227–233
household
    domestic table vs. Temple altar, 70–71, 72
    and vows, 15, 17
Hullin, 65, 68–70, 72–86, 125

I
The Incarnation of God: The Character of Divinity in Formative Judaism (Neusner), 207n3

intentionality
    definition, 150–160
    and freedom of will, 160–166
    gentiles, 74
    and slaughter of animals, 74
    taxonomy and, 100–116
    and transactions of power, 166–175
    and uncleanness, 102–106
    and vows, 14, 22, 25–27, 31–32
    will of God/Man, 175–176
    and words, 3
Isaac, submission of, 207n2
Israel
    foundational writings, 216–218
    in Mishnah, 49–51, 75
    sanctity inheres in people, 59–68, 75–76, 80–81, 84–86
    social order, 206–211
    zekhut and, 192–199

J
Judaism, and Christianity, 215–216
Judaism: The Evidence of the Mishnah (Neusner), 179n1
Judaism and Scripture (Neusner), 193n10
Judaism as Philosophy: The Method and Message of the Mishnah (Neusner), 179n1
Julian, 216

K
Keritot, 91
Ketubot, 15, 16, 30
Kila'yim, 132–133

L
language, and meaning, 17–18, 21–22, 25–27, 31
Levy, S., 207n2
liquids. *See* mixtures; uncleanness

M
Ma'aser Sheni, 133–134
Ma'aserot, 134–135
Makhshirin, 102, 127–128
marriage
    and vows, 14–17, 19, 23, 29–30
meat preparation. *See* Hullin

Index of Subjects

merit, 190n7. *See also zekhut*
Messiah-theme, in Mishnah, 55–58, 217–218
Miqvaot, 125–127
Mishnah
    classification and monotheism, 89–97
    deductive reasoning in, 97–100
    history and time in, 47–49
    Israel's history, 49–51
    Messiah-theme in, 55–58
mixtures, 98–99, 117–123, 149
    Bikkurim on, 128–129
    Dema'i on, 129–130
    Hallah on, 130–132
    Hullin on, 125
    Kila'yim on, 132–133
    Ma'aser Sheni on, 133–134
    Ma'aserot on, 134–135
    Makhshirin on, 127–128
    Miqvaot on, 125–127
    Orlah on, 135–137
    Pe'ah on, 137–140
    Shebi'it on, 140–144
    Temurah on, 125
    Terumot on, 144–148
    Zebahim on, 123–124
monotheism, 89–97

N
Nazir, 20
Nazirite vow, 20–29, 33–34
Nedarim, 17–18, 20

O
oaths
    Aggadic treatment, 9–12
    Halakhic treatment, 9–10, 13–14
    and intentionality, 155
    speciation of, 95–96
    types, 6–7
offerings, and intentionality, 155
O'Meara, John, 220n12
omnipotence, 3–5
Original Virtue and Other Studies (Levy), 207n2
Orlah, 135–137

P
paganism, 216–217
patterning events
    Augustine's and sages' conceptions of, 227–233
    in history of cult, 51–55
    and Mishnah, 47–49
    and Scripture, 44–47
Pe'ah, 137–140
Pentateuch, 48
Platonism, Middle, 221n16, 223
The Political and Social Ideas of St. Augustine (Deane), 220n12, 221n15
The Political Aspects of St. Augustine's 'City of God' (Figgis), 220n12
politics, 163, 166–175
power, transactions of, and intentionality, 166–175
prayer, 154, 159
produce, preparation and use, 69–70. *See also* food-preparation
property, and oaths, 6

Q
Qiddushin, 16, 17, 30
Qorban, 25, 29

R
rash oaths, 5, 6, 12
rationality, 206–211
rebellion, and will, 161–162
religious obligations, and intentionality, 159
repentance, and intentionality, 155
restraint, 213

S
Samson-vows, 22
sanctification
    gradations of, 80–82
    grid of, 120
    of Israel, 61–62
    and vows, 27–28
sanctions, and intention, 164–175
Sanhedrin-Makkot, 6
Scripture
    patterning events in, 44–47
    temporal considerations, 37–44

self-control, 212, 213
sexual sin, 10–11
Shebi'it, 140–144
Shebuot, 6, 7, 94
sin, sanctions against, 164–175
sincerity, 153
slaughtering an animal. See Hullin
Smith, Jonathan Z., 232–233
Sotah, 55–58
speciation, 18
St. Augustine of Hippo: Life and Controversies (Bonner), 220n12
Stoicism, 121–122

T
Talmud, 218
Tamid, 38
taxonomies. See classification
Temple, 59
    altar slaughter, 70–71, 72, 83–86
temporal order, 35–44, 47–49
Temurah, 125
Ten Commandments, 9
terefah-beast, 69–70
Terumot, 144–148
Teselle, Eugene, 220n12
testimony, oath of, 6, 12–13
Theodosius, 216–217
Torah, history and time in, 47–49
Torah-study, 153, 180, 199
Tosefta, 188n6

U
uncleanness
    cultic contamination, 62–63
    gradations of sanctification, 80–82
    grid of, 120
    and intentionality, 27–28, 102–106, 157–158
    virulence of sources of, 63–64

V
vain oaths, 6, 12, 13
Van der Meer, F., 220n12
Vanquished Nation, Broken Spirit: The Virtues of the Heart in Formative Judaism (Neusner), 211n5

virtue, 207n2, 213, 214n6
vows, 14–34
    and intentionality, 14, 22, 25–27, 31–32
    located in household, 14–17
    nullification of, 18, 19–20, 23

W
Weber, Max, 206n1
will
    of God and Man, 175–176
    power of, 3
    transactions of, 160–166
women, and vows, 19–20, 23
word, man's and God's, 7, 12

Y
Yebamot, 16
Yerushalmi, 21n2, 218, 219

Z
Zebahim, 123–124
zekhut
    about, 180–184
    deeds that generate, 199–203
    defining, 184–186
    in Genesis Rabbah, 193–199
    in Israel's social order, 206–211
    meanings in context, 186–193
    as political economy of Judaism, 203–205
    response to power and politics changes, 219–220
Zeraim, 128–148
zob-uncleanness, 29

www.ingramcontent.com/pod-product-compliance
Lightning Source LLC
Chambersburg PA
CBHW062014220426
43662CB00010B/1321